Collins *practical ga*

CONTAINER GARDENING

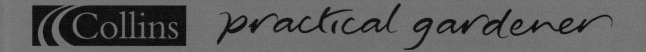

Collins *practical gardener*

CONTAINER GARDENING

JENNY HENDY

First published in 2004 by HarperCollins*Publishers*

77–85 Fulham Palace Road, London, W6 8JB

The Collins website address is:

www.collins.co.uk

Text by Jenny Hendy; copyright © HarperCollins*Publishers*

Artworks and design © HarperCollins*Publishers*

Photography by Tim Sandall and Jenny Hendy

Cover photography by Tim Sandall

Photographic props: Coolings Nurseries, Rushmore Hill,
Knockholt, Kent, TN14 7NN, www.coolings.co.uk

Design and editorial: Focus Publishing, Sevenoaks, Kent

Project editor: Guy Croton

Editor: Vanessa Townsend

Project co-ordinator: Caroline Watson

Design & illustration: David Etherington

For HarperCollins

Managing Editor: Angela Newton

Art Direction: Luke Griffin

Editor: Alastair Laing

Editorial assistant: Lisa John

Production: Chris Gurney

A CIP catalogue record for this book is available from the
British Library

ISBN 0007164041

Colour reproduction by Colourscan

Printed and bound in Italy by L.E.G.O.

Contents

Introduction

The key word in container gardening is flexibility. It does not matter if you do not have the right kind of soil in which to grow rhododendrons, for example – you can simply grow them in pots of ericaceous or lime-free compost. And if your beds and borders are not ideally situated, or the garden is fully paved, containers provide the means to plant just about anything you like anywhere that you want.

Patio gardening

Container gardening is perhaps the most dynamic branch of horticulture, in that scores of new varieties specifically bred and marketed for use in pots and planters appear ever year. Many of these plants are not hardy and do best in the more sheltered environs surrounding the house, perhaps overwintering in the conservatory. The phrase 'patio living' is used to describe life on the terrace, especially during the summer months, when containers overflow with colourful annuals, tender perennials and exotic foliage plants. You will often find an area in the garden centre devoted to 'patio plants', which has tempting, instant-

colour displays of flowers, foliage plants, fruits and berries throughout the year.

Easy care pots

With the right selection of hardy, long-lived, low-maintenance plants, you can design whole gardens in containers that will require very little attention from one year to the next.

Such pot groupings are perfect for softening the hard lines of the house and driveway, especially in the front garden, or in areas where you want to add interest but at the same time wish to minimize the amount of gardening that you have to undertake. You will find plenty of planting suggestions for containers of every description in the A–Z directory of this book.

Gardening with containers means that you can have interesting displays whenever you like

How to Use This Book

Container Gardening is divided into three main sections. The first covers practical matters such as choosing and buying plants and containers, potting up, and essential information on watering, feeding and general plant maintenance. It also includes aspects of design such as using colour effectively, placing pots for best effect and creating seasonal and permanent planting schemes.

There then follows an illustrated A–Z of more than 200 different groups of container plants, divided into the categories of flowers, foliage plants, architectural plants and evergreens. The final section outlines the pests and diseases you are likely to come across in container gardening, with tips on how to deal with them, as well as a handy 'Troubleshooting' key for quick reference.

latin name of the plant genus, followed by its **common name**

detailed descriptions give specific advice on care for each plant, including pruning and pests and diseases

alphabetical tabs on the side of the page, colour-coded to help you quickly find the plant you want

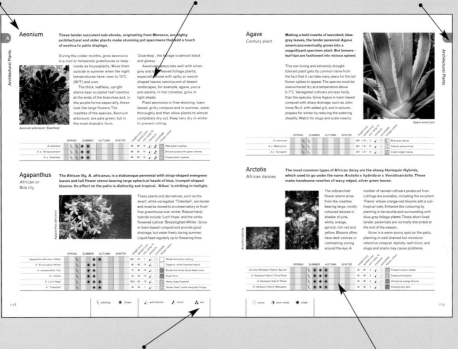

a key at the bottom of the page explains what each symbol means

variety charts list popular, recommended species and cultivars most suitable for container growing. These display key information about plants, showing:

• when the plant is in flower during the year
• the time to plant for the best results
• the height and spread of the plant in centimetres
• the minimum temperature the plant will withstand
• the plant's watering and light/shade requirements
• a rough approximation of the flower or berry colour
• additional comments by the author

7

Assessing Your Garden

The garden presents a wide range of differing growing environments, and knowing about the pros and cons of each will greatly increase your chance of success. For pot work, choosing the right plant for the right place and mixing only plants with similar requirements is a major key to success.

Around the house

Using baskets and windowboxes is one of the principal ways of softening the bare walls of a house and decorating adjacent areas of hard landscaping, such as paved patios or wooden decks. In these 'outdoor rooms' most of us want an abundance of colour and variety – particularly during the summer months – and use a mixture of bedding plants, tender perennials and bulbs for maximum impact. There is potentially a lot of work involved with watering, feeding and deadheading such displays, so it is wise to group pots together placing them close to a convenient water supply.

Sunny, sheltered aspects benefit tender, sub-tropical and mediterranean plants because the heat absorbed by walls and paving is radiated back into the surrounding atmosphere at night. Even during the colder months of winter, temperatures are often appreciably higher within the confines of sheltered patios than in the open garden, sometimes enabling plants that require frost-free conditions to remain outside permanently. The downside is that during the summer, temperatures can soar, baking the roots and causing rapid water loss. Here, heat and drought tolerant plants such as silverlings, plants with succulent, waxy leaves and many of the aromatic herbs become essential ingredients.

KEY

The yellow line denotes the sunniest area of the garden. The sun will shine on both sides of the line for most of the day.

This blue arrow denotes the direction of wind. In this case, the wind swirls over the top of the fence and down the garden.

choose tough, drought resistant plants for windowboxes on a sunny wall

tender plants and overwintering topiary benefit from the shelter of a warm wall

watch for wind turbulence that might damage delicate shoots, especially in hanging baskets

use plants that thrive in shade for containers that do not get much sun

heat is radiated back from flagstones and house walls at night, keeping temperatures appreciably higher

Shady walls and fences

Many of the common bedding plants and tender perennials perform poorly in shade – notable exceptions being fuchsias, busy Lizzies and begonias. In the gloom, sun worshippers may produce fewer flowers and the blooms of plants like osteospermums and gazanias may fail to open. Variegated foliage may turn all green and growth could become thin and leggy. Choose woodland bulbs, herbaceous perennials, ferns and shrubs that relish the cool, shady conditions created by buildings, fences and hedges. You might think that pots will need less frequent watering because moisture does not evaporate so quickly, but beware the rain shadow effect at the base of walls and under tree canopies where pots and planters remain dry even after a downpour.

Vertical gardening

Conditions on the walls of a house may be extreme. Turbulence created by surrounding buildings causes the wind to whip around baskets and wall planters, tearing at vulnerable shoots and stripping the moisture from leaves. Containers used for decorating walls do not often hold

Plants like these *Hydrangea paniculata* cultivars thrive in shade

Choose tough, flexible plants for windowboxes on exposed walls

very much compost because of the difficulty in fixing up something large and heavy. On hot, sunny walls, a lot of heat is thrown back onto the plants and even quite tolerant specimens may become overcooked. Choose the most sheltered parts of the house for siting windowboxes, baskets and wall planters and concentrate on drought tolerant plants with wiry, flexible stems, such as trailing geraniums and Bidens, rather than brittle, fleshy shoots which can easily be snapped off.

Away from the house

Further from the sheltering effects of buildings, plants need to be hardier to withstand winters without extra protection. In addition to placing pots of spring or summer bedding to fill temporary gaps in the flower borders, you could also use large containers planted with year round schemes that utilize tough deciduous and evergreen shrubs, conifers, perennials, bulbs, grasses and ground cover plants. Organise a hose reel or be prepared to go to and fro with a watering can.

Choosing Pots & Planters

You can now choose from a huge range of pots and planters designed for every style of garden. But some containers are more suited to certain situations and plantings than others. For example, in colder gardens, permanent displays should be made in large pots with good thermal insulation to protect the roots from frost – heavy wooden barrels are a good choice. Non-porous pots, including glazed terracotta, are useful in hot, dry spots, because the plants in them will need less frequent watering. And for balconies and roof gardens with a limited load bearing capacity, lightweight plastic containers are ideal.

Metal pots need thermal lining

Terracotta

Clay pots and planters are porous and so dry out quickly. Combat this by lining with plastic sheeting, keeping the drainage holes uncovered. Look for stoneware and terracotta with a frost proof guarantee as opposed to planters carrying only a frost-resistant label. When the latter absorbs moisture, which then freezes, the expansion causes pots to crack or shatter. Check for chips and flaking and lightly tap the side listening for a bell like ringing tone. A dull thud indicates hidden cracks likely to weaken the integrity of the pot.

Glazed ceramic

Characterized by beautifully coloured and patterned glazes, pots vary in quality but are generally frost proof because the glaze prevents moisture from permeating the clay. Check for crazing or blistering of the glaze and be wary about purchasing pots from hot countries like Thailand and Vietnam that may not perform as well in exposed conditions.

Metal

Galvanized metal planters have become very fashionable in recent years often coming in very modern, minimalist shapes ideal for the urban look.

There is a very wide choice of terracotta and glazed ceramic pots now available

Metal conducts heat most efficiently and in hot weather there is a danger that the root ball will 'cook'. Likewise in winter, there is very little insulation and roots are vulnerable to frost damage. Before planting, line with layers of bubble plastic insulation or polystyrene sheeting and for convenience use a plastic pot insert.

Wood

Large hardwood barrels such as those made from oak look at home in country and cottage settings and are ideal for permanent plantings because there is plenty of space for root development and they are naturally rot resistant. Traditional square Versailles planters have a much more formal look. Extend the life of softwood planters, troughs and window boxes by painting the inside with wood preservative that is harmless to plants or, in the case of barrels, try waterproofing the inside with bituminastic paint. Finish exteriors with coloured wood stain, yacht varnish or microporous paint. Lining with plastic sheeting or, for windowboxes, using plastic troughs as inserts, helps prevent rotting.

Plastic

Quality varies but you can now buy reasonably lifelike reproductions of classical lead and metalwork urns, terracotta pots and stonework. The great advantage of plastic is that it is lightweight, though in windy gardens this may be a disadvantage as pots may blow over when

Wooden barrels are perfect for permanent plantings

dry. You can paint or 'age' pots with artist's acrylics, matching colours to reflect elements in your garden. Check that the pots are UV stabilized, as otherwise they will become brittle on exposure to sunlight.

Stone

Copies of antique carved stone planters made from concrete or reconstituted stone are far cheaper than the real thing and only need a little weathering to make them look convincing. Encourage algae by painting with live yoghurt, liquid manure or manufacturers' own ageing compound. Containers that look like polished granite are available in simple shapes – such as cubes – and suit modern, minimalist settings very well. Remember that top-heavy stone pots may be pulled over by young children.

Reproduction stone can suit period settings

11

Designing with Containers

The impact of pots and planters can be greatly enhanced by careful positioning or by making attractive groupings. Pots are not only vessels for planting, but can also act as sculptural elements within the garden.

Getting the size right

Size and proportion are all important factors that affect whether a planter looks right in a particular spot. Generally speaking, if in doubt, buy something bigger. This may sound irrational, but it is especially true when dealing with a small space like a courtyard, where the surrounding high walls dominate. You can check beforehand by piling up cardboard boxes or by using something like a kitchen bin or dustbin.

Pot groupings

Small pots set out on their own can look insignificant and out of proportion with their surroundings. The answer is to group them together and use one or two larger pots to visually 'anchor' the collection. You might even consider a tiered pot stand or staging to give them extra prominence. Groupings of pots painted the same colour or made from the same material, e.g. terracotta, tend to have the most impact. On a large plain wall, you can make a hanging gardens effect by combining lots of different sized black ironwork planters and baskets or try a collection of terracotta pots attached with special holders.

Group pots together for more impact

In the border

Pots containing striking architectural plants or colourful flowers and foliage can boost interest in borders, especially at times when the planting is looking a little tired or 'between seasons'. They can also be used to plug gaps created when bulbs die back or when a plant has not performed well. Use containers with a contrasting colour – for example a blue pot in a yellow border, or something that tones like a white cast iron vase in a bed of whites and silvers. If the planter is becoming lost in amongst the foliage and flowers, consider raising it up on a plinth for a more dramatic effect. Shady areas, especially under trees, are notorious for being predominantly green, and just a few pots of fuchsias or boldly variegated hostas could lift the whole display.

Doors and entranceways

Use a pair of matching pots or planters to add extra emphasis to a doorway or gate, or to mark the passage from one distinct area of the garden into the next. Paired topiaries such as spiral clipped box or lollipop headed

This flight of steps has been transformed into a stage set for pots

standards are perfect for a period or formal setting. Also consider using a pair of metalwork obelisks set into matching planters to mimic the height and structure of topiary and plant with a flowering climber such as clematis.

Rhythm and repetition

A line of matching pots placed equidistantly along a pathway, topping a retaining wall, edging a paved terrace or running either side of a formal pool, creates a pleasing visual rhythm. Keep the planting simple and for stylish effect use just one type of plant in each. A flight of steps can also be dramatically enhanced with a run of identical pots from top to bottom but make sure they are properly secured and that they do not interfere with safe foot traffic. You can also take advantage of wide steps and terracing to help create a theatrical stage set where a large collection of containers is arranged to maximum effect, perhaps incorporating statuary or garden lighting. For an elegant and formal border edging, try setting matching pots in alcoves created at regular intervals in a low clipped hedge, such as dwarf box.

Alternative containers

Gardeners have always improvised by putting plants in anything that will hold compost. Sometimes our inspiration comes from recycling old items – a leaking milk churn, a worn out boot and so on – but these items often work better in a more rustic, cottage garden setting. Many ceramic artists and other craftspeople now create sculptural pieces that are designed with planting in mind – from quirky heads just waiting to be

Experiment with unusual containers

planted with grass 'hair', to stylish abstract or geometric forms. These must be displayed with the same care as other decorative elements and given space to be appreciated. Above all, the planting should be kept simple in order to be effective.

Choosing & Buying Plants

Some plants fare better than others in containers. For example, yew dislikes being restricted in a pot for any length of time. Good container plants are compact and quick to mature – that is, flower, or produce fruit. They have a long season of interest, are drought tolerant once established and have excellent disease resistance. Plants for year-round use should be hardy and not require frequent division or any special cultivation techniques. Unless they are being grown for their sculptural or architectural qualities, they should also have attractively shaped evergreen, and variegated or coloured foliage, preferably in addition to flowers or berries.

Where to find plants

For more imaginative displays you will need to look at the whole range of plants on offer through the year. Don't just rely on the bedding and patio plant areas of the garden centre for your blooms. In the A–Z section of this book you will find suggestions for flowering and

foliage plants drawn from the catergories of herbs and alpines, shrubs and climbers, as well as those of herbaceous perennials, ground cover plants and ferns.

In 'Architectural Plants' (pages 106–31), specimen-sized examples of some of the sub-tropical plants listed – for example, cannas, palms, bananas and astelia – do not normally appear until early summer and can often be found in protected, under-cover areas. The houseplant section can also be an excellent source of sculpted leaves and exotic blooms.

From mid-spring you will also find tender specimens such as standard marguerites (Argyranthemum), fuchsias and abutilons in the houseplant section, but if you buy them for the patio you will have to find room to keep them under cover until the risk of frost has passed.

Autumn, winter and spring bedding plants, and bulbs for spring flowering, all start to come in from the end of summer. You will also find a wide range of small potted evergreens, including herbs, shrubs, conifers and heathers grown for their attractive foliage, winter blooms or berries.

Spotting a good buy

Look for plants with plenty of buds that are just coming into flower rather than those covered in fully open or fading blooms. Avoid any plants showing signs of pest or disease or those with wilted or discoloured foliage – perhaps a sign of faulty watering, nutrient deficiency or chilling injury. The plants should be compact, balanced in overall shape and well clothed in leaves. Ones that have been grown in containers for a long time often have exposed roots showing through the compost and may be potbound. Gently remove the pot to check.

Saving money

Early in the growing season, many bedding and patio plants or tender perennials are available as seedlings, plugs or little plants in plastic mesh pots. You can buy them from garden centres and nurseries or by mail order. These are much cheaper than larger plants available later in spring, and are ideal if you have the time and space to nurture them.

Prick out seedlings straight away. When tiny, especially if the variety is all one colour, don't worry too much about pricking out singly – small clumps are fine. Transfer to trays or modular units filled with seed compost. Plugs and rooted cuttings in net pots can be used to plant up a liner for a pot or windowbox directly or to make up a hanging basket. Grow the arrangement on under heated glass until ready for hardening off a couple of weeks before the last likely frost date for your area. Alternatively, plant into larger pots of multi-purpose compost and keep on a warm, light window ledge.

A cold frame is a convenient way to harden off tender plants in spring

You can get a head start with pots and baskets by planting early using plug plants and tots

Using Colour & Form Effectively

Two of the essential elements of good container planting are colour scheming and the combination of different forms, shapes and textures.

Overall shape

The various styles of containers suit different combinations of plant shapes. Narrowly upright pots often need a horizontal element to balance them – for example, a spreading plant like Bidens, or something with a pendulous habit such as *Fuchsia* 'Swingtime'. Heavy formal designs including Versailles planters are perfect for geometric topiary – cones, spirals or mop-headed standards and because of their bold lines, sculpted specimens including New Zealand flax (Phormium), silver spear (Astelia) and Agapanthus look just right in modern architectural planters. Offsetting upright or columnar plants like flame-shaped conifers and combining them with a variety of lower growing elements makes for a more interesting display than going for the more traditional central placing. However, fountain shapes such as Cordyline do work best when positioned symmetrically in, for example, a classical urn.

Grassy foliage works well against galvanized metal

Bold architectural plants create a subtropical atmosphere

Make sure that the size of container is in proportion with the size of planting, avoiding top-heavy arrangements or planting that seems dwarfed by the container.

Texture

Maximize textural contrast when combining plants by using different sized and shaped leaves and flowers. Plants consisting of bold, solid shapes, for example tuberous begonia, look well complemented by diaphanous flowers like trailing lobelia or filigree foliage such as *Senecio cinerea* 'Silver Dust'. The glossy foliage of Bergenia contrasts pleasingly with furry textured lamb's ears (*Stachys byzantina*) and plants with large rounded shaped leaves look stunning with grassy or narrow, strap-like foliage. The texture of the pot is also influential – for example, a high sheen pot would suit matt or felted foliage whilst a rough finish, raw terracotta pot might enhance a plant with waxy or silvery metallic leaves.

Coleus leaves pick up the colour of terracotta

Colour

You can be dramatic or subtle with colour, choosing contrasting shades or those that blend. The artist's colour wheel provides a useful guide to combining colours. Ones taken from opposite sides – cool and hot – provide the most dramatic contrasts – for example, blue with orange, purple or magenta with yellow, and red with green.

The way in which you work with the colour of the pot can also have a large influence on the success of the scheme. Ceramic glazes now come in a surprising range of colours, including metallics like pewter and bronze. The latter looks particularly rich with brown grasses and sedges, maroon-purple heucheras and steely blue foliage plants like *Acaena* 'Blue Haze'. For a note of vibrancy, try adding burnt orange in the form of the daisy flowered *Arctotis* x *hybrida* 'Flame'.

Colour-coordinated schemes

The following recipes giving seasonal ideas for three different pots showing how the colour and finish of a container can be used to strengthen the overall scheme

TERRACOTTA (traditional)

Spring: Vivid blue grape hyacinth (*Muscari armeniacum*) or *Scilla siberica* with the dwarf daffodil *Narcissus* 'Jetfire' (yellow with orange centre) and gold variegated ivy
Summer: blue Scaevola; silver helichrysum; orange and yellow bicoloured *Lantana camara* and maroon purple *Cordyline australis* centrepiece
Autumn: Orange berries (*Solanum capsicastrum*); orange and lime green heather foliage (*Calluna vulgaris* cultivars); creamy-yellow marbled ivy
Winter: Mix of clear orange and deep purple violas and *Heuchera* 'Palace Purple'

GALVANIZED METAL

Spring: white *Tulip* 'Purissima'; white double daisies; green and white marbled ivy
Summer: metallic, silver-green *Astelia chathamica*; metallic silver-grey *Convolvulus cneorum* with white 'bindweed' flowers; finely cut silver leaved *Rhodanthemum hosmariense* with white daisies; trails of silvery-grey *Plechostachys sepyllifolia*
Autumn: white-tinged-pink mini cyclamen; white, pink and green ornamental kale; pale green-white *Carex* 'Frosted Curls'; pink and cream variegated trails of *Ajuga reptans* 'Burgundy Glow'
Winter: White berried *Gaultheria mucronata*; white *Erica carnea*; green, cream and white marbled Leucothoe (use ericaceous compost)

DEEP BLUE GLAZE

Spring: Bright creamy-yellow variegated *Vinca minor* 'Illumination'; blue polyanthus with a yellow eye; *Narcissus* 'Tête à Tête'
Summer: Cerise pink *Verbena* 'Tapien Series'; grey-green and cream variegated helichrysum; magenta osteospermum; *Tanacetum ptarmiciflorum* 'Silver Feather'
Autumn: Deep cerise Aster 'Jenny'; red-berried *Gaultheria procumbens*; green and gold ivy trails; gold-variegated *Artemisia vulgaris* 'Oriental Limelight'
Winter: creamy yellow-variegated *Euonymus fortunei* 'Blondy'; cream Viola 'Sorbet Series'; silvery-blue fluffy *Chamaecyparis pisifera* 'Boulevard'

Pick flower and foliage shades that complement one another

Seasonal Plantings

Container arrangements using colourful bedding and bulbs are an ideal way of introducing seasonal highlights to the garden and to ring the changes throughout the year.

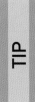
Spring

Many spring arrangements require forward planning, especially when using hardy bedding and bulbs that perform best if planted by early autumn of the previous

Plant bulbs in layers for successive colour

year. It is more interesting to overlay bulbs with winter and spring flowering plants and evergreens to avoid having pots of bare soil. Try planting bulbs at different depths to provide a succession of flowers from early to late spring, using varieties with relatively fine, unobtrusive foliage that dies away gracefully. Small, early flowering bulbs including varieties of *Crocus chrysanthus*, Scilla and *Iris reticulata* could be planted towards the surface with larger, later flowering bulbs that require deeper planting beneath – for example, dwarf daffodils and tulips.

Summer

There is a wealth of flower and foliage to choose from when planning summer containers. Tempting displays of bedding plants, tender perennials or patio plants in bud or flower often coming into the garden centres surprisingly early in spring. Most of these plants will be frost sensitive and cannot be put out permanently until after the last likely frost date for your area, so if you don't have space to grow them under cover, it is best to wait. In any case there is no rush, because invariably winter and spring bedding varieties such as pansies and polyanthus are putting on their best flowering displays from mid- to late spring.

Autumn

Though summer flowers may still be in full bloom well into autumn, they can look incongruous against the backdrop of the autumn garden and turning leaves. Some bedding only appears in the garden centres in autumn, including dwarf Michaelmas daisies; pot chrysanthemums; miniature cyclamen and the tender cape heaths, orange-berried winter cherries and ornamental peppers. Combine flowers and fruits with ivies and other hardy foliage plants, including the colourful ornamental kales and cabbages and shelter displays as much as possible to keep them unblemished by frost.

Winter

There will be continued supplies of hardy, weather-resistant pansies and violas right through autumn and into the first half of winter. In addition you can buy jewel-coloured hardy primroses and polyanthus as well as double daisies. But winter flowering bedding rarely has the same impact as summer and should be augmented with sparkling evergreen foliage plants. Try using strongly defined colour schemes to make displays more eye-catching.

Use liners to slot fresh displays into permanent troughs

Permanent Planting Ideas

Hard surfaces around the house and garden – including driveways – can be softened with large pots and planters containing plants for year-round interest. Such permanent arrangements may not be as eye-catching as seasonal displays because the focus is on foliage rather than flower, but they help to take away the starkness of walls and paving.

Ideal plants

Permanent displays should be low maintenance using easy-care plants that perhaps only need annual pruning or the occasional deadheading or clipping over. Because displays need to look good year round, the majority of plants will be evergreen (see the 'Evergreen' section of the A–Z, pages 132–51). Mix different leaf shapes and textures and incorporate plenty of variegated and coloured leaf types as well as flowering evergreens like the winter flowering heathers (*Erica carnea* varieties).

Avoid vigorous spreaders, as they will rapidly outgrow their containers and exhaust the soil. Instead choose smaller more compact-growing versions. A few deciduous shrubs with attractive foliage, coloured stems, berries or a long flowering season should also be mixed in along with perennials and bulbs to avoid displays appearing too static. Herbaceous plants must be compact and not require staking or frequent division – hostas are perfect candidates for pots where they often escape slug damage and look wonderful combined with ferns, ivies and bulbs for illuminating shady corners. Flowering perennials should also have a long season in bloom to avoid 'holes' in your displays.

Gardens without borders

In some garden spaces the soil is completely covered over. This means that all planting has to be in containers, including screening plants for creating privacy and climbers for covering bare walls, fencing and trellis. Introduce structure and a feeling of maturity by growing: small trees; columnar or conical conifers; topiary; bamboos and architectural grasses, together with taller shrubs. Mount heavy pots on castors so that you can ring the changes from time to time – for example, moving flowering plants or shrubs coming into autumn colour into a more prominent position.

On balconies and roof terraces, there may be weight restrictions, and so in addition to using lightweight

containers made from plastic and fibreglass resin, plant in soil-less media such as peat-substitute or coir-based composts. Use tough, drought and wind tolerant plants to screen and protect more vulnerable types in what is quite often a hostile, high-rise environment.

Alpines and succulents

Stone or stone-effect troughs make attractive additions to gravelled areas of the garden and can be planted up with alpines, including miniature shrubs, conifers and bulbs. Seek advice from an alpine specialist to obtain a range of suitably sized plants for a display that will last well beyond spring and early summer. Shallow bowls and traditional terracotta half pans could also be used to showcase a collection of houseleeks (Sempervirens) or other hardy evergreen succulents like sedums.

Gardens with lots of hard surfaces cry out for bright pots

Many drought-tolerant alpines are are perfect for pots

Preparing Pots & Containers

Good drainage and soil structure are foundations for strong healthy root growth. Picking the right compost and following some straightforward rules when preparing your pots will get plants off to a great start.

Compost selection

Most seasonal plantings including bedding and bulbs can be grown in peat-based multipurpose compost or a peat-free type such as coir or recycled compost. Mixtures that don't contain peat are more environmentally friendly, but the quality may vary so go for a good brand. Coir composts may be more difficult to keep evenly moist and the plants in them are best fed with fertilizers designed for coir. Some multi-purpose composts are now also available pre-mixed with a proportion of John Innes loam, creating better conditions for plants that require good drainage. More sophisticated mixtures are suitable for longer term planting, for example for shrubs, conifers, perennials, etc., and incorporate chipped bark and/or a proportion of loam to help retain the soil structure, prevent compaction and maintain adequate drainage. Many composts sold specifically for container work also now contain a wetting agent and moisture-retentive component to aid watering and help prevent the mix drying out too quickly. In addition, they may incorporate a controlled release fertilizer to last all season. The loam based John Innes No. 3 compost is used for long-term rather than seasonal planting and is ideal for drought tolerant

architectural plants like palms and yuccas. Avoid buying compost that has been stored outside and exposed to the elements for any length of time – rain saturated compost can start to break down and release substances that are harmful to plants.

Specialist mixtures

Multi-purpose and John Innes composts both contain lime. For acid loving plants, for example rhododendrons and azaleas, Pieris, Camellia and Skimmia, use lime-free or ericaceous compost. Alpines and succulents require a very free draining mix. If you can't buy one ready-prepared, combine a 50:50 mix of peat-based potting or multipurpose compost with John Innes No 3 and add a good quantity of coarse grit.

Easy feed compost

The soil-less multipurpose composts are designed for short term, seasonal plantings and therefore usually contain only a limited amount of fertilizer. After a few weeks plants will have used up available supplies and will require regular feeding. However,

Cover the holes in the base of the pot with crocks

one way to avoid this extra maintenance task is to incorporate slow-release fertilizer granules or powder in the container before planting, mixing in the specified amount thoroughly before putting the plant in the pot. The granules are affected by heat and moisture and release more nutrients when the plants are in active growth, providing a controlled supply throughout the growing season.

Preparing the pot

• Soak plants whose rootballs are not already thoroughly wetted. Fully immerse the pot or tray in a bucket of water and wait till the stream of escaping air bubbles has almost stopped. If the compost you are using is dry, turn it out into a wheelbarrow and mix some water with it.

• Ensure that the container has sufficient drainage holes – with plastic pots you may have to punch out the pre-marked holes in the base with a screwdriver and hammer, or for neater holes, drill through. Metal containers often come without any drainage but are usually thin enough to punch through several times with a hammer and nail. Wicker baskets may be pre-lined with plastic and these also need a drainage hole cutting to avoid problems with waterlogging.

• Cover holes with large pieces of broken clay pots. This is a process known as crocking, which is designed to prevent the holes from blocking with compost. You could also use flat stones or pieces of broken up polystyrene plant trays.

• Cover the crocks with a layer of gravel several centimetres (inches) deep. The larger the pot, the greater the depth of drainage required.

• If your compost does not contain a water-retaining agent, you can add gel crystals according to the manufacturer's instructions. These are best mixed with water beforehand. Stir in the gelatinous compound thoroughly to ensure even distribution.

Add gravel or broken polystyrene plant trays for extra drainage

Water retaining gel crystals can keep compost moist

Planting Pots & Containers

By following a few simple steps you can avoid many of the common pitfalls in planting and ensure that your creations look good from the start, perform well and are easier to maintain.

Step-by-step planting

With a relatively small planter like the one illustrated below, you won't need very much drainage, provided the holes in the base are well covered with crocks. Check the state of your compost before planting. If it is very dry, turn it out into a wheelbarrow or large container and mix some water with it. It should be just moist, not overly wet. Pour some compost into your planter, breaking up the large lumps as you go and firm down very lightly [A].

Try the largest plant for size. You may have to add or take away compost at this stage, because what you are aiming for is to leave a gap 6–10cm (2–3in) between the surface of the compost and the rim of the pot. This gap allows for watering and mulching the plant. Without it, when you come to water, it will bounce straight off the top of the compost and does not have the chance to soak in. Most plants should be planted no deeper than they were in their original containers, as this can cause the neck to rot. Also ensure that you do not bury leaves when you plant – gather them up in one hand whilst you work the compost around the neck of the plant [B].

Continue to add in plants, building up the composition to achieve a good balance of contrasting leaf and flower shapes and different plant habits – for example, upright and trailing – as well as a pleasing mix of colours. It is always a good idea to do a mock up of the planting on the ground before you start, so that you can check out how the plants might look together. Work in more compost to fill the gaps and firm gently. When using young plants in late spring and early summer, leave sufficient space between them to allow for growth in the coming weeks [C].

Water the planting thoroughly and leave to settle. Check the compost levels a little later on, as they may have gone down in places after watering [D].

A

B

C

D

PLANTING LARGE AND AWKWARD CONTAINERS

It can take a lot of compost to fill a large, deep container, and if you plan only to use bedding plants, for example, that root into just the top layer, you may be wasting money. Fill the bottom third to a half with broken up polystyrene plant trays, old bricks or rubble. Pour on coarse gravel or chippings until the surface is levelled and cover with fine plastic mesh to prevent soil washing down between the cracks. This method also ensures excellent drainage. Another solution, useful with a Greek pithoi or any container with a relatively narrow opening, is to fit a smaller pot inside the neck, hidden by the rim and if necessary supported on a column of bricks.

Planting a Trough

It can be a little more tricky to make troughs and windowboxes look good because there is not very much room from front to back to allow for creative planting. The trick is to stagger the plants in more of a zig-zag formation, so that they don't end up looking like they are all standing in a single line. For window boxes and wall-mounted troughs, you have the ideal opportunity to create a 'hanging gardens' look with trailing plants cascading down the wall in colourful, luxuriant curtains.

Step-by-step planting

Firstly ensure that the drainage holes of the trough are properly covered with crocks to prevent them from blocking up [A].

> **TIP**
>
> Pots of ivy sold in the house or bedding plant section of the garden centre usually contain numerous cuttings. These can be separated off and planted individually to grow on or to use in the sides of hanging baskets or simply split apart to create one long straight run of cuttings. This gives a good edge effect for the front of troughs or the rim of circular planters, and is far more economical than buying several separate pots.

Add some compost [B], but do not overfill the trough at this stage as the rootballs will take up a good deal of space once the plants have been set in position. If your compost doesn't contain a water retaining compound, consider mixing in gel crystals as narrow troughs, particularly more exposed, wall-mounted ones, tend to dry out quite quickly.

After having worked out your scheme beforehand so that you know roughly where each plant is to go, take one of the larger plants and try it for depth [C]. Adjust the level so that the surface of the root ball is 6–10 cm (2–3in) down from the rim of the trough. Put in the rest of the taller back row of plants leaving gaps at the front for lower growing flowers and foliage plants as well as trailers.

Plant the foreground of the trough. You can gently squeeze the rootballs into a different shape if it makes it easier to fit them into the available spaces [D]. Check that there are no gaps between the plants by feeding more compost into the cracks. Water thoroughly.

Removable plastic troughs are convenient for planting fixed windowboxes

23

Planting Hanging Baskets & Wall Pots

There are many different styles of wall planter and hanging basket. Those with solid sides including self-watering types are relatively straightforward to plant up but open mesh hanging baskets and manger-style planters are more tricky.

Planting a basket with moss

The traditional wire hanging basket allows for planting through the sides as well as in the top so that you can create some very imaginative displays.

Line the basket sides with plenty of moss

Before you begin planting, pre-soak sphagnum moss so that it is well saturated. Select a 36 or 42cm (14 or 16in) diameter basket (smaller sizes dry out too rapidly) and place in the top of a pot to steady it. Temporarily unclip one or two of the three or four chains and lay to one side. This just makes it a lot easier to plant otherwise you will always be having to lift the chains out of the centre of the basket.

Cut a dinner plate sized piece of thick polythene (an old compost bag is ideal) and place it black side down in the bottom of the basket.

Taking large handfuls of moss, tuck it under the edges of the plastic and continue to build a thick lining part way up the sides of the basket [A]. Fill the resulting 'nest' with compost. Ideally, pick a mixture designed for hanging baskets which contains moisture-retaining compounds and wetting agents that make it easier to rescue dried out compost. Alternatively, mix in pre-soaked water retaining gel crystals.

Using a combination of trailing, spreading or low, bushy plants, start to plant up the sides. If the rootball is small enough, pull it through the wire from the outside in [B]. With larger rootballs, gently feed the shoots through to the outside, leaving the roots resting well inside the basket on the compost surface. Pack the neck of the plant around with moss to prevent soil leaking out when watering.

Add more compost and moss then place more plants around the rim. Angle the plants or lay them on their sides so that the foliage is already beginning to trail over the edge [C].

Use a more substantial upright specimen in the centre [D] – one with large leaves and flowers would be ideal, for example, tuberous begonia or zonal pelargonium – to

The basket may be hung in position once acclimatized

A wick extends into the reservoir and draws moisture up

Solid baskets

Baskets with solid sides include plastic and self-watering types as well as plastic lined wicker baskets, which now come in a range of novel shapes, including the cornucopia and cone. These are simple to plant up, though rarely as luxuriant as open-sided baskets which allow a wider variety of plants to be used.

Large solid baskets do have the advantage of not drying out as quickly, especially ones containing a self-watering reservoir. These have a base covered with capillary matting below the compost and plants, and a wick that extends from that and dips into the reservoir. There are seep holes at the top of the reservoir so that excess water can drain away and more sophisticated models usually have a watering tube which directs water straight into the compartment. If you follow the manufacturer's instructions, once a good root system has established, you should be able to leave the basket unattended for a couple of days – a boon if you are frequently away from home.

provide a solid contrast to the more diaphanous flowers and foliage.

Fill in remaining gaps with compost and mulch with a thick layer of moss giving the water a chance to soak in to prevent soil erosion. Take care not to smother drought tolerant succulents or they may rot off.

Water thoroughly and stand baskets in the top of a bucket to allow them to acclimatize in a sheltered shady spot for around ten to fourteen days. This enables them to build a sufficiently strong root system to withstand the water loss caused by exposure to wind, strong sunlight and heat and to recover from any damage.

A similar technique is used to plant up manger style baskets but you need to cut a piece of plastic to form a lip or small reservoir that folds part of the way up the front of the planter and then continues up the back to prevent moisture soaking into the wall.

Alternatives to moss

Fresh moss is sometimes difficult to get hold of and there are environmental concerns about its use. Alternatives include green-dyed wool waste or coir fibre and black polythene lining with cross-shaped holes cut for planting. You can also get prefabricated soft wool or coir liners with pre-cut holes. For an attractive natural looking winter lining, use conifer hedge clippings. Take pieces about 20cm (8in) long and overlap them thickly. Place a dinner plate sized piece of plastic on top to form a mini reservoir. The clippings stay green right through the season.

Permanent baskets enable the installation of full-time watering devices

Watering

When plants run short of water they won't grow or flower as well. Don't allow the compost to completely dry out as it can be difficult to re-wet and by this time some of the plants may be beyond help. Check pots, troughs and baskets daily from spring to mid autumn and water when the surface has become dry. Fill the space between the compost surface and rim of the pot with water so that it seeps through gradually and moistens the compost to its full depth. Baskets and small pots may need watering twice a day during hot, dry, summer weather.

Cutting down on watering

Moisture loss is one of the biggest problems to manage in container gardening and the most labour intensive aspect, but there are plenty of things you can do to cut down on watering and make life easier.

- Select large containers which will hold a greater volume of soil
- Use moisture-retentive compost or add a water retaining gel at planting time
- Mulch to slow evaporation from the compost surface
- Plant in non porous containers, for example glazed ceramic, plastic or metal, and use self-watering plastic hanging baskets and troughs
- Soak new terracotta before use or line pots with plastic sheeting – don't cover up drainage holes
- If you know you won't be able to water regularly, plant with a large proportion of drought resistant varieties.

DROUGHT RESISTANT PLANTS

The following list includes some of the best flowering and foliage plants for drought tolerance and recovery from wilting after missed waterings

- Agave (century plant)
- Artemisia (silver leaf varieties)
- *Begonia semperflorens* (fibrous-rooted begonias)
- *Bidens ferulifolia*
- Dorothenanthus (ice plant)
- Echeveria
- Felicia (kingfisher daisy)
- Gazania
- Hedera (ivy)
- *Helichrysum petiolare*
- Juniperus (juniper)
- Lavandula (lavender)
- *Lotus berthelotii* (parrot's beak)
- Pelargonium (geranium)
- *Plecostachys serpyllifolia*
- *Plectranthus madagascariensis* (variegated mint leaf)
- Portulaca
- *Salvia farinacea*
- Sedum
- Sempervirens (houseleek)
- *Senecio cineraria* (cineraria)

Easy watering

Group containers together so that you can water them all together. In summer, saucers placed underneath pots can catch drainage water giving it more time to be absorbed by thirsty plants. Remove at the end of summer, as otherwise plants could become waterlogged. When you have a lot of containers, consider attaching a hosepipe to an outside tap and use a spray gun attachment to give a soft spray that will not erode the compost.

Overhead watering

Don't struggle with a heavy watering can. A 2 litre (4 pint) plastic water bottle delivers about the right amount of water for a 36cm (14in) basket and is much easier to lift. A long lance attachment on a hosepipe is another efficient method. Alternatively, fit a spring-loaded pulley device so that you can bring baskets down to your level with ease.

A trickle watering system works well with multiple containers

Types of Mulch

Covering the surface of compost after planting conserves moisture and provides a decorative finish. This is known as mulching. It also helps to prevent erosion of the compost from the root system and sharp or gritty mulches may also deter slugs and snails. The only downside is that you have to scrape away some of the mulch if you want to check how dry the compost is beneath. Depending on the size of pot, use a 2–8cm (1–3in) layer of your chosen mulch spreading it over the surface of moist compost. Avoid piling it up round the necks of plants.

Types of mulch

Different types of mulch suit different planting and container styles. Here are some good combinations:

Chipped bark ideal for topdressing woodland style plantings e.g. ferns and hostas in a wooden barrel or surrounding a specimen rhododendron or pieris.

Iridescent glass marbles are highly decorative

Granite chips make an elegant container mulch

Slate shards contrast well with aluminium pots

Cocoa shells These smell strongly of chocolate when first applied. Similar to bark chips in appearance and use, they seem to be a good deterrent for slugs and snails.

Gravel Available in different grades and colours so it should be easy to find one to match your container. Fine golden gravel works well in classical terracotta and stone reproduction containers planted with Mediterranean style plants, especially silver and blue-green leaved types. Some plants are very sensitive to excess moisture and a fine grit or gravel mulch can improve the growing conditions of drought loving herbs like thyme as well as many other alpines and succulents.

Slate shards This material comes in several shades including plum, charcoal and green and provides an excellent mulch for contemporary style containers especially metallic, modern ceramic or reconstituted stone planters. It is a perfect foil for architectural plants and grasses.

Pebbles Rounded pebbles and cobbles come in different shades and a variety of sizes to match the scale of the container and its planting. They work well in hi-tech environments, in eastern style settings as well as seaside plots. The rounded shapes complement grasses and plants with spiky or long strap-shaped foliage.

Glass and acrylic aggregates This is the fastest growing area of decorative mulching. You can now get a very wide range of colours and grades with shades to match or to contrast with the brightly coloured glazes of ceramic pots. The mulches can also reflect the colours used in your planting. Coloured glass chips and other fine aggregates work well with metallic and modern glazed ceramic pots.

Feeding

Most potting and multipurpose composts contain a limited amount of fertilizer sufficient to last for about the first eight weeks after planting, by which time bedding and patio plants in particular may have begun to struggle. Tell tale signs include slowing down of growth, leaves and flowers getting smaller and foliage becoming pale or discoloured.

Plant food basics

Plants need nitrogen (whose chemical symbol is N) for leaf and shoot growth; phosphorous (P) for healthy root growth and potassium (K) to support flower and fruit production. Different fertilizer products have these elements in varying proportions written as the N:P:K ratio. Products with a high value for nitrogen are best for foliage plants, whilst those with relatively high levels of potassium favour the production of flowers.

Getting the balance right

If your planters are producing all leaf and no flower, switch to a fertilizer with a higher proportion of potassium. If possible, look for products that also contain trace elements – e.g. manganese, zinc, boron and copper – it's a bit like giving plants a good multivitamin tablet! As well as general, all-purpose fertilisers there are specialist products better suited to certain types of planting e.g. ones for hanging baskets and ericaceous plants. When a plant has suffered some form of stress, such as being re-potted, or is suffering

from a specific nutrient deficiency, try a foliar feed tonic, for example seaweed-based or sequestered iron. This is sprayed directly onto the leaves from where it is readily absorbed.

How to feed

Follow the manufacturer's directions carefully and do not overfeed, as this can lead to all kinds of pest and disease problems. The compost must already be moist before applying feeds or it could scorch and damage the root system. The regular application of dilute liquid feeds often gives the best results. Here, powdered or concentrated liquid plant food is dissolved or diluted in water and applied directly to the roots, typically once a week though you can also use a very diluted rate every time you water. Low-maintenance options include:

• Granular, slow-release fertilizer mixed into the compost prior to planting. The rate at which the feed is dispersed is governed by temperature and moisture and so it keeps pace with the demands of the growing plants.

Measure carefully – don't overfeed!

• Organic fertilizer applied as a top dressing two or three times a year and watered in. For example, the general purpose 'Fish, Blood and Bone' which is suitable for long term plantings.
• Fertilizer blocks that operate within an automatic watering system and give the same diluted dose to each container.
• Feeders that fit onto the end of the hosepipe and automatically dilute a specifically named soluble plant food.
• Fertilizer spikes or pellets that push into the compost providing a controlled release of feed through the season.

Foliar feeds are administered with water

General Care

In addition to routine watering and feeding, there are a number of regular jobs as well as less frequent seasonal tasks that need taking care of.

Maintaining displays

Clearing away spent blooms, yellowing leaves, dead plants and other debris helps to reduce disease problems and keeps displays in top condition. Remove fading heads with thumb and forefinger, a task known as deadheading, to prevent energy being diverted away from flower into seed production. Use scissors or secateurs for tough stems.

Remove fading blooms with thumb and forefinger

Deadheading tips

- Take care with plants like gazania, dahlia and verbena, where the green seedpods resemble buds. Also, plants like pansies, whose newly opening blooms can look like fading heads.
- Violas and pansies hide their seedpods low amongst the foliage. Deadhead just as the flowers are going over, but before they've dropped their petals. Remove the whole flower stem to avoid unsightly brown stalks.
- In wet weather, the spent blooms of busy Lizzie (Impatiens) stick to the plant's foliage. Pick off before they dry and turn brown.
- Tuberous rooted begonias have a central double male bloom surmounted by two winged female flowers. Nip off the insignificant female buds to encourage more showy males.
- Use nail scissors to snip out dead patches in flowerheads consisting of many smaller blooms, e.g. Ageratum, sweet white alyssum, Heliotrope and Pelargonium.

Keeping a balance

Some plants are a lot more vigorous than others and in a mixed display can smother their neighbours. Trim back plants like *Helichrysum petiolare*, *Bidens ferulifolia* and *Verbena* 'Homestead Purple'. Trailing plants such as *Glechoma hederacea*, ivy and Surfinia petunias may also grow so long that they throw containers out of balance. Cut back as necessary. Petunias and pansies sometimes produce long stems devoid of leaves and flowers. To encourage them to branch and produce fresh flowers, cut back growth by about half at mid-season and water and feed well.

Re-cycling plants

When dismantling seasonal bedding ready for autumn and winter plantings, discard annuals but consider overwintering tender perennials either as cuttings or stock plants if you have frost-free storage space. Salvage ivies and other evergreens including ground cover plants e.g. *Lamium* 'White Nancy'; shrubs e.g. *Euonymus fortunei* varieties and lavender as well as alpines, e.g. *Rhodanthemum hosmariense*. These plants will have put on a lot of growth during the summer and will add maturity to autumn and winter displays.

Winter displays

Move pots of winter bedding close to house walls to minimize frost damage and encourage flowering. During frosty weather, bring hanging baskets into a greenhouse or porch. Ensure adequate drainage by standing pots on 'feet'. Empty out terracotta that is not guaranteed frost proof and store under cover.

Move hanging baskets under glass when it is frosty

Checking for pests and diseases

The easiest way to keep on top of problems with pests and diseases is to check over plants whenever you are carrying out deadheading or watering. For example, dry compost and overheated growing conditions can promote powdery mildew in summer and early detection and action could save the display. Some pests are hard to spot and you might need to look underneath leaves and at the soil surface to discover camouflaged caterpillars, slugs and the like. Slugs and snails are nocturnal feeders, so the easiest approach is to go out with a torch at night when you will spot them out in the open. During the day, search for them in their roosting sites.

Sap sucking insects like aphids, whitefly, scale insect and red spider mite may be controlled using systemic insecticides which are taken up through the plant's roots. Those watered directly onto the compost are less likely to harm bees and other pollinating insects. If you don't have much time, you can now buy products that last the whole season with a single application.

Sometimes the problem is below soil level. Sudden collapse of plants or discolouration and unhealthy pallor of the leaves of evergreens such as ivies, could indicate that the roots are being eaten away by vine weevil grubs (see page 155). Carefully lift the affected plants out of the pot to examine the roots. If grubs are discovered, empty the whole pot, gently shake off loose compost from each plant, as a precaution rinsing the roots in a bucket of water and replant in fresh compost. Use a soil insecticide to safeguard against further infestation.

Seek out slug and snail roosting sites

Overwatering

It may seem unlikely, but it is possible to give container grown plants too much water – especially those drought tolerant types that prefer free-draining conditions! Checking that the soil surface is dry before watering is a good test. It is a mistake for most plants to keep the compost constantly moist or wet or to stand pots for

Check rootballs for vine weevil grubs

Wheeled platforms aid drainage as well as making it easy to move pots around

prolonged periods in saucers of water. This can cause the roots to rot through lack of oxygen. Plants like fuchsias show signs of overwatering in their leaves which drop prematurely after developing yellow patches. If the compost has a green film over the surface then you are probably keeping it too moist. Providing adequate drainage in the base of the pot at planting time and raising the pot on 'feet' should ensure that excess moisture drains away freely. Another alternative to feet would be a wheeled pot stand, allowing you to move the container around the patio with ease, so that a plant does not get unduly drenched by heavy rain.

Replenishing seasonal displays

At various times through the year, you may find one or two plants in a scheme die out or become unattractive. If this happens, carefully dig out the affected plant and replace it with a reasonably vigorous substitute that will grow to fill the gap quite quickly. Alternatively, if space allows, use a larger specimen sized plant that's already in flower. Use an unrelated plant rather than trying to make a direct swap as there may be something in the compost or to do with the growing conditions that would adversely affect that specific variety. In spring, pots of dwarf bulbs bought in bud can easily be slotted in to fill any gaps.

End of season jobs

Certain tender plants can be salvaged for use the following year provided you take action before the first frosts. These include pelargoniums, fuchsias, Helichrysum, Lotus, Bidens, Argyranthemum, and Osteospermum. If you have frost free greenhouse facilities, you can pot up the plants after trimming back some of the top growth and bring them under cover. These plants can be used as large specimens for the next summer season or as stock plants to provide lots of cuttings in the spring. Use seed compost which contains only a very small amount of fertiliser for potting as this will discourage new, vulnerable growth. Keep compost on the dry side. Some plants need very little heat provided they are kept almost completely dry through the winter. Pelargoniums for example will be perfectly happy on the windowledge of an unheated bedroom. Fuchsias don't need light once they have dropped their leaves and could be overwintered in a frost-free windowless garage. Cover up with bubble wrap insulation to provide rootballs with added protection against cold. There is no need to water until new growth begins to

appear on shoots in spring. When you have very little space, it may be easier to root little pots of tender perennial cuttings in late summer and early autumn. Keep these in virtual suspended animation by keeping them cool with very little water until they are potted up in the spring and started into growth. Lift tender tubers, bulbs, corms and rootstocks, for example Canna and Dahlia after cutting down top growth. Store frost free in deep trays or pots of barely moist peat or sand and check occasionally through the winter for signs of pest or disease.

Move tender plants back into the greenhouse in autumn before the frosts

Maintaining Permanent Plantings

Plantings of trees, shrubs, perennials and bulbs should be relatively easy to care for, but there are a few techniques that benefit plants being grown in containers from one year to the next.

Topdressing

Long term watering causes the surface layer of compost to be eroded exposing vulnerable roots. Top up the levels every now and then. Use topdressing as an annual tonic for a plant that has grown in the same pot for some time. To do this, simply scrape away loose surface compost and replace it with new soil mixed with some slow release fertilizer. Water well.

Potting on

When a plant gets too big for its pot and looks unbalanced, particularly if the compost is full of roots, it's time to pot on. Tell tale signs that a plant is root bound are when excessive amounts of water are needed to prevent wilting and roots are coming out of the drainage holes. If the roots have adhered to the inside of

the container, turn the pot on its side and knock it several times as you rotate it, using cushioning material to prevent damage. Avoid pulling the plant out by its neck! Use a pot only one to two sizes larger since an excess of cold, wet, airless compost can cause the new roots to rot off. Put drainage and some fresh compost in the base, try the plant for depth and then fill in the sides. Water thoroughly.

Re-potting

To keep a plant in its original pot and to control its size, you need to rejuvenate it every few years otherwise the plant slows down and begins to decline. Remove the plant and shake and tease off any loose soil from around the roots. Trim back some of the old woody roots or cut off 3–6 cm (one to two inches) of dense, matted roots with a sharp knife or machete if the root ball is very congested. Re-pot using fresh compost. Water and keep in a sheltered shady spot for a couple of weeks to allow for recovery.

Winter care

Container plants are vulnerable to frost damage because the root system is less well insulated above ground. If the root ball freezes, evergreens and conifers can suffer scorching or death when exposed to strong winds because the moisture stripped from the leaves

Plant pockets of bulbs to brighten up permanent containers using a lining of plastic mesh. This allows the fading bulbs to be lifted out in one piece after flowering so that something else can be planted in their place. Alternatively, sink pots of bulbs into containers just as they are coming into bud.

cannot be replaced. Below are some suggestions for helping vulnerable plants to survive the winter unscathed.

- Bring house or conservatory plants, that have spent the summer outdoors, under cover before night temperatures drop close to freezing.
- Move evergreens and borderline hardy specimens into the relatively warm, protected zone close to the house.
- Protect pots too heavy or awkward to move, wrapping them where they stand with thick layers of insulation e.g. hessian sacking packed with straw or bubble wrap/ greenhouse insulation.
- Apply plumber's foam pipe insulation to the stems of standard plants like bay and box.
- Wrap the top growth of vulnerable evergreens with horticultural fleece, which is breathable, lets in light and protects from wind and cold.
- With the exception of shade loving woodland plants that need to be kept evenly watered, maintain compost on the dry side for other evergreens, succulents and silverlings – it is the combination of overly wet compost plus the cold that kills many plants.
- Ensure good drainage for all winter planters through the use of pot feet or pot stands.

Pruning

Just as deciduous and evergreen shrubs grown in the border need pruning, so too do ones grown in containers. For compact, slow growing evergreens, this may simply be a case of trimming off errant shoots to bring the plant back into balance.

- Tackle evergreens between late spring and late summer as delayed pruning can encourage regrowth at a time when it will be vulnerable to frost damage.
- To keep small-leaved, domed hebes growing neatly, use a pair of small hand shears or pruners to clip over annually.
- Clip or trim potted lavenders and heathers after the flowers have faded, removing a couple of centimetres (1in) of new shoot growth to encourage branching further back.
- Ground covering conifers such as junipers may start to grow larger than intended but will take judicious pruning. Trim so that the cut end is hidden by foliage.
- Deciduous shrubs grown for their spring or early summer flowers are pruned immediately after flowering.
- Late summer and autumn flowering shrubs including many clematis are pruned in early spring.
- Plants producing autumn berries e.g. cotoneaster, are all the more attractive if excess growth is cut back to reveal the fruiting stems.
- Cut back hard *Alchemilla mollis* and *Lamium maculatum* cultivars in mid-summer, to encourage a fresh crop of attractive foliage and further flushes of flower.

Water and treat the plant with liquid feed to promote speedy re-growth.

Prune evergreen shrubs between late spring and late summer

Topiary Effects

The decorative effect of plants can be enhanced by training or clipping to a more formal shape. Use potted topiary to add emphasis to the garden's design, for example, placing a matching pair of standards to strengthen a doorway or a row of clipped globes to create a pleasing rhythm along the edge of a path.

Green sculpture

Many small leaved evergreens can be clipped into simple geometric forms, such as balls, domes and cones. You only need a few simple tools – secateurs, small or ladies hand shears or one-handed 'sheep' shears. Box (*Buxus sempervirens*), is a classic topiary plant that's sufficiently fine textured and dense to allow for more complex forms including spirals. Also consider:

Euonymus fortunei 'Emerald Gaiety' and 'Emerald 'n' Gold'
Hebe, e.g. *H. topiaria*; *H. rakaiensis*
Ilex aquifolium
Ilex crenata
Laurus nobilis
Ligustrum delavayanum
Myrtus communis
Osmanthus heterophylla (forms)
Osmanthus x *burkwoodii*
Pittosporum tenuifolium (forms)
Pittosporum tobira
Santolina chamaecyparissus
Viburnum tinus

Clipped bay standards

Use secateurs to shape larger leaved plants like bay, holly and viburnum. To clip balls or domes, stand above the plant and turn the shears upside down so that the shape of the blade follows the curve. Keep walking round and standing back to view. Trim flowering and berrying shrubs after the display and avoid shaping evergreens between the end of summer and mid to late spring otherwise the soft re-growth might not withstand frosts.

Training standards

Flowering and foliage standards have a clean, vertical 'leg' topped with a shaped head. Start with a young plant e.g. a rooted cutting and prune away side branches to reveal a single straight stem. Support with a cane to keep it vertical. Allow the shoot to continue growing to just below the desired height then pinch out the tip. This causes a proliferation of shoots at the top which can then be shaped. Initially, leave intact any foliage that grows directly off the main stem as this helps to feed and strengthen the wood. Clean up the stem when training is nearing completion. Many woody-based herbs and tender perennials can be used but you need to get the proportions right, for example standards of lavender or heliotrope would only have short stems, whilst the more vigorous bay or holly standards could have a stem measuring a metre (3ft) or more. For flowering standards also consider marguerite, rosemary, abutilon, fuchsia, *Hydrangea paniculata* and Lantana.

Mark the line of the spiral with string or ribbon to guide your first cut

> **TIP**
>
> To get more speedy results with plants such as box, for example when creating an animal shape like a chicken, use several plants together in the same pot. Make sure they are the same clone otherwise differences in foliage and hardiness may become apparent. Clip as a single plant.

Decorative supports

Topiary frames are often very decorative and allow the finished shape to be instantly appreciated. Place over the plant and snip off branches that grow through. Avoid using very small frames that have to remain in position through the life of the plant as these soon become congested with foliage. Grow climbers like clematis and sweet peas over supports ranging from formal metalwork or trellis obelisks to rustic willow wigwams.

Ivy topiary

Varieties of plain green English ivy (*Hedera helix*) may be grown over wire topiary frames to create the effect of traditional topiary in a much shorter time. Avoid variegated cultivars which fail to create a well-defined

Annual climbers like *Ipomoea lobata* can be trained up a wicker frame

Clipped box cones and standards look good singly or in pairs flanking entrances

profile. Simply plant around the rim of the pot and twine the long trails around the wires of the frame. The leaves hold the stems in place. Once completely covered, snip off any unwanted shoots.

For this technique, use ivy with small foliage and short joints (length of stem between the leaves). Plants like 'Duckfoot' and 'Très Coupé' remain compact and give a finish closer to that of clipped box or yew than more vigorous types that rapidly outgrow the frame and begin to look threadbare. Regularly treat with liquid foliar feed that is relatively high in nitrogen to promote leafy growth.

Flowering Plants

What would our pots and baskets be like without flowers? It doesn't bear thinking about... From late winter, bulbs begin to emerge among the hardy bedding plants, their delicate blooms seemingly impervious to the cold. By summer, there's a veritable extravaganza of flower – with old favourites often mixed in with the latest, trendiest plants.

Then, just as the season seems to be drawing to a close, the garden centres offer a stunning, if ephemeral, array of autumn gems. Thinking ahead at this time, planting up containers with bulbs overlaid with winter bedding – violas, pansies, primroses – virtually guarantees colour in sheltered corners of the house and garden right through the coldest months.

Modern varieties of bedding plants and tender perennials – the latter often sold under the umbrella heading of patio plants – often have improved flowering performance and uniformity, better weather resistance, and also come in a wider range of shades. Increasingly, plants are also being persuaded to grow in a novel way, too – for example, dwarf sweet peas that need no support and violas and snapdragons that trail over the sides of hanging baskets.

Compact herbaceous perennials and alpines like thrift (Armeria) and *Scabious* 'Butterfly Blue' are also frequently seen in mixed container plantings. In bedding and tender perennials, you now have a fantastic selection – anything from vivid, larger-than-life blooms with more than a hint of exotica, to delicate, old-fashioned looking flowers that come in soft pastels or 'antique' blends. The latter would be perfect for a period property, but the choice of plants and the availability of single colours makes colour scheming and styling to suit your individual taste so much easier. But let's not forget fragrance, which has sadly been overlooked in the past. Perfume is now a significant factor in whether we choose to grow a plant.

Abutilon

At one time viewed solely as plants for the conservatory, these tender shrubs with their exotic-looking blooms make dramatic additions to patio displays. There are two distinct forms. The main group of half-hybrids are bushy plants that can be trained into woody-stemmed standards.

The flowers, produced over a long period, are reminiscent of hibiscus. There are many colours to choose from, but one of the best is the primrose-yellow 'Canary Bird'. These eventually grow much larger than indicated in the table but can be pruned to keep to a manageable size.

Try combining potted abutilons with bold foliage plants such as cannas, *Cordyline australis* and brightly coloured phormiums and add a Riviera feel to your terrace. 'Cannington Carol' is a dwarf hybrid suitable for baskets with bright red blooms and yellow spotted leaves and plants in the Bella Series are also dwarf and compact with large, waxy blooms. *Abutilon pictum* 'Thompsonii' adds a lush, tropical note, with its large, maple-like, yellow-blotched leaves.

In the second group are the moderately hardy *A. megapotamicum* (a red and yellow bicolour) and the peachy flowered cultivar 'Kentish Belle'. Both have an elegant, lax habit and are best trained over a frame or against a warm wall. Their pendulous flowers are tubular with protruding stamens and the foliage is slender and tapering. There are variegated forms of both. Watch for whitefly, red spider mite and scale. Use compost with a high proportion of loam. Insulate plants left outside for winter.

Abutilon megapotamicum

	SPRING	SUMMER	AUTUMN	WINTER	height (cm)	spread (cm)	min. temp °C	moisture	sun/shade	colour	
Abutilon 'Bella Series'		● ● ● ● ●			45	30	1°	💧	☼	▦	Dwarf variety
Abutilon 'Canary Bird'		● ● ● ● ●			90	60	1°	💧	☼	▢	Glossy foliage
Abutilon 'Cannington Carol'		● ● ● ● ●			45	45	1°	💧	☼	▩	Dwarf. Yellow mottled leaves
Abutilon 'Kentish Belle'		● ● ● ● ●			150	150	-5°	💧	☼	▥	Wall shrub. Dark purple stems
Abutilon megapotamicum		● ● ● ● ● ● ●			150	150	-5°	💧	☼	▤	Wall shrub. Semi-evergreen
Abutilon pictum 'Thompsonii'		● ● ● ● ● ● ●			90	60	1°	💧	☼	▦	Yellow blotched leaves

✂ *planting*   ❋ *flower*   💧 *well drained*   ☼ *sunny*

Ageratum
Flossflower

These low-growing half-hardy bedding plants are a useful source of soft blues and purples though shades of pink and white as well as mixtures are available. The fluffy heads are composed of tightly packed flowers forming a posy effect.

Container gardeners may find the rather stiff, low growing and uniform habit of ageratums a challenge when putting together schemes. These plants are best used as foreground or edging, especially in formal trough and windowbox arrangements.

Ageratums work best in pastel schemes, combining well with plants having a bushy or upright structure, especially those with well-defined flower shapes like petunias, fuchsias and tobacco plants. The range of blue-flowered ageratums has been expanded and now includes pale blues like 'Adriatic' to deep blues such as 'Atlantic Plus'. 'Pacific' is just one of a range of attractive purple-violet varieties. The widely sold 'Blue Danube' is known for its free flowering qualities and the new compact Hawaii Series offers a range of pretty pastel shades. This series is best used on its own and would look beautiful in a large deep blue or purple glazed bowl.

Wet weather and overhead watering can cause flowers to rot. Darker shades hide the brown patches caused by fading flowers more readily, but you can snip out unsightly bits and deadhead with nail scissors to maintain displays and encourage further flowering.

These plants are good in pastel arrangements as a foreground or edging for more well-defined flower shapes such as Petunia, Fuchsia and tobacco plant (Nicotiana). Overwatering causes foot rot.

Ageratum 'Blue Danube'

	SPRING	SUMMER	AUTUMN	WINTER	height (cm)	spread (cm)	min. temp °C	moisture	sun/shade	colour	
Ageratum houstonianum 'Adriatic'					20	20	1°				Early flowering
A. h. 'Atlantic Plus'					20	20	1°				Improved form
A. h. 'Blue Danube'					20	20	1°				Abundant flowers, compact
A. h. 'Blue Mink'					30	30	1°				More open habit. Strong
A.h. 'Hawaii Series'					15	15	1°				Long flowering period
A. h. 'Pacific'					20	20	1°				Deeper colour hides deadheads

planting · flower · well drained · moist · wet

Alonsoa
Mask flower

The mask flower is a relative of Nemesia, snapdragon and Diascia, with hot coloured blooms having a similar shape and habit to the latter.

Bushy, spreading forms of this half-hardy perennial are well suited to planting on the edge of a large pot or basket. Try *A. warscewiczii*, *A. meridionalis* 'Firestone Jewels Series' and for soft single colours, *A. m.* 'Salmon Beauty' and *A. warscewiczii* 'Peachy-keen'. Best combined with cool blues, and white, mask flowers would work well with white variegated *Felicia amelloides* or *Salvia* 'Strata'. Watch for aphids.

Alonsoa warscewiczii

	SPRING	SUMMER	AUTUMN	WINTER	height (cm)	spread (cm)	min. temp °C	moisture	sun/shade	colour	
A. meridionalis 'Firestone Jewels Series'		●●●	●●		30	30	1°	💧	☀	▨	Hot colours predominate
A. m. 'Salmon Beauty'		●●●	●●		60	30	1°	💧	☀	▢	Light salmon pink
A. warscewiczii		●●●	●●		60	30	1°	💧	☀	■	Good for baskets
A. w. 'Peachy-keen'		●●●	●●		60	30	1°	💧	☀	▢	Best mixed with other trailers

Antirrhinum
Snapdragon

Antirrhinum majus cultivar

The familiar snapdragon has undergone many changes over the years, with more and more dwarf, compact strains being developed that are suitable for pot work.

A. majus 'Magic Carpet Series' and the rust resistant strains 'Sweetheart' and 'Tahiti' are especially good for containers. There are also a number of 'trailing' snapdragons that make unusual additions to hanging baskets. Though snapdragons are short-lived perennials, treat as half-hardy annuals and discard plants at the end of the season to reduce disease problems.

	SPRING	SUMMER	AUTUMN	WINTER	height (cm)	spread (cm)	min. temp °C	moisture	sun/shade	colour	
Antirrhinum majus Magic Carpet Series		●●●	●●		15	22.5	0°	💧	☀	+	Low, spreading – good for baskets
A. m. Sweetheart Series		●●●	●●		30	22.5	0°	💧	☀	+	Double flowers; rust resistant
A. m. Tahiti Series		●●●	●●		20	20	0°	💧	☀	+	Rust resistant
A. Chinese Lanterns		●●●	●●		30	25	0°	💧	☀	+	Ideal for baskets grow from seed
A. Lampion Series		●●●	●●		30	25	0°	💧	☀	+	Cascading habit
A. Luminaire Series		●●●	●●		30	25	0°	💧	☀	+	Cascading habit

☀ *sunny* ◑ *semi-shady* ● *shady* | + *many colours*

Argyranthemum

Marguerite

These tender perennials or sub-shrubs have one of the longest flowering periods of any patio plant and thrive in pots of loam-based compost. Different flower forms and colours are available, but the single white daisies of *Argyranthemum frutescens* and the superior *A. foeniculaceum*, whose larger blooms are set against blue-grey, finely cut foliage, have a simple purity and elegance.

Marguerites look best grown singly in pots. For smaller containers, use dwarf types such as the pink, double flowered 'Summer Melody', single 'Petite Pink', pure white 'Snow Storm' or yellow 'Butterfly. More vigorous, tall-growing types can be trained into standards – for example, the single yellow 'Jamaica Primrose' or for a short, compact alternative, 'Cornish Gold'.

The anemone centred 'Vancouver' is another excellent candidate for training, its sugar pink flowers fading to very pale flesh pink over time, producing an attractive mix.

Argyranthemum 'Butterfly'

Argyranthemum 'Petite Pink'

'Chelsea Girl' also looks well trained on a leg, making a show of its blue, thread-like foliage but the white flowers are sparse.

Deadheading keeps plants looking neat and encourages continued flowering throughout summer and autumn. Use scissors or secateurs for deadheading, as the stems of argyranthemums are quite tough. Alternatively, after each main flush of flowers, clip over lightly with small shears removing the faded blooms and creating a more formal rounded or domed profile. Watch for leaf minor. Otherwise, pests and diseases are not really a problem.

	SPRING	SUMMER	AUTUMN	WINTER	height (cm)	spread (cm)	min. temp °C	moisture	sun/shade	colour	
Argyranthemum 'Butterfly'	planting	flower	flower		45	35	1°	well drained	sun		Compact form
A. 'Cornish Gold'	planting	flower	flower		60	60	1°	well drained	sun		Compact form
A. foeniculaceum	planting	flower	flower		60	90	1°	well drained	sun		'Royal Haze' has blue-grey leaves
A. frutescens	planting	flower	flower		70	90	1°	well drained	sun		Robust, free-flowering
A. gracile 'Chelsea Girl'	planting	flower	flower		60	60	1°	well drained	sun		Thread-like leaves
A. 'Jamaica Primrose'	planting	flower	flower		100	100	1°	well drained	sun		Superseded by 'Cornish Gold'
A. 'Petite Pink'	planting	flower	flower		30	30	1°	well drained	sun		Dwarf, grey-green foliage
A. 'Snow Storm'	planting	flower	flower		30	30	1°	well drained	sun		Dwarf
A. 'Summer Melody'	planting	flower	flower		60	60	1°	well drained	sun		Dwarf, double flowers
A. 'Vancouver'	planting	flower	flower		90	90	1°	well drained	sun		Anemone-centred flowers

planting   *flower*   *well drained*   *moist*   *wet*

Armeria

Though traditionally plants for the rock garden, these hardy, drought tolerant alpines flowering between late spring and summer make attractive additions for permanent container gardens, and not just alpine troughs.

Armeria maritima

With their drumstick heads held singly over hummocks of narrow evergreen foliage, armeria have quite a contemporary look, especially when planted singly and mulched with slate shards. Most have rich pink blooms, but there is a white flowered form, *Armeria maritima* 'Alba'. Named varieties such as 'Dusseldorfer Stolz' are usually selected for larger or more vividly coloured blooms. 'Vindictive' has an unusually long flowering period, from late spring to mid-summer. Deadhead to encourage sporadic repeat flowering after the main flush.

	SPRING	SUMMER	AUTUMN	WINTER	height (cm)	spread (cm)	min. temp °C	moisture	sun/shade	colour	
Armeria maritima		● ●			20	30	-15°	◊◊	☼	▢	Wind tolerant evergreen
A. m. 'Alba'		● ●			20	30	-15°	◊◊	☼	▢	White form of species
A. m. 'Düsseldorfer Stolz'		● ●			15	20	-15°	◊◊	☼	▪	Deeper flowers than species
A. m. 'Vindictive'		● ● ●			15	20	-15°	◊◊	☼	▪	Longer flowering period

Asarina

Twining snapdragon

These unusual tender perennial climbers, usually grown as half-hardy annuals, are gaining popularity as trailing basket plants.

The tubular flared flowers of *Asarina antirrhiniflora* are vivid red-purple set against bright green ivy-shaped leaves. *A.* 'Victoria Falls' is similar, but with contrasting lime green bracts. Meanwhile 'Red Dragon' has larger blooms of carmine red. The mixture *A. scandens* 'Jewel Mixed' is a pretty combination of white, pink, red, blue and maroon. Try growing with trailing lobelia, lilac sutera or *Verbena* 'Blue Cascade'.

Asarina 'Red Dragon'

	SPRING	SUMMER	AUTUMN	WINTER	height (cm)	spread (cm)	min. temp °C	moisture	sun/shade	colour	
Asarina antirrhiniflora		● ● ●	● ●		120	30	1°	◊◊	☼	▪	Also known as *Maurandella antirrhiniflora*
A. 'Red Dragon'		● ● ●	● ●		60	30	1°	◊◊	☼	▪	Large blooms
A. scandens 'Jewel Mixed'		● ● ●	● ●		180	30	1°	◊◊	☼	▥	Also known as *Lophospermum s.* 'Jewel Mixed'
A. 'Victoria Falls'		● ● ●	● ●		60	30	1°	◊◊	☼	▪	Also known as *Maurandya* 'Victoria Falls'

☼ sunny   ☀ semi-shady   ● shady

Aster novae-angliae 'Harrington's Pink'

Aster x frikartii 'Mönch'

Asteriscus maritimus

A

Flowering Plants

Aster
Michaelmas daisy

The asters are a welcome addition to the selection of plants available for autumn pot work.

The bushy little plants are smothered in single or double blooms and you can choose from a range of jewel colours – rich pinks, blues and purples – as well as white.

These hardy perennials flower from late summer to around the middle of autumn. Keep the compost evenly moist, deadhead with scissors and look out for slugs and snails.

Grow mildew resistant strains if possible. The varieties listed are amongst the best available. Try combining with gold-variegated trailing ivies and heaths and heathers (Calluna and Erica) with lime-green or flame coloured foliage.

	SPRING	SUMMER	AUTUMN	WINTER	height (cm)	spread (cm)	min. temp °C	moisture	sun/shade	colour	
Aster novi-angliae 'Harrington's Pink'	planting	●●●	●●● planting		120	45	-15°	moist	sun/shade	▮	Double flowers
A. novi-belgii 'Schneekissen'	planting	●●	●● planting		30	45	-15°	moist	sun/shade	□	Semi double flowers
Aster x frikartii 'Mönch'	planting	●●●	●● planting		70	45	-15°	moist	sun/shade	▨	Single flowers

Asteriscus
Gold Coin

The low-growing *Asteriscus maritimus* is a tender perennial that enjoys full sun and good drainage. If this plant is deadheaded regularly, it will flower for much of the summer.

Plants are well clothed in spoon-shaped, grey-green silken leaves, making an attractive foil for the large golden yellow daisies.

Try planting Asteriscus in the sides of hanging baskets and combine with other sun lovers such as cerise pink trailing pelargoniums and *Scaevola aemula* 'Blue Wonder'.

Alternatively, use this plant to soften the edges of pots, contrasting the rounded flowers with grassy foliage such as the blue-leaved *Festuca glauca*. Height 25cm (10in), spread 30cm (12in).

 planting   ● flower   ◗ well drained   ◖ moist   ◗ wet

Begonia

Bedding and patio begonias fall into two groups – the tuberous rooted types which have large, jaggedly cut leaves and showy blooms in a wide range of colours and the compact, fibrous rooted kinds (strains of *Begonia semperflorens*) with rounded, fleshy leaves in green, bronze or dark brown and a profusion of small flowers in shades of pink and white, depending on the variety.

Begonia 'Illumination Rose'

The tuberous rooted begonias are further sub divided between the upright types – for example, the widely grown Nonstop Series with their pompon flowers, the Picotee Series in which the petals have a dark margin, and the cascading Pendula begonias. The latter are excellent for hanging baskets, tall pots and urns on pedestals. Good examples include the Illumination and Sensation Series, as well as the Show Angels Series, in which the petals are pointed, a proportion having picotee edging. If you want cascades of small flowers in hanging baskets, choose varieties like *B. semperflorens* 'Pink Avalanche' and 'Stara Mixed'. The clear apricot coloured species *B. sutherlandii* also looks lovely tumbling over the sides of pots and planters. Combine with cool blues, lavender and white flowers, for example pansies, *Sutera cordata* and white-variegated foliage, such as variegated spider plant (Chlorophytum).

Begonia Multiflora Nonstop Series

Begonia semperflorens 'Olympia Red'

For containers in shade, mix tuberous begonias with plants that enjoy similar conditions, for example busy Lizzies, fuchsias and golden creeping Jenny (*Lysimachia nummularia* 'Aurea'). Wait until plants bought as mixtures are just showing some flower colour to avoid clashes.

Keep a look out for slugs and snails, vine weevil activity, and be vigilant over removing fading flowers and foliage to reduce the risk of grey mould and stem rot.

Fibrous begonias are very difficult to raise from seed and so it is advisable to buy plugs or trays of plants. Unlike the tuberous begonias, they are highly weather resistant.

	SPRING	SUMMER	AUTUMN	WINTER	height (cm)	spread (cm)	min. temp °C	moisture	sun/shade	colour	
Begonia Multiflora Nonstop Series		● ● ● ● ● ●			30	30	5°	●●	☀	+	Large pompon heads
B. Pendula Illumination Series		● ● ● ● ● ●			60	30	5°	●●	☀	+	Cascading double blooms
B. Pendula Sensation Series		● ● ● ● ● ●			60	30	5°	●●	☀	+	Cascading double blooms
B. Pendula Show Angels Series		● ● ● ● ● ●			60	30	5°	●●	☀	☐	Cascading, some flowers picotees
B. Picotee Series		● ● ● ● ● ●			60	60	5°	●●	☀	+	Large pompon flowers, picotee edged
B. semperflorens Ambassador Series		● ● ● ● ● ●			20	20	1°	●●	☀	▮	Green foliage
B. s. Excel Series		● ● ● ● ● ●			20	20	1°	●●	☀	▯	Dark bronze and green foliage
B. s. Olympia Series		● ● ● ● ● ●			20	20	1°	●●	☀	▮	Green leaves
B. s. 'Pink Avalanche'		● ● ● ● ● ●			20	20	1°	●●	☀	▣	Good for baskets
B. s. 'Stara Mixed' F1		● ● ● ● ● ●			20	20	1°	●●	☀	▮	Good for baskets
B. sutherlandii		● ● ● ● ● ●			45	45	1°	●●	☀	▣	Tumbling habit

☼ sunny   ☀ semi-shady   ● shady   + many colours

43

Bellis
Double daisy

These early flowering bedding plants are relatives of the common lawn daisy, *Bellis perennis*. Bellis has a long history: it was a popular garden flower in Medieval times and many still have an old fashioned, cottage garden appeal.

The simple semi-double and pompon flowered miniature types are the most weather resistant and are easier to combine with other plants than the giant headed daisies like Goliath, which can look a little ungainly. Colours range from white through pink to deep red.

Bellis perennis 'Tasso Red'

Although some of the hardier, early flowering Series produce a few blooms during mild periods in winter, the main display is in spring. You can often buy trays of daisies in separate colours, which makes colour scheming easier, and these neat little plants are ideal for edging large containers and windowboxes or for combining with compact forget-me-nots (Myosotis), violas, blue or white polyanthus and spring bulbs. Deadhead regularly and watch for aphids.

	SPRING	SUMMER	AUTUMN	WINTER	height (cm)	spread (cm)	min. temp °C	moisture	sun/shade	colour	
Bellis perennis Carpet Series	● ● ●		✿ ✿ ✿	●	15	15	-17°	◊◊	☀	▮	Even habit, free flowering
B. p. Goliath Series	● ● ●		✿ ✿	●	20	20	-17°	◊◊	☀	▮	Large double blooms
B. p. Pomponette Series	● ● ●		✿ ✿	●	15	15	-17°	◊◊	☀	▮	Button-like, quilled petals
B. p. Tasso Series	● ● ●		✿ ✿	●	20	20	-17°	◊◊	☀	▮	Early flowering, button-like
B. p. Tasso 'Strawberries and Cream'	● ● ●		✿ ✿ ✿	●	20	20	-17°	◊◊	☀	▮	Early; flowers change from pink to white

Bidens

One of the easiest of all basket plants, bidens is a tender perennial producing masses of honey-scented golden yellow blooms along its spreading branches. This versatile plant can be used for any number of different purposes in containers.

With finely cut foliage and an airy habit, it combines easily with other trailers of equal vigour – for example, Tapien verbenas, Surfinia petunias and golden helichrysum – but it can swamp weaker plants and may need occasional cutting back to maintain balance. If wilted through drought, plants will usually recover well after a long soak. *Bidens ferulifolia* is often available as a named variety, such as the prostrate growing 'Golden Eye' or 'Golden Goddess', which has more finely divided foliage and slightly larger flowers than the species.

Bidens ferulifolia

	SPRING	SUMMER	AUTUMN	WINTER	height (cm)	spread (cm)	min. temp °C	moisture	sun/shade	colour	
Bidens ferulifolia		✿	● ● ● ● ●			50	60	0°	◊◊	☀	▮	Trim back over-vigorous shoots
Bidens ferulifolia 'Golden Eye'		✿	● ● ● ● ●			30	60	0°	◊◊	☀	▮	Low, spreading habit
B. f. 'Golden Goddess'		✿	● ● ● ● ●			60	60	0°	◊◊	☀	▮	Excellent basket plant

✿ planting   ✿ flower   ◊ well drained   ● moist   ● wet

Brachyscome
Swan river daisy

Breeders have worked on the half-hardy annual Swan river daisies to create compact, long flowering and scented plants that are ideal for patio pots.

Mixtures like 'Bravo' contain purple-blue, violet and white flowers, often with a striking dark eye. For single colours choose members of the Splendour Series, for example, 'Purple Splendour', 'White Splendour' or the diminutive 'Blue Star'. One newcomer to watch out for is *Brachyscome* 'Strawberry Mousse', which has large, vivid pink blooms, bold foliage and excellent garden performance.

Amongst the best of the cascading plants for basket work to appear in recent years is the mossy leaved tender perennial *Brachyscome multifida* – a plant with real flower power and reasonable drought tolerance. *Brachyscome multifida* mingles well with other basket plants in pastel schemes, such as varieties of *Sutera cordata* and trailing verbena, and it makes a soft foil for stiff, solid plants like ivy-leaved geraniums.

B. iberidifolia 'Bravo Mixed'

	SPRING	SUMMER	AUTUMN	WINTER	height (cm)	spread (cm)	min. temp °C	moisture	sun/shade	colour	
Brachyscome iberidifolia 'Blue Star'		●●●●			30	30	1°	💧	☀		Very floriferous
B. i. 'Bravo Mixed'		●●●●			23	30	1°	💧	☀		Vivid colours
B. i. Splendour Series		●●●●			30	45	1°	💧	☀		'Purple Splendour' especially good
B. multifida		●●●●●			45	45	1°	💧	☀		Free flowering, with mossy foliage
B. m. Mist Series		●●●●●			45	45	1°	💧	☀		'Lemon Mist' not so compact
B. 'Strawberry Mousse'		●●●●●			40	75	1°	💧	☀		Large blooms

Calceolaria
Slipper *or* Pouch flower

The half-hardy shrubby perennial *Calceolaria integrifolia* has given rise to a number of compact varieties, usually treated as annuals, that are well suited to growing in container and baskets.

'Midas', 'Golden Bunch' and 'Sunshine' are very similar but bloom at slightly different times. The flowers are like clusters of bright golden yellow bubbles and make a striking effect in baskets contrasted with vivid violet-purple or magenta verbenas and petunias or dark blue trailing lobelia. 'Kentish Hero' is an older variety that is best suited to pots.

Calceolaria integrifolia 'Kentish Hero'

	SPRING	SUMMER	AUTUMN	WINTER	height (cm)	spread (cm)	min. temp °C	moisture	colour	
Calceolaria integrifolia 'Kentish Hero'		●			25	25	1°	💧		Compact
C. i. 'Midas'		●			25	25	1°	💧		Weather tolerant, upright
C. i. 'Sunset Mixed' F1		●●●			20	25	1°	💧		Benefits from an early sowing
C. i. 'Sunshine'		●			30	30	1°	💧		Good in hanging baskets

☀ sunny   ☀ semi-shady   ● shady

Calendula
Pot marigold

This ancient herb has spawned a number of interesting varieties, but most are too tall for container gardening and are better suited to the cottage border. The flower petals are edible and can be used to garnish soups and salads.

Pot marigolds are very easy to grow from seed and are also available as plants early on in the summer bedding season. Look for the compact 'Fiesta Gitana' (30cm/12in tall) with double flowers in shades of orange, yellow and gold, usually with a dark 'eye'. Try growing it on its own in bright blue painted or glazed pots for a vivid splash of colour. Deadhead regularly to keep plants flowering and maintain even watering to lessen the risk of powdery mildew. Deal with aphids as soon as they are noticed.

Calendula officinalis 'Fiesta Gitana'

Campanula
Bellflower

Most bellflowers are herbaceous perennials that are too tall for container work, but some of the alpine varieties have just the right combination of a neat, compact habit and long flowering period.

Campanula carpatica 'Karl Foerster'

Amongst the hardy *Campanula carpatica* cultivars – which have large, bell-shaped blooms held over a spreading mound of foliage – 'White Clips' and 'Karl Foerster' are two of the best and most widely available, along with 'Blue Clips'.

Campanula isophylla 'Stella Blue' is often sold as a houseplant with long trailing branches covered with starry lilac-blue or sometimes white flowers. Though not reliably hardy, it will bloom happily outdoors in baskets during the summer months and is perfect for pastel schemes.

For tumbling over the sides of larger containers, consider the ultra-vigorous ground cover bellflower, *Campanula poscharskyana* and *C. p.* 'Stella', which both bear abundant starry, lilac-blue flowers in phases through summer into autumn and can look very effective on the patio.

	SPRING	SUMMER	AUTUMN	WINTER	height (cm)	spread (cm)	min. temp °C	moisture	sun/shade	colour	
Campanula carpatica 'Blue Clips'	planting	flower			20	50	-15°	moist	sun		Large bell flowers
C. c. 'Karl Foerster'	planting	flower			20	50	-15°	moist	sun		Large bell flowers
C. isophylla 'Stella Blue'	planting	flower			30	50	-15°	moist	part shade		Excellent for hanging baskets
C. poscharskyana	planting	flower	flower		15	60	-15°	moist	part shade		'Stella' is a more vivid shade

planting 🌼 flower 💧 well drained 💧 moist 💧 wet

Celosia
Prince of Wales Feathers

The fluffy, vividly coloured Prince of Wales Feathers have an unreal quality that makes them ideal for fantasy or subtropical arrangements.

Plant celosia singly in pots for more impact, setting them against a backdrop of dramatic foliage plants such as canna. Alternatively, try blending them with coleus (Solenostemon) and large-flowered New Guinea hybrid impatiens. Celosia need shelter and warmth to thrive. Watch out for foot rot and leaf spot.

Celosia spicata
Flamingo Series

	SPRING	SUMMER	AUTUMN	WINTER	height (cm)	spread (cm)	min. temp °C	moisture	sun/shade	colour	
C. argentea Plumosa Group 'Dwarf Geisha'		● ● ●			20	20	1°	◐	☼		Uniform and very compact
C. spicata Flamingo Series		● ● ●			60	60	1°	◐	☼		Branching habit

Cerastium
Snow-in-summer

Like many plants that are too vigorous for a garden situation, the evergreen snow-in-summer makes an excellent container plant, producing a spreading carpet of fine, silvery, felted foliage studded with white stars for weeks on end in summer.

Cerastium tomentosum

In large, permanent containers placed in a hot spot, use this drought tolerant alpine to cover the bare earth around a tree or standard shrub – especially on gritty, loam-based soil – and watch it cascade over the sides with its dramatic, free-flowing form. The plant will need plenty of room in a good-sized pot to fulfil its true potential.

Try underplanting Cerastium with dwarf bulbs, including *Scilla sibirica*. This plant would also work well as an edge softener for Mediterranean style herb planters containing sun lovers such as purple sage, French lavender, trailing rosemary and shrubby thymes.

Alternatively, use Cerastium to cascade over the sides of hanging baskets and wall planters that are designed for easy maintenance. For example, you could mix it with plants like trailing pelargoniums, bidens, ivy and *Sedum lineare* 'Variegatum', all of which are drought and heat resistant.

Cerastium grows to a height of 20cm (8in), and will spread over 1m (1yd) or more.

☼ *sunny*   ☼ *semi-shady*   ● *shady*

Chrysanthemum

Pot mums

During late summer and early autumn, garden centres take delivery of a range of chrysanthemums smothered in buds. You'll find dwarfed plants that have been treated with growth regulating hormone – these make useful additions to mixed autumn planters.

Chrysanthemum hybrid

Chrysanthemum hybrid

You can also buy impressive dome-shaped specimens that look spectacular when planted singly in blue-glazed patio pots. Try a matching pair either side of a doorway. Deadheading and removal of yellowing leaves keeps plants neat and healthy and encourages continued flowering, but frost will finish the display overnight, so either move plants temporarily under cover or protect them with fleece. Colours include white, pink and yellow, but for the most part there are smouldering oranges, tawny reds and browns.

Clematis

Compact growing clematis make excellent pot subjects, trained up simple cane tripods, obelisks or topiary frames. If your garden is paved, potted clematis also enable you to cover walls and trellis panels.

Clematis hybrid

Clematis alpina

Plant in a large, wide pot – for example, a wooden half-barrel filled with John Innes No 3, setting the plant about 10cm (4in) below the compost surface. This encourages shooting from below the soil level, which thickens up the plant to provide greater coverage. When training the new shoots over a framework, try to guide the stems close to the horizontal to promote abundant vertical side shoots. On frames, wrap the stems around, taking them to the top and then back down again to get the best coverage of leaf and flower, otherwise a bulky mass of leaves will form at the top only. Mulch with organic matter like bark chippings. Very light shade is preferable to leaving pots where they will bake on a sun-drenched patio, since clematis are principally woodlanders that prefer a cool root run. Start the season off with dainty *Clematis alpina* and *C. macropetala* forms which have ferny foliage and for later displays pick some of the showy, large flowered hybrids.

	SPRING	SUMMER	AUTUMN	WINTER	height (m)	spread (m)	min. temp °C	moisture	sun/shade	colour	
Clematis alpina 'Pamela Jackman'	● ●	●	✂ ✂		3	1.5	-15°	♦♦	☼		Nodding bells, fluffy seedheads
C. 'Arctic Queen'		● ● ● ●	✂		2	1	-15°	♦♦	☼		Double flowers. Light pruning in autumn
C. 'Dr Ruppel'		● ● ● ●	✂		2	1	-15°	♦♦	☼		Striped flowers. Light pruning in autumn
C. 'Lady Northcliffe'	● ●	● ● ●	✂		1.5	2.5	-15°	♦♦	☼		Wavy 'petals', contrasting cream stamens
C. 'Pink Fantasy'		● ● ● ●	✂		1.8	1	-15°	♦♦	☀		Best in partial shade
C. 'Vyvyan Pennell'	● ●	●	✂		2	1	-15°	♦♦	☼		Double flowers only in early summer

✂ *planting*   ● *flower*   ♦ *well drained*   ♦♦ *moist*   ♦♦♦ *wet*

costaler

Convolvulus
Bindweed

Unlike the dreaded bindweed, garden forms of convolvulus are normally very well behaved. Even the potentially invasive *Convolvulus althaeoides*, a pink flowered carpeting or trailing plant, is no trouble when confined to a pot.

Convolvulus sabatius

Of similar habit though much less vigorous is the pretty lavender blue flowered *C. sabatius*, a tender perennial which given time will cascade over the edge of a pot or basket. Meanwhile in *C. cneorum*, it is the silken, metallic silver leaves of this dome shaped shrub that feature most strongly – the large, white-tinged-pink blooms being an added bonus. Like all of the plants so far described it enjoys full sun and sharp drainage. Varieties of the hardy annual *C. tricolor* have large funnel shaped blooms all summer and are a magnet for beneficial insects like hover flies. You can get mixtures with white and pink flowers, but the vivid 'Royal Ensign' is particularly eye-catching, with its white and yellow centres. Try it in hanging baskets with yellow bidens or in pots with Afro-French marigolds and deadhead regularly to encourage repeat flowering.

	SPRING	SUMMER	AUTUMN	WINTER	height (cm)	spread (cm)	min. temp °C	moisture	sun/shade	colour	
Convolvulus althaeoides					15	100	-15°				Grey-green leaves
C. cneorum					60	90	-5°				Metallic silver foliage
C. sabatius syn. *C. mauritanicus*					15	45	-5°				Overwinter under glass
C. tricolor 'Royal Ensign'					50	50	-15°				Hardy annual

Cosmos

The aptly named chocolate cosmos is a tender, tuberous rooted perennial with dish shaped dark maroon flowers that smell just like the real thing!

This plant is not particularly floriferous, but the elegant, single blooms carried on long stems stand out well against a lighter backdrop of flower and foliage. Try planting it in a pale, weathered terracotta pot with tawny coleus, bronze leaved *Fuchsia* 'Thalia' and cascading silver-grey *Lotus berthelotii*. *Cosmos bipinnatus* is a bushy, half-hardy annual with a long flowering period and beautiful feathery green foliage. Choose members of the dwarf Sonata Series for container plantings. Deadhead regularly.

Cosmos atrosanguineus

	SPRING	SUMMER	AUTUMN	WINTER	height (cm)	spread (cm)	min. temp °C	moisture	sun/shade	colour	
Cosmos atrosanguineus					75	45	-4°				Chocolate scent
C. bipinnatus Sonata Series					50	30	1°				Compact

☼ *sunny*   ☀ *semi-shady*   ● *shady*

Crocus

Spring flowering crocus are ideal for planting in clumps between other plants in pots or spring baskets and to push up through creeping or ground-covering varieties. They bring a breath of spring freshness wherever they are planted.

Because they only require shallow planting, these plants can also be used to form the uppermost level of a layered arrangement where bigger, later flowering bulbs are set at intervals lower down. Forms of *Crocus chrysanthus* flower very early in the year and their weather-resistant multiple blooms, held close to soil level, are one of the harbingers of spring. In full sun, they open out almost flat to reveal the prominent stigma. Try planting 'Cream Beauty' or the subtle 'Blue Pearl' amongst pink or purple winter flowering heathers or shrubs in permanent planters.

The larger flowered Dutch crocus, *C. vernus* have single blooms shaped like wine glasses and they bloom slightly later than *C. chrysanthus*. 'Pickwick' is beautifully marked with purple and white streaks. You could plant a cheerful pot of mixed colours or use individual varieties to enhance colour-schemed arrangements.

Crocus chrysanthus 'Cream Beauty'

Crocus vernus 'Jeanne d'Arc'

	SPRING	SUMMER	AUTUMN	WINTER	height (cm)	spread (cm)	min. temp °C	moisture	sun/shade	colour	
Crocus chrysanthus 'Blue Pearl'	flower flower		planting planting planting	flower	8	5	-17°	well drained	sun		Subtle colouring
C. c 'Cream Beauty'	flower flower		planting planting planting	flower	8	5	-17°	well drained	sun		Orange stigma
C. c. 'Lady Killer'	flower flower		planting planting planting	flower	8	5	-17°	well drained	sun		Dark purple blotches at base of petals
C. c. 'Zwanenburg Bronze'	flower flower		planting planting planting	flower	8	5	-17°	well drained	sun		Brown/purple markings on petals
C. vernus 'Jeanne d'Arc'	flower flower flower		planting planting planting		10	8	-17°	well drained	sun		Vigorous, showy
C. v. 'Pickwick'	flower flower flower		planting planting planting		10	8	-17°	well drained	sun		Striped petals

Cuphea

If you're looking for something unusual, try Cuphea, and especially the Mexican cigar plant, *Cuphea ignea*, a shrubby evergreen perennial with little red tubular flowers tipped with black and white that is normally found in the houseplant section.

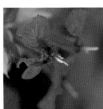

Cuphea llavea 'Tiny Mice'

For a hot colour scheme, try combining Cuphea with a bronzy leaved orange dahlia and flame-coloured Coleus. New on the scene is the aptly named 'Tiny Mice', perfect for planting singly as a bushy little specimen. The false heather, *C. hyssopifolia* has quite a different character, with spreading branches covered with rows of gleaming dark green leaves and tiny lilac or in the case of 'Alba', white flowers. Plant singly in small containers or in baskets.

	SPRING	SUMMER	AUTUMN	WINTER	height (cm)	spread (cm)	min. temp °C	moisture	sun/shade	colour	
Cuphea ignea		planting	flower flower	flower flower		30	30	7°	well drained	sun		Taller if overwintered
C. hyssopifolia		planting	flower flower	flower flower		60	75	5°	well drained	sun		Good for baskets
C. h. 'Alba'		planting	flower flower	flower flower		60	75	5°	well drained	sun		Good for baskets
C. llavea 'Tiny Mice'		planting	flower flower	flower flower		38	22	1°	well drained	sun		Unusual bicoloured blooms

planting   flower   well drained   moist   wet

Cyclamen
Florist's
cyclamen

In early autumn, hardier forms of the indoor plant *Cyclamen persicum* appear outdoors in the patio plants section of garden centres.

The nodding blooms with sweptback petals are beautifully sculpted. Colour scheming is easy because the plants come individually potted and in bloom. There are pure white, pale and deep pink, scarlet red and deep wine red flower colours to choose from and some of the reds and pinks are perfumed.

Cyclamen persicum

	SPRING	SUMMER	AUTUMN	WINTER	height (cm)	spread (cm)	min. temp °C	moisture	sun/shade	colour	
C. persicum Miracle Series			● ● ●		15	15	-1°	💧	☀	▦	Marbled foliage
C. p. Lazer Series			● ● ●		20	20	-1°	💧	☀	▢	More substantial plants

Dahlia

A wide variety of dahlias in bud and flower can be found in the garden centres from mid-summer through till autumn. These perennially popular plants have a multitude of uses, either in bedding schemes or a wide variety of containers.

These tender, tuberous rooted perennials range from taller plants of substance such as the dramatic black leaved 'Bishop of Llandaff' and 'Moonfire' – whose bronzed foliage makes the perfect foil for the pale orange blotched flowers – to compact bedding types including Dahlietta Series and 'Rigoletto', which are seed raised and come in a wide and vibrant range of colours. You can also widen your selection by buying tubers in spring and potting them up to grow on frost-free until it is safe to put them out permanently in early summer.

Dahlias in hot colours, especially those with bronze or purple-black leaves, are ideal for creating a sub-tropical feel on the patio in combination with architectural plants like cannas and cordyline. Watch out for slugs, earwigs and aphids. Avoid hot dry conditions which make plants susceptible to powdery mildew and red spider mite. Deadhead regularly.

Dahlia 'Dahlietta'

Dahlia 'Bishop of Llandaff'

	SPRING	SUMMER	AUTUMN	WINTER	height (cm)	spread (cm)	min. temp °C	moisture	sun/shade	colour	
Dahlia 'Bishop of Llandaff'		🌱 ●	● ●		90	45	1°	💧	☀	▦	Purple-black foliage
D. Dahlietta Series		🌱 ●	● ●		22	40	1°	💧	☀	▢	Dwarf bedding dahlia
D. 'Moonfire'		🌱 ●	● ●		60	45	1°	💧	☀	▦	Dark central zone to flowers
D. 'Redskin' (annual)		🌱 ●	● ●		60	60	1°	💧	☀	▦	Bronze foliage, double flowers
D. 'Rigoletto' (annual)		🌱 ●	● ●		38	30	1°	💧	☀	▦	Semi-double and double
D. 'Roxy'		🌱 ●	● ●		45	40	1°	💧	☀	▦	Bronze-purple leaves. Single flowers

☀ *sunny*   ◐ *semi-shady*   ● *shady*

Dianthus
Pinks *and* Carnations

Many of the evergreen perennial and alpine dianthus have a sweet spicy fragrance. The Modern Pinks produce a succession of large double blooms in a wide range of colours over a clump of narrow grey-green leaves during summer.

Dianthus chinesis 'Strawberry Parfait'

These flowers work well in mixed permanent plantings of lime-loving subjects, including herbs such as dwarf lavender. Dwarf carnations are also well scented with large double blooms, but the plants are petite and can be mixed with other bedding such as diascias and silver cineraria and are ideal in pots and window boxes. The new Sunflor series is available in flower from garden centres as soon as early spring and Lillipot Series bloom from mid-summer till the first frosts. The Indian pinks (varieties of *Dianthus chinensis*), are annuals or short-lived perennials, usually with single flowers and fringed petals. Plant in lime-rich compost, deadhead regularly and watch for aphid, leafspot, slugs and snails.

	SPRING	SUMMER	AUTUMN	WINTER	height (cm)	spread (cm)	min. temp °C	moisture	sun/shade	colour	
D. chinensis 'Strawberry Parfait'	✂✂✂	●●●			15	15	-17°	◗◗	☼	▦	Large single flowers
D. 'Doris' (Modern Pink)	✂✂✂	●●●			30	30	-17°	◗◗	☼	▦	Fragrant
D. 'Lillipot' (dwarf carnation)	✂	●●●	●●		23	20	1°	◗◗	☼	■	Fragrant doubles, some bicolours
D. 'Princess Mixed' F1 (annual)	✂				20	15	1°	◗◗	☼	■	Continuous flowering
D. Sunflor Series	✂●●●	●●●			30	15	-17°	◗◗	☼	☐	Repeat-flowering
D. Telstar Series (annual)	✂	●●●●	●		20	20	-17°	◗◗	☼	▦	Long flowering

Diascia

These South African trailing perennials have become extremely popular basket plants in recent times with new varieties being added to the collection every year.

Colour scheming is simple with varieties like 'Coral Belle,' 'Ruby Field' and 'Salmon Supreme' providing orangey pinks – great with true blues, white and lime green and 'Lilac Belle', 'Little Dancer' and 'Twinkle' with blue-pink flowers more suited to pastel schemes. Cut back flowered stems to encourage repeat blooming and do not let the compost dry out.

Diascia 'Lilac Belle'

	SPRING	SUMMER	AUTUMN	WINTER	height (cm)	spread (cm)	min. temp °C	moisture	sun/shade	colour	
Diascia 'Coral Belle'	✂✂✂	●●●	●●		45	45	-4°	◗◗	☼	▦	Good for baskets
D. 'Lilac Belle'	✂✂✂	●●●	●●		45	45	-4°	◗◗	☼	▦	Good for baskets
D. 'Little Dancer'	✂✂✂	●●●	●●		45	45	-4°	◗◗	☼	■	Good for baskets, dark foliage
D. 'Ruby Field'	✂✂	●●●	●●		45	45	-4°	◗◗	☼	▦	One of the most hardy
D. 'Salmon Supreme'	✂✂✂	●●●	●●		45	45	-4°	◗◗	☼	☐	Unusual shade
D. 'Twinkle'	✂✂✂	●●●	●		45	45	-4°	◗◗	☼	▦	Good basket plant

✂ planting   ● flower   ◗ well drained   ◗◗ moist   ◗◗◗ wet

Dicentra
Bleeding Heart

With ferny foliage and arching sprays of little heart-shaped flowers, these woodlanders are a delight in spring and early summer.

Many of the low growing carpeting dicentras are useful for large permanent pots and planters located in a sheltered, shady spot where the wind can't scorch the foliage.

The compost also needs to be rich in organic matter to make it moisture retentive. Add a thick mulch of bark chippings or cocoa shells after planting up the container and watering thoroughly. Colours range from the deepest red of 'Bacchanal' and 'Adrian Bloom',

Dicentra spectabilis 'Alba'

Dicentra spectabilis

though mid-pinks such as the glowing 'Luxuriant' and the pure white of 'Snowflakes'.

Quite different in character, the taller growing *Dicentra spectabilis*, commonly called bleeding heart or Dutchman's breeches, is a magnificent sight in late spring or early summer when the 1.2m (4ft) high stems bear arching sprays of flowers that look just like heart shaped lockets. The white form 'Alba' is particularly elegant. Dry conditions may cause powdery mildew.

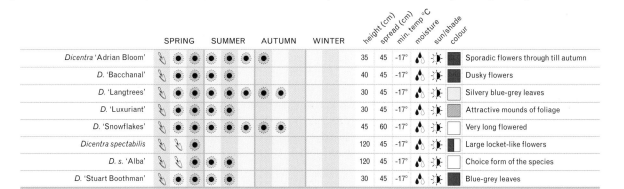

	SPRING	SUMMER	AUTUMN	WINTER	height (cm)	spread (cm)	min. temp °C	moisture	sun/shade	colour	
Dicentra 'Adrian Bloom'					35	45	-17°				Sporadic flowers through till autumn
D. 'Bacchanal'					40	45	-17°				Dusky flowers
D. 'Langtrees'					30	45	-17°				Silvery blue-grey leaves
D. 'Luxuriant'					30	45	-17°				Attractive mounds of foliage
D. 'Snowflakes'					45	60	-17°				Very long flowered
Dicentra spectabilis					120	45	-17°				Large locket-like flowers
D. s. 'Alba'					120	45	-17°				Choice form of the species
D. 'Stuart Boothman'					30	45	-17°				Blue-grey leaves

Dimorphotheca

Dimorphotheca annua 'Glistening White'

These sun-loving plants are normally grown from seed and treated as half-hardy annuals. They are closely related to the osteospermums and have the same characteristic of closing their large daisy-like blooms when the sun goes behind a cloud, giving rise to the common names of 'Rain daisy' and 'Weather prophet'.

Mostly white varieties are available from seedsmen, for example the compact 'Glistening White' and the somewhat taller 'Tetra Pole Star' but you can sometimes also find soft orange shades. Most have a

violet blue reverse and eye colouring. Despite flowering from early summer to the first frosts, Dimorphotheca benefits from regular deadheading. Watch for grey mould.

	SPRING	SUMMER	AUTUMN	WINTER	height (cm)	spread (cm)	min. temp °C	moisture	sun/shade	colour	
Dimorphotheca annua 'Glistening White'					30	15	1°				Dark eye
D. pluvalis 'Tetra Polar Star'					40	20	1°				Dark eye. Slightly taller.

☼ *sunny*   ☀ *semi-shady*   ● *shady*

Dorotheanthus
Livingstone daisy

Fluorescent coloured daisies, each with a dark centre and sparkling succulent leaves, make this sun lover an eye-catching plant for the summer patio. Try mixtures like 'Harlequin' and 'Magic Carpet' for an array of shades that look as though they have come from a child's paint box.

You will find mostly mixtures but also a few single colours in the seed catalogues – try looking under the former name of Mesembryanthemum. If you have shallow or small pots that other bedding plants don't thrive in because of the dry conditions, give the Livingstone daisy a try – it loves poor, shallow and sharply drained soil. Deadhead to prolong flowering. Protect against slugs and snails, avoid overwatering which can cause plants to rot and watch out for aphids on young plants.

Dorotheanthus bellidiformis

	SPRING	SUMMER	AUTUMN	WINTER	height (cm)	spread (cm)	min. temp °C	moisture	sun/shade	colour	
D. bellidiformis 'Harlequin Mixed'	planting	flower flower flower flower			15	30	1°	well drained	sun	+	One of the best colour ranges
D. bellidiformis 'Magic Carpet'	planting	flower flower flower flower			15	30	1°	well drained	sun	+	An established variety
D. occulatus 'Lunette'	planting	flower flower flower			15	30	1°	well drained	sun	+	May stay open in dull weather for longer

Erigeron
Fleabane

Most erigerons are plants of the herbaceous border or alpine garden with large, solid, daisy-like blooms in a range of blue, pink or purple shades, but one plant is very different in character and has become a popular choice for baskets.

Erigeron karvinskianus syn. 'Profusion'

Erigeron karvinskianus, often found in garden centres as *E.* 'Profusion', has masses of tiny white daisies that gradually darken to pink, giving a pretty two-tone effect in hanging baskets. It looks good with pink diascias. 'Dimity' is an herbaceous perennial low enough to use to soften the edge of a large permanent container. Pick up on the pink by combining it with *Ajuga reptans* 'Burgundy Glow'. 'Elstead Pink' flowers for longer and the blue-green foliage is an attractive feature after flowering. Deadhead, divide plants every couple of years to maintain vigour and watch for slugs, snails and powdery mildew.

	SPRING	SUMMER	AUTUMN	WINTER	height (cm)	spread (cm)	min. temp °C	moisture	sun/shade	colour	
E. 'Dimity'	planting planting	flower flower			25	30	-17°	well drained	sun	■	Semi-double, orange centres
E. glaucus 'Elstead Pink'	planting flower	flower flower			30	45	-17°	well drained	sun	■	Bluish-green leaves
E. karvinskianus syn. 'Profusion'	planting	flower flower flower flower flower flower			30	80	-17°	well drained	sun	■	Seeds around

planting   flower   well drained   moist   wet

Erodium
Stork's bill

A number of these little hardy alpine plants that resemble miniature herbaceous geraniums are suitable for permanent container plantings, where they enjoy the extra drainage. Combine with other compact and slow-growing subjects to avoid competition.

Selected forms of the hybrid *Erodium* x *variabile* make cushions of little scalloped leaves studded with pink, five-petalled blooms all summer. 'Album' has white flowers and the double flowered 'Flore Pleno' blooms over a long period. The divided leaves of *E. glandulosum* are grey green and aromatic and the summer flowers are produced in small clusters on airy stems.

Erodium x variabile 'Album'

	SPRING	SUMMER	AUTUMN	WINTER	height (cm)	spread (cm)	min. temp °C	moisture	sun/shade	colour	
Erodium glandulosum					20	20	-17°				Petals have darker markings
E. manescaui					45	60	-17°				Leaves blue-green
E. x variabile 'Album'					20	40	-17°-				White flowers
E. x v. 'Bishop's Form'					20	40	17°				More open habit
E. x v. 'Flore Pleno'					20	40	-17°				Double blooms

Erysimum
Wallflower

Bedding wallflowers, forms of *Erysimum cheiri*, are grown as biennials and planted in late summer and autumn for spring flowering. Dwarf varieties are most suitable for containers and as well as mixtures such as 'Prince' and 'Tom Thumb', the Bedder Series provides a range of single shades useful for colour schemed pots.

Erysimum altaicum 'Apricot Twist'

Erysimum cheiri Bedder Series

The Siberian wallflowers are also used for bedding, notably the compact 'Orange Queen'. In spring, garden centres now also stock pot grown perennial wallflowers such as the subtly shaded 'John Codrington'. The perennials are relatively short lived but can be propagated from cuttings. Cut back flowered stems to encourage further blooms. Wallflowers are renowned for their fragrance and work well with taller spring and early summer flowering bulbs. Wallflowers prefer alkaline soil which helps to minimize club root disease but they are susceptible to many other pests and diseases.

	SPRING	SUMMER	AUTUMN	WINTER	height (cm)	spread (cm)	min. temp °C	moisture	sun/shade	colour	
Erysimum x allionii 'Orange Queen'					30	30	-17°				Spicy scent
E. altaicum 'Apricot Twist'					40	40	-17°				Ideal for pots and windowboxes
E. cheiri 'Bedder Series'					30	30	-17°				Primrose Bedder is a soft yellow
E. c. 'Prince Mixture'					20	20	-17°				Very free flowering and compact
E. 'John Codrington'					25	30	-17°				Pretty pastel flowers

☼ *sunny*   ◑ *semi-shady*   ● *shady*   + *many colours*

Euryops pectinatus

This tender, sub-shrubby patio plant is a native of South Africa and enjoys good drainage and full sun.

The grey-tinged ferny foliage of this plant is a perfect foil for the bright yellow daisy flowers with narrow ray petals produced from early summer to mid-autumn. The habit is bushy (1 x 1m/3 x 3ft) but plants may become rather woody and leggy and benefit from a light trim after flowering. Overwinter whole plants frost-free under glass, take cuttings in early autumn, or discard at the end of the season. Try planting singly in a blue glazed pot.

Euryops pectinatus

Felicia
Blue daisy *or* Kingfisher daisy

The tender perennial blue daisy, *Felicia amelloides*, and the half-hardy annual Kingfisher daisy, *F. bergeriana*, provide some of the best true blue-coloured flowers for container work.

Given a hot sunny position, these drought tolerant plants flower all summer into autumn – the flowers close up in shade. Variegated forms are not so floriferous, but the bright leaf colouring is adequate compensation. For daisies up to 5cm (2in) across, grow the variety *F. a.* 'Santa Anita'. However, if you want a mix of colours, try growing the dainty little *F. heterophylla* varieties such as 'Spring Marchen' raising them from seed.

The short stature and stiff upright habit of felicias makes them ideal for creating an edging for window boxes and troughs. Combine blue felicias with other sun lovers including silverlings such as artemisias and *Senecio cineraria*; white, salmon pink, or red pelargoniums or the larger, daisy blooms of compact growing osteospermums in shades of yellow, white or vivid pink. Or for a zingy combination grow in terracotta pots with gazanias and lime green helichrysum. These mix mostly blue with scatterings of pink, rose and purple.

Deadhead regularly and clip over *F. amelloides* varieties after the initial flush to promote further blooms. Take cuttings in early autumn to overwinter.

Felicia amelloides 'Santa Anita'

	SPRING	SUMMER	AUTUMN	WINTER	height (cm)	spread (cm)	min. temp °C	moisture	sun/shade	colour	
Felicia amelloides	🪴	● ● ● ● ●	● ●		30	30	5°	💧	☀	⬜	Drought tolerant
F. a. 'Santa Anita'	🪴	● ● ● ● ●	● ●		30	30	5°	💧	☀	⬜	Larger blooms
F. a. 'Variegated'	🪴	● ● ● ● ●	● ●		30	30	5°	💧	☀	⬜	Cream variegated
F. bergeriana	🪴	● ● ● ● ●	● ●		30	30	1°	💧	☀	⬜	Seed raised
F. heterophylla 'Spring Marchen'	🪴	● ● ● ● ●	● ●		20	15	1°	💧	☀	▨	Also try 'Blue and Rose Mixed'

🪴 *planting*   ● *flower*   💧 *well drained*   💧 *moist*   💧 *wet*

Fuchsia

Fuchsias are sumptuous summer flowering shrubs with hundreds of varieties to choose from, many of which are perfect for pots and baskets where they combine effortlessly with other shade lovers such as trailing lobelia, busy Lizzies, trailing tuberous begonias and violas.

For shaded baskets and wall pots, try the showy doubles like the white-tinged-pink 'Pink Marshmallow' or striking magenta purple and white 'La Campanella'. Elegantly cascading singles include the vibrant rose pink 'Red Spider' and widely available 'Jack Shahan' as well as the gold variegated 'Golden Marinka' which has deep red blooms. The frilly pink and white 'Swingtime' is semi-trailing and can be trained into an excellent standard. For upright plants in the centre of a hanging basket or in patio pots, choose the so-called bush fuchsias such as the free-

Fuchsia 'Red Spider'

flowering pink and lavender blue double, 'Winston Churchill', or a single like the pretty pastel 'Love's Reward'. Orange and orange-red colouring is unusual in fuchsias, but *F. triphylla* hybrid 'Thalia' has orange-red tubular flowers set off by bronzy foliage and has an altogether sub-tropical feel. Try it in an Italianate terracotta pot with purple cordyline and trailing pelargoniums.

Fuchsia stock plants may be overwintered frost-free after leaf drop, or as cuttings taken in late summer. Watch for aphids, grey mould, red spider mite, rust and vine weevil. Yellowing and leaf spot may be caused by overwatering and poor drainage.

Fuchsia 'Eva Boerg'

	SPRING	SUMMER	AUTUMN	WINTER	height (cm)	spread (cm)	min. temp °C	moisture	sun/shade	colour	
F. 'Eva Boerg'		● ● ●	● ●		15	45	1°				Semi-double flowers
F. 'Golden Marinka'		● ● ●	● ●		15	45	1°				Gold variegated foliage; single
F. 'Jack Shahan'		● ● ●	● ●		45	60	1°				Single; trailer
F. 'La Campanella'		● ● ●	● ●		30	45	1°				Double; trailer
F. 'Lady Thumb'		● ● ●	● ●		30	45	-5°				Borderline hardy dwarf bush
F. 'Love's Reward'		● ● ●	● ●		45	45	1°				Single; bush
F. 'Pink Marshmallow'		● ● ●	● ●		50	45	1°				Double; trailer
F. 'Red Spider'		● ● ●	● ●		30	60	1°				Single; trailer
F. 'Swingtime'		● ● ●	● ●		60	75	1°				Double; good for standards
F. triphylla 'Thalia'		● ● ●	● ●		90	90	1°				Bronzy leaves
F. 'Winston Churchill'		● ● ●	● ●		60	60	1°				Double; bush

☼ *sunny*   ☀ *semi-shady*   ● *shady*

Gazania
Treasure flower

Gazanias are tender perennials normally grown as half-hardy annuals with big daisy like flowers that have wide petals and which are usually prominently marked with darker rings or stripes that really make them stand out.

Gazania 'Daybreak Red Stripe'

In recent years, extensive breeding work has been carried out to develop new bedding varieties that are more compact and weather resistant and whose blooms stay open longer in overcast weather, for example, 'Gazoo' and 'Kiss'. Gazanias are normally bright orange or yellow, but many selections now offer colours from cream through purple-pink to dark mahogany red. The handsome jaggedly cut leaves are normally grey-green, but in the Talent Series they are an attractive silver shade. Gazanias are easy to care for, drought tolerant plants, but they do benefit from regular deadheading. Grow orange and yellow colours with sky blue Felicia or purple heliotrope.

	SPRING	SUMMER	AUTUMN	WINTER	height (cm)	spread (cm)	min. temp °C	moisture	sun/shade	colour	
Gazania Chansonette Series	planting	flower flower flower flower	flower flower			25	20	1°	well drained	sun		Compact, zoned flowers
G. Daybreak Series	planting	flower flower flower flower	flower flower			20	20	1°	well drained	sun		Zoned or striped flowers
G. 'Gazoo'	planting	flower flower flower flower	flower flower			25	20	1°	well drained	sun		Extra large blooms. No zoning
G. Kiss Series	planting	flower flower flower flower	flower flower			20	20	1°	well drained	sun		Early, free flowering
G. Mini-Star Series	planting	flower flower flower flower	flower flower			20	20	1°	well drained	sun		Compact, some zoning
G. Talent Series	planting	flower flower flower flower	flower flower			20	20	1°	well drained	sun		Silvery leaves

Geranium
Cranesbill

These herbaceous perennials range from compact alpines like 'Ballerina' to invasive giants, but some of the more compact types are ideal for growing in permanent containers because they combine handsome lobed foliage with abundant blooms.

Geranium cinereum 'Ballerina'

Geranium 'Johnson's Blue'

One of the earliest to flower is 'Johnson's Blue', whose large, bowl-shaped blooms are a terrific bee magnet. Try it with creamy yellow tulips or golden yellow *Euonymus fortunei* cultivars. The fresh young leaves of 'Ann Folkard' are bright lime green, making a striking combination with the magenta, black-eyed flowers. Both thrive in a sunny or lightly shaded spot with moisture-retentive loam to lessen the risk of powdery mildew.

	SPRING	SUMMER	AUTUMN	WINTER	height (cm)	spread (cm)	min. temp °C	moisture	sun/shade	colour	
Geranium 'Ann Folkard'	planting planting	flower flower flower	flower flower		30	60	-17°	well drained	sun		Lime green foliage
G. 'Johnson's Blue'	planting planting	flower flower flower flower			30	45	-17°	well drained	part shade		Luminous blue flowers
G. cinereum 'Ballerina'	planting planting	flower flower flower flower flower			15	30	-17°	well drained	sun		Long flowering
G. renardii	planting	flower			30	30	-17°	well drained	sun		Handsome foliage
G. sanguineum 'Album'	planting planting	flower flower flower flower			25	30	-17°	well drained	sun		Fine cut foliage

planting | flower | well drained | moist | wet

Helianthemum
Rock rose

Small, summer flowering shrubs suitable for containers are few and far between so the low growing evergreen rock roses are a boon. Throughout late spring and early summer, these lime-loving Mediterranean alpines are studded with dish-shaped blooms.

Most cultivars come in hot colours, such as 'Fire Dragon' and 'Henfield Brilliant', making a bright show when combined with the gentian coloured alpine *Lithodora* 'Heavenly Blue'. Try white and pastel shades like the light, carmine pink 'Rhodanthe Carneum' with purple leaf sedums and *Artemisia stelleriana* 'Boughton Silver'. Grow in gritty, free-draining loam as rock roses dislike winter wet. Clip over lightly after flowering.

Helianthemum 'Wisley Primrose'

	SPRING	SUMMER	AUTUMN	WINTER	height (cm)	spread (cm)	min. temp °C	moisture	sun/shade	colour	
Helianthemum 'Fire Dragon'					30	30	17°				Grey-green foliage
H. 'Henfield Brilliant'					25	30	17°				Grey-green foliage
H. 'Jubilee'					30	30	17°				Double flowers
H. 'Rhodanthe Carneum'					30	45	17°				Grey foliage
H. 'The Bride'					30	45	17°				Silver-grey foliage
H. 'Wisley Primrose'					30	45	17°				Grey green foliage

Helianthus
Sunflower

Dwarf varieties of the hardy annual sunflower still have larger than life flowerheads and large, coarse leaves, but the height is much reduced compared with the giant relatives that most people associate with the name of this plant.

These plants have a distinctive cottage garden character and it is fun to plant them in novel containers such as old-fashioned watering cans. Also try them singly in simple clay pots ranged in a row against a wall or in a windowbox with other bright annuals. Most are yellow, but for an autumnal mix try 'Music Box' or the bronze flowered 'Sundance Kid'. 'Teddy Bear' has furry golden flowerheads like flattened pompons.

Watch for slug and snail damage and powery mildew. Otherwise, diseases are not a problem.

Helianthus annuus 'Teddy Bear'

	SPRING	SUMMER	AUTUMN	WINTER	height (cm)	spread (cm)	min. temp °C	moisture	sun/shade	colour	
Helianthus annuus 'Big Smile'					60	30	-17°				Darker yellow centres
H. a. 'Music Box Mixed'					60	30	-17°				Multi-branched, free flowering
H. a. 'Sundance Kid'					45	30	-17°				Unusual colour
H. a. 'Sunspot'					60	30	-17°				Large heads
H. a. 'Teddy Bear'					90	45	-17°				Double flowers

☼ *sunny*   ☼ *semi-shady*   ● *shady*

Flowering Plants · H

Heliotropum
Heliotrope *or*
Cherry pie

This old fashioned bedding plant with the fragrance of vanilla, is really a tender shrub but with seed raised varieties like 'Marine', most people treat the plants as half-hardy annuals.

The domed flowerheads are made up of many tiny blooms that are tightly packed. The foliage makes an attractive foil, having a crinkled appearance due to its deep veining, and is often glossy with a bronzy tinting. Compact forms such as 'Dwarf Marine' and the diminutive 'Baby Blue' are useful for hanging baskets and window boxes. All heliotropes attract butterflies. Watch for aphids, red spider mite and whitefly as well as grey mould.

Heliotropium hybrid

	SPRING	SUMMER	AUTUMN	WINTER	height (cm)	spread (cm)	min. temp °C	moisture	sun/shade	colour	
Heliotropium arborescens 'Baby Blue'					30	23	1°				White star eye
H. a. 'Chatsworth'					45	30	1°				Suitable for standards
H. a. 'Dwarf or Mini Marine'					40	30	1°				Dark leaves
H. 'Marine'					45	45	1°				Attractive crinkled foliage

Helleborus
Hellebore

Though not ideally suited to being grown in containers, these winter and spring flowering woodlanders look at home in large wooden half barrels combined with dwarf, early flowering bulbs and trailing ivy.

The most reliable are the garden hybrids, which usually have beautiful streaks and speckles inside the nodding flowers. Buy in bloom to be sure of the colour. The hybrid, *Helleborus* x *sternii*, and selected 'Blackthorn Group', have creamy green flowers with the reverse suffused pinkish purple. The choice *H. lividus* needs a warm, sheltered spot. Use John Innes no 3 mixed with peat, leaf mould or ground, composted bark and mulch. Watch for aphids, slugs and snails.

Helleborus x hybridus

	SPRING	SUMMER	AUTUMN	WINTER	height (cm)	spread (cm)	min. temp °C	moisture	sun/shade	colour	
Helleborus lividus					45	45	-5°				Purple suffusion. Marbled leaves
H. x *hybridus* cultivars					45	45	17°				The most reliable cultivars
H. x *sternii*					60	45	15°				Suffused pinkish purple

planting   flower   well drained   moist   wet

Hyacinthus
Hyacinth

These powerfully fragrant spring bulbs are wonderful to grow on the patio so that their perfume can be detected through open windows.

For the best visual effect, plant close together in groups of three, five and so on, or in a staggered row in troughs and window boxes. There are many excellent varieties to choose from with colours mainly in the blue, purple and pink range. Departing from that are the creamy white 'L'Innocence', primrose yellow 'City of Haarlem' and salmon-apricot 'Gypsy Queen'. Try planting with double daisies, violas, pansies, white- or yellow-variegated ivy. Allow foliage to die down before dismantling the display, feeding weekly with liquid fertilizer after flowering.

Hyacinthus orientalis 'Pink Pearl'

	SPRING	SUMMER	AUTUMN	WINTER	height (cm)	spread (cm)	min. temp °C	moisture	sun/shade	colour	
H. orientalis 'Anna Marie'	●		🌱🌱🌱		20	8	-17°	💧	☀		Unusual pink
H. o. 'City of Haarlem'	●		🌱🌱🌱		20	8	-17°	💧	☀		Late flowering
H. o. 'Delft Blue'	●		🌱🌱🌱		20	8	-17°	💧	☀		Pretty pastel blue
H. o. 'Gipsy Queen'	●		🌱🌱🌱		20	8	-17°	💧	☀		Unusual colour
H. o. 'L'Innocence'	●		🌱🌱🌱		20	8	-17°	💧	☀		Deadhead promptly
H. o. 'Pink Pearl'	●		🌱🌱🌱		20	8	-17°	💧	☀		A good strong pink

Iberis
Perennial candytuft

This drought tolerant evergreen alpine softens the edges of large permanent containers. In spring and early summer the plants are covered in rounded clusters of pure white flowers.

Iberis variety

There are two excellent iberis cultivars. 'Weisser Zwerg' or 'Little Gem' is much smaller and hummock forming, whilst 'Schneeflocke' is like a low growing version of the parent plant. Grow iberis in free-draining compost in a hot, sunny spot with other alpines and Mediterranean shrubs, herbs and silverlings. Clip plants over lightly after flowering. Watch for slugs and snails.

	SPRING	SUMMER	AUTUMN	WINTER	height (cm)	spread (cm)	min. temp °C	moisture	sun/shade	colour	
Iberis sempervirens	🌱 ● ● ● ● ●				30	60	-17°	💧	☀		Narrow leaves
I. s. 'Schneeflocke' syn 'Snowflake'	🌱 ● ●				25	60	-17°	💧	☀		Low carpeter
I. s. 'Weisser Zwerg' syn. 'Little Gem'	🌱 ● ●				15	25	-17°	💧	☀		Mound forming

☀ *sunny*   🔆 *semi-shady*   ● *shady*

Impatiens
Busy Lizzie

For flowering performance in shade, it is hard to beat the well known busy Lizzie, a half hardy annual or tender perennial that flowers non stop throughout summer until the first frosts. Compact, weather-resistant veterans in a wide range of colours include Accent and the dwarf Super Elfin. The blooms of Novette Star and Mega Orange Star are highlighted by a broad white cross.

On a more subtle note, the new Mosaic series has petals flecked with white. It doesn't have as much flower power as some of the standard bedding varieties, but it is a very pretty strain of the plant. Equally attractive is the pastel Swirl Series, one of several picotee busy Lizzies with a darker pink edging.

For large blooms, pick members of the Blitz 2000 series or one of the New Guinea Hybrid impatiens, such as the eye-catching 'Tango', which has vivid orange blooms complemented by bronze foliage. The New Guinea Hybrids are not as robust or as weather resistant as varieties of *Impatiens walleriana* and prefer some direct sunshine and a warm, sheltered spot. They come in many colours and have bold variegated, bronze or green, lance shaped leaves. They have a distinctly sub-tropical look and appear even more exotic when planted with cannas, abutilon and dahlias such as 'Bishop of Llandaff'.

Double-flowered busy Lizzies have recently made a comeback. You can grow your own from seed with 'Carousel' – a mix of singles and semi-doubles – or buy individual plants in the Fiesta series. These are relatively upright plants, smothered with rose-like blooms. Avoid overhead watering, which can knock off flowerheads and also cause the plants to rot.

One of the most recent developments has been the Fanfare Series of trailing

Impatiens New Guinea Group

planting   flower   well drained   moist   wet

impatiens. These need similar conditions to the New Guinea Hybrids to promote increased growth of the slowly trailing stems. Of the group, Fanfare Orange is the most vigorous. But for hanging baskets any of the more compact *I. walleriana* types will perform well and

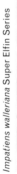

Impatiens walleriana Super Elfin Series

can look stunning used as a single subject. Otherwise, mix with trailing fuchsias and begonias. The new 'Tempo' is particularly good for baskets, because it branches freely low down. Many of the pastel blooms have a darker eye.

Dark coloured busy Lizzies tend to bleach if left in full sun. After rain the petals of these plants can stick to the foliage and it is worth picking them off before they turn brown. Although busy Lizzies have some ability to recover from drought, bedding impatiens prefer evenly moist compost, but in wet summers, watch out for grey mould.

Flowering Plants

	SPRING	SUMMER	AUTUMN	WINTER	height (cm)	spread (cm)	min. temp °C	moisture	sun/shade	colour	
Impatiens 'Tango' (New Guinea Group)					45	30	1°				Large flowers and bronze foliage
I. Fanfare					8	50	1°				New. Slowly trailing habit
I. New Guinea Hybrids					60	40	1°				Larger flowers; variegated leaves
I. walleriana Accent Series					20	20	1°			+	Compact F1 hybrid
I. w. Blitz 2000 Series					25	30	1°			+	Large blooms
I. w. 'Carousel'					30	30	1°			+	Double and semi doubles from seed
I. w. Fiesta Series					40	25	1°			+	Double blooms. Olé are shorter
I. w. 'Mega Orange Star'					23	30	1°				Large, weather-resistant blooms
I. w. Mosaic Series					25	20	1°				Mottled petals
I. w. Novette Star Series					25	30	1°			+	White star marking
I. w. Super Elfin Series					15	15	1°			+	Dwarf strain
I. w. Swirl Series					20	30	1°				Petals edged darker pink
I. w. Tempo Series					20	30	1°				Branch low down. Dark eye

☼ *sunny*   ◐ *semi-shady*   ● *shady*   ⊞ *many colours*

Ipomoea
Morning glory

Given a sheltered sunny position, the twining morning glories will quickly reach the top of a wigwam of canes or a decorative obelisk fixed into a pot. Foliage cover is quite poor, though, so wind the stems back down once they have reached the top.

Ipomoea tricolor 'Heavenly Blue'

The large circular blooms of *Ipomoea tricolor* are electric blue, whilst those of 'Flying Saucers' are marbled blue and white. In marked contrast, 'Crimson Rambler' is a deep crimson red and 'Scarlett O'Hara' as the name suggests, is bright red. Set apart from the group is *Ipomoea lobata*, formerly know as *Mina lobata*, which is a real show stopper, with arching flower stems carrying numerous orange-red to cream blooms.

Plant morning glories out well after the risk of frost has passed, as the plants are highly temperature sensitive. Watch out for red spider mite and powdery mildew and counter attack both these conditions by watering regularly.

	SPRING	SUMMER	AUTUMN	WINTER	height (cm)	spread (cm)	min. temp °C	moisture	sun/shade	colour	
I. lobata syn *Mina lobata*		planting/flower	flower		300	100	7°	well drained	sun		Unusual flower shape
I. nil 'Scarlet O'Hara'		planting/flower	flower		300	100	7°	well drained	sun		White throat
I. tricolor 'Crimson Rambler'		planting/flower	flower		300	100	7°	well drained	sun		White throat
I. t. 'Flying Saucers'		planting/flower	flower		300	100	7°	well drained	sun		Striped petals
I. t. 'Heavenly Blue'		planting/flower	flower		300	100	7°	well drained	sun		White throat

Iris

The bulbous Reticulata irises flower in late winter and early spring and, being mainly blue, combine very effectively with white and yellow *Crocus chrysanthus* cultivars, especially in windowboxes.

They are also able to push up through low growing heathers such as *Erica carnea* 'Springwood White'. In fact, wherever you have space in permanent containers, it is worth planting clusters of these dainty irises. Another idea is to plant different varieties in weathered clay pots – especially half pots, which suit the proportions well. Some like the deep blue species, *Iris reticulata* and the plum purple cultivar 'George', have narrow petals – grow the latter with a golden gravel mulch, as the flowers do not stand out well against dark compost.

Iris reticulata 'Harmony'

	SPRING	SUMMER	AUTUMN	WINTER	height (cm)	spread (cm)	min. temp °C	moisture	sun/shade	colour	
Iris 'George' (Reticulata type)	flower		planting	flower	15	8	-17°	well drained	sun		Plant through pale mulch
I. 'Harmony' (Reticulata type)	flower		planting	flower	15	8	-17°	well drained	sun		Prominent yellow markings
I. 'Joyce' (Reticulata type)	flower		planting	flower	15	8	-17°	well drained	sun		Showy, broad petals
I. foetidissima 'Variegata'	planting		planting	flower	45	30	-17°	well drained	sun		Evergreen, variegated, rarely flowers
I. histrioides 'Major' (Reticulata)	flower		planting	flower	15	8	-17°	well drained	sun		Vigorous cultivar
Iris reticulata	flower		planting	flower	15	8	-17°	well drained	sun		May not flower well the following year

planting   flower   well drained   moist   wet

Kalanchoe
Flaming Katy

In colder climes, the succulent plant, flaming Katy, is treated as a houseplant, but in recent years it has been promoted for summer use in patio containers and windowboxes, where it has a strong and individual decorative presence.

Bearing domed heads of many tiny flowers in a wide range of shades from tropical reds and oranges to yellow, pink and cream, *Kalanchoe blossfeldiana* remains in flower for many weeks. It flowers naturally towards the end of the year, being a short day plant, but growers can bring plants into bloom at any time. Take care not to overwater as the roots may rot and do not plant out until early to mid-summer, because the fleshy leaves and stems are highly temperature sensitive, requiring a minimum night temperature of around 10°C (50°F). Grow in full sun using free-draining compost, allowing it to dry out a little between waterings. Hot coloured kalanchoes look particularly good with other succulents and drought tolerant plants such as Aloe, Sedum, Echeveria and *Dichondra* 'Silver Falls', but the range of colours ensures that you can blend plants into a wide variety of schemes. Buy in bud with just a few blooms open, deadhead regularly and discard after flowering. Height and spread is variable but generally around 30 x 23cm (12 x 10in).

Kalanchoe blossfeldiana

Lantana
Yellow sage

This prolific flowering tender shrub is in many ways an ideal patio plant, thriving in full sun and enjoying the good drainage afforded by pot cultivation.

The rounded flowerheads are made up of many tightly clustered blooms and these often change colour with age or have two-tone shading. Colour scheming is easy with such a range of colours to choose from – white through mauve and pink to yellow orange and red. Due to its vigour, Lantana is ideal for filling the base of a large potted specimen tree or topiary piece in summer.

Lantana camara

K
L

Flowering Plants

	SPRING	SUMMER	AUTUMN	WINTER	height (cm)	spread (cm)	min. temp °C	moisture	sun/shade	colour	
Lantana camara 'Cream Carpet'		●●●	●		30	75	10°	◌◌	☼	☐	Low, spreading
L. c. 'Fabiola'		●●●	●		120	120	10°	◌◌	☼	▨	Pretty bicolor
L. c. 'Feston Rose'		●●●	●		120	120	10°	◌◌	☼	▨	Touches of yellow
L. c. 'Radiation'		●●●	●		120	120	10°	◌◌	☼	■	Intense, 'hot' shade, darker round the edge
L. c. 'Snow White'		●●●	●		120	120	10°	◌◌	☼	☐	White with a yellow eye
L. c. 'Spreading Sunset'		●●●	●		120	120	10°	◌◌	☼	▨	Colour darkens to reddish pink with age

☼ *sunny*   ☼ *semi-shady*   ● *shady*

Lathyrus

The delicate winged flower of the hardy annual sweet pea has an old fashioned, cottage garden appeal.

Although traditionally grown on tall frames for cutting, compact sweet peas make delightful container plants, some requiring no support at all.

Try growing medium sized sweet peas such as the fragrant *L. o.* 'Jet Set' in deep tubs or wooden barrels using a simple cane wigwam for support. 'Snoopea' and 'Bijou' are smaller but need no support. 'Patio' is particularly fragrant. 'Pink Cupid' and the cascading 'Sweetie' are recommended for single subject hanging baskets. Plant in loam-based compost such as John Innes No 3. For windowboxes and hanging baskets add water-retaining gel. Feed regularly.

Lathyrus odoratus 'Pink Cupid'

	SPRING	SUMMER	AUTUMN	WINTER	height (cm)	spread (cm)	min. temp °C	moisture	sun/shade	colour	
Lathyrus odoratus 'Bijou'	planting	flower			40	20	-17°	well drained/moist	sun	■	Requires support; fragrant, frilled petals
L. o. 'Jet Set'	planting	flower			90	20	-17°	well drained/moist	sun	□	Large flowers; no support needed
L. o. 'Patio'	planting	flower			38	20	-17°	well drained/moist	sun	■	Needs no support; well scented
L. o. 'Pink Cupid'	planting	flower			23	45	-17°	well drained/moist	sun	■	Good fragrance; spreading habit
L. o. 'Sweetie'	planting	flower			30	20	-17°	well drained/moist	sun	□	Cascading habit; good for baskets
L. o. 'Snoopea'	planting	flower			75	20	-17°	well drained/moist	sun	■	No tendrils; needs no support

Laurentia

The starry Laurentia is a tender perennial that is normally grown as an annual. Both the flowers and slender tooth-edged leaves give the plants quite a delicate appearance, but there is a lot of flower power.

Laurentia axillaris

Try Laurentia in baskets or on the edge of patio containers, where it will trail over the sides. Use the blue species and varieties such as the deeper 'Fantasy Blue' as a foil for pink, purple and white flowered container plants e.g. small flowered Surfinia petunias, single flowered fuchsias and busy lizzies or to contrast with yellows and oranges such as Calceolaria.

	SPRING	SUMMER	AUTUMN	WINTER	height (cm)	spread (cm)	min. temp °C	moisture	sun/shade	colour	
Laurentia axillaris	planting	flower	flower		30	30	5°	well drained/moist	sun	■	Long-flowering
L. a. 'Fantasy Blue'	planting	flower	flower		30	30	5°	well drained/moist	sun	■	Deeper blue than the species
L. a. 'Pink Charm'	planting	flower	flower		25	30	5°	well drained/moist	sun	■	Pretty mauve pink
L. a. 'Shooting Stars'	planting	flower	flower		25	30	5°	well drained/moist	sun	□	Pure white
L. a. Star Series	planting	flower	flower		30	30	5°	well drained/moist	sun	▨	Pastel mixture

Flowering Plants

planting | flower | well drained | moist | wet

Lobelia

Traditionally, trailing lobelia has been one of the main ingredients in hanging baskets, the deep blue of 'Sapphire' being the perfect backdrop for red, white, orange and yellow trailing begonias. Possibilities broadened with pretty mixtures from the Cascade Series which make a lovely foil for trailing petunias, as well as individual pastel shades such as 'Lilac Fountain' and 'Regatta Blue Splash'.

Lobelia erinus 'Mrs Clibran'

Compact lobelias – including the aptly named 'Cambridge Blue' and dusky 'Crystal Palace' – are useful for edging window boxes and containers in shade and combine beautifully with busy Lizzies and the moisture loving mimulus. Although the plant doesn't have a great deal of vigour, the double rosebud flowers of 'Kathleen Mallard' are intriguing. All plants so far described are derived from *Lobelia erinus*, a half-hardy annual. This has minute seed, is quite difficult to handle and for convenience it is best to buy plants as plugs or in modular trays. Don't pick trays that are already in flower – they will almost certainly be rootbound and that makes them harder to establish.

Lobelia erinus 'Crystal Palace'

Lobelia erinus 'Cascade Mixed'

Lobelia richardsonii is a tender perennial, normally discarded at the end of the season, with an open habit, wiry stems and relatively large individual blue blooms. Use it in a hanging basket or to trail over the edge of a pot. Quite different in character are the strongly upright herbaceous perennials of the Fan and Kompliment Series. The former are particularly good in pots because they branch from the base and are more compact. They have large, fan-shaped blooms and flower for months given a steady supply of moisture. Grow with tender perennials and bedding or try combining them with blue-leaved hostas and yellow splashed *Artemisia* 'Oriental Limelight'.

Lobelias tolerate full sun provided they have a constant supply of moisture, but they are happier in semi-shade. Use moisture retentive compost and, if necessary, mix in water retaining gel. If *Lobelia erinus* varieties suffer missed waterings they rarely recover properly. Watch for slugs and snails.

L

Flowering Plants

	SPRING	SUMMER	AUTUMN	WINTER	height (cm)	spread (cm)	min. temp °C	moisture	sun/shade	colour	
Lobelia erinus 'Cambridge Blue'	🐛 🐛	● ● ●	● ●		15	15	1°	💧💧	☀️		Compact
L. e. Cascade Series	🐛 🐛	● ● ●	● ●		30	15	1°	💧💧	☀️		Trailing. Some flowers have a white eye
L. e. 'Crystal Palace'	🐛 🐛	● ● ●	● ●		15	15	1°	💧💧	☀️		Compact, bronze foliage
L. e. 'Kathleen Mallard'	🐛 🐛	● ● ●	● ●		15	15	1°	💧💧	☀️		Tiny double rosette flowers
L. e. 'Mrs Clibran'	🐛 🐛	● ● ●	● ●		30	15	1°	💧💧	☀️		Compact bushy habit
L. e. Regatta 'Blue Splash'	🐛 🐛	● ● ●	● ●		25	15	1°	💧💧	☀️		Semi-trailing. White tinted blue
L. e. 'Sapphire' syn 'Blue Basket'	🐛 🐛	● ● ●	● ●		30	15	1°	💧💧	☀️		Trailing. Flowers have a white eye
L. Fan Series	🐛 🐛	● ● ●	● ●		60	20	-17°	💧	☀️		Herbaceous, with green or bronzed foliage
L. Kompliment Series	🐛 🐛	● ● ●	● ●		75	20	-17°	💧	☀️		Herbaceous, with unbranched stems
L. richardsonii syn. 'Richardii'	🐛 🐛	● ● ●	● ●		30	15	1°	💧💧	☀️		More open, wiry habit, trailing

☀️ *sunny*　☀️ *semi-shady*　● *shady*

Lobularia
Sweet alyssum

The delicious honey scent of sweet white alyssum, a long-established hardy annual, is a major reason for growing this easy plant.

One of the best of the many whites available is 'Snow Crystals', which is a hybrid with extra large flowers that never runs to seed. It has a spreading domed habit. But white is no longer the only type of alyssum available; a range of other shades and several series now exist, with a wide variety of pastels punctuated by darker crimson reds and purples.

Lobularia maritima 'Snow Crystals'

	SPRING	SUMMER	AUTUMN	WINTER	height (cm)	spread (cm)	min. temp °C	moisture	sun/shade	colour	
Lobularia maritima Aphrodite Series	planting	flower			10	30	-17°	well drained	sun	▨	Wide pastel colour range
L. m. 'Rosie O'Day'	planting	flower			10	20	-17°	well drained	sun	▨	Compact
L. m. 'Oriental Night'	planting	flower			10	23	-17°	well drained	sun	▨	Compact
L. m. 'Snow Crystals'	planting	flower			22	45	-17°	well drained	sun	▢	Large blooms. Very long flowering
l. m. pendula 'Wandering Star'	planting	flower			22	30	-17°	well drained	sun	▨	New. Cascading habit
L. m. Easter Bonnet Series	planting	flower			10	20	-17°	well drained	sun	▨	Early into flower

Mimulus

Most bedding for shady containers has flowers in the white, pastel pink and purple range, but the moisture loving forms of *Mimulus* x *hybridus* offer vibrant oranges, yellows and reds.

Mimulus x hybridus 'Viva'

In addition, the flared, funnel shaped blooms often have exotic speckles, streaks and blotches in the throat. This half-hardy bedding plant is easy from seed and comes into flower relatively quickly, and this is especially true of the Magic Series. The 'Calypso' mixture has large blooms some of which are bicoloured, blotched or spotted. Meanwhile the showy 'Viva' has large, orchid like blooms of light yellow, boldly marked with deep burgundy. But if you want clear colours and a neat, compact habit try Mystic Series. Quite different is the tender perennial *M. aurantiacus*, which has large, unmarked blooms with wavy margins and a lax, vigorous habit.

	SPRING	SUMMER	AUTUMN	WINTER	height (cm)	spread (cm)	min. temp °C	moisture	sun/shade	colour	
Mimulus aurantiacus	planting	flower			90	90	1°	well drained	sun	▨	Sticky. Large wavy edged blooms
M. x hybridus Calypso	planting	flower			30	30	-17°	moist	part	▨	Some bicolors. Large velvety blooms
M. x h. Magic Series	planting	flower			20	30	-17°	moist	part	▮	Early to bloom. Some bicolors
M x h. Malibu Series	planting	flower			15	20	-17°	moist	part	▢	Superseded by later Series
M. x h. Mystic Series	planting	flower			20	20	-17°	moist	part	▨	Blooms clear, rarely blotched or speckled
M. x h. 'Viva'	planting	flower			30	30	-17°	moist	part	▨	Large flowers with bold maroon blotch

L

M

Flowering Plants

| planting | ● flower | well drained | moist | wet |

Mirabilis

Four o'clock flower *or* Marvel of Peru

Anyone holidaying in the Mediterranean will have seen this tender tuberous-rooted perennial. The leafy plants form rounded bushes (90 x 90cm/3ft x 3ft), which during the day would be easily overlooked.

Later in the afternoon, however, they are transformed with magenta-purple or crimson and sometimes orange, yellow or striped flowers. Bizarrely, you can get a mixture of these colours all together on the same plant! Blooms remain open all night and the perfume is lovely. This is certainly a plant to grow on a sheltered sunny patio or in a courtyard where you sit out in the evenings after work. The flowering period is mid- to late summer. If you have a conservatory, move plants undercover for the winter. Otherwise, store the tubers frost free as you would tuberous begonias and plant out again

Mirabilis jalapa

in spring when there is no risk of frost. Use a well-drained loam based compost such as John Innes No. 3 and feed and water regularly during the growing season.

Muscari

Grape hyacinth

For an abundance of fragrant, true blue spring flowers, it is hard to beat the common grape hyacinth (*Muscari armeniacum*). The plant gets its name from the bunch of grapes effect of the tiny rounded blooms crowded together on each spike.

Muscari armeniacum

If you look closely you'll see that the rim of the flower is edged in white. For the most dramatic effect, plant in dense clumps in pots or in a broad band along the front of troughs and window boxes. Try combining with white or yellow dwarf daffodils, double daisies or polyanthus for a fresh display. The showy flowers of 'Blue Spike' are double and a more intense blue, but this plant doesn't bulk up as quickly as the species. For pure white flowers grow *M. botryoides* 'Album'. The fluffy heads of the tassel hyacinth, *M. comosum* 'Plumosum' appear later than the rest and being slightly taller make perfect partners for elegant lily flowered tulips.

	SPRING	SUMMER	AUTUMN	WINTER	height (cm)	spread (cm)	min. temp °C	moisture	sun/shade	colour	
Muscari armeniacum	●		🌱 🌱 🌱		20	2	-17°	💧💧	◐		Spreading clumps, fragrant
M. a. 'Blue Spike'	●		🌱 🌱 🌱		20	2	-17°	💧💧	◐		Double flowers, fragrant
M. botryoides 'Album'	● ●		🌱 🌱 🌱		20	2	-17°	💧	◐		Fragrant
M. comosum 'Plumosum'		●	🌱 🌱 🌱		30	2	-17°	💧💧	◐		Large, fluffy heads, fragrant

☼ *sunny*   ◑ *semi-shady*   ● *shady*

Narcissus
Dwarf daffodil

To achieve the right scale or balance in a container, it is better to go for the more delicate looking dwarf narcissi rather than the large trumpet daffodils, which can look rather clumsy in pots and windowboxes.

Narcissus 'Dove Wings'

Narcissus 'February Gold'

These belong to several different groups or divisions within the genus, most notably the hardy, weatherproof, early flowering Cyclamineus types such as 'February Gold', 'Dove Wings' and 'Jetfire' that produce a single flower per stem, and often have elegantly swept back petals. 'Peeping Tom' is taller than most in its group, but with great character, having a very narrow, elongated trumpet. Several other good pot cultivars belong to the dainty Triandrus group, for example 'Hawera' and the exquisite, creamy-white 'Thalia', recognizable by the small cluster of nodding blooms per stem. Another multi-headed type is 'Tête à Tête', one of the most reliable for container planting.

The name narcissus refers to the narcotic effect that the fragrance can have on the nose. Some dwarf daffodils are deliciously scented.

Narcissus 'Tête-à-Tête'

These include the hardy but delicate looking 'Sweetness' (a member of the Jonquilla) division, usually referred to as jonquils; and the more robust looking double flowered 'Cheerfulness' and 'Sir Winston Churchill'.

Combine early flowering types with *Crocus chrysanthus* varieties, dwarf Reticulata irises and vivid blue *Scilla siberica* or Muscari. Hardy primroses and polyanthus, violas, double daisies and winter flowering heathers also make good companions. Dwarf daffodils can also be planted as part of a permanent arrangement for a splash of spring colour. With seasonal arrangements, if you want to keep the bulbs for next year, dead head after flowering.

	SPRING	SUMMER	AUTUMN	WINTER	height (cm)	spread (cm)	min. temp °C	moisture	sun/shade	colour	
Narcissus 'Cheerfulness'	●		🌱🌱🌱		40	15	-17°	💧💧	☼		Frilly double, fragrant
N. 'Dove Wings'	●		🌱🌱🌱		30	8	17°	💧💧	☼		Swept back petals
N. 'February Gold'	●		🌱🌱🌱		30	8	-17°	💧💧	☼		Yellow trumpets
N. 'Hawera'		●	🌱🌱🌱		18	8	-5°	💧💧	☼		Multiple heads
N. 'Jenny'	●		🌱🌱🌱		30	8	-17°	💧💧	☼		Similar to 'Dove Wings' but later
N. 'Jetfire'	●		🌱🌱🌱		20	8	-17°	💧💧	☼		Showy with orange cups
N. 'Minnow'	●		🌱🌱🌱		18	8	-5°	💧💧	☼		Petite, multiple heads
N. 'Peeping Tom'	●		🌱🌱🌱		40	10	-17°	💧💧	☼		Long narrow trumpets
N. 'Sir Winston Churchill'	●		🌱🌱🌱		40	15	-17°	💧💧	☼		Frilly double. Fragrant
N. 'Sweetness'	●		🌱🌱🌱		40	8	-17°	💧💧	☼		Very fragrant
N. 'Tête à Tête'	●		🌱🌱🌱		20	8	-17°	💧💧	☼		Multiple heads, early and long lasting
N. 'Thalia'	●		🌱🌱🌱		35	8	-17°	💧💧	☼		Elegant, starry nodding heads

🌱 *planting*   ● *flower*   💧 *well drained*   💧💧 *moist*   💧💧💧 *wet*

N

Flowering Plants

Nemesia

Though forms of the tender perennial *Nemesia caerulea* only began to appear in garden centres in the 1990s, they are almost as popular now as their South African relatives, the diascias. These plants are quite different to the long established annual *Nemesia strumosa*, which though it has larger blooms, can be tricky to keep flowering all summer long.

Most come in pastel shades of blue-tinged-purple, pale pink or white, often with a prominent yellow 'eye', and some have a peppery sweetness. The plants are usually compact but may be strongly upright or spreading and bushy in habit. Many are suitable for hanging baskets or for softening the rim of a container, including the white flowered 'Compact Innocence', pale pink 'Blushing Bride', pale lavender 'Blue Bird' and cascading 'Ravello'. 'Blue Lagoon' is a clear lavender blue with larger than normal flowers and 'Aromatica Deep Blue' is unusually dark for this soft shaded group. Some pretty pinks include the rose coloured 'Honey Girl' and 'Candy Girl' whose fading flowers create a lovely two-tone effect. The pale sugar pink 'Fragrant Cloud' is hardier than the rest of the group and forms a larger plant with a domed profile.

Combine tender perennial Nemesia with similarly delicate plants having a contrasting flower shape, for example trailing verbenas, brachyscome and heliotrope. Trim back lightly after flowering flushes and keep the compost evenly moist. Plants may overwinter unprotected on a sheltered patio.

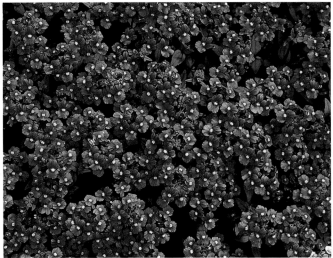

Nemesia 'Blue Lagoon'

	SPRING	SUMMER	AUTUMN	WINTER	height (cm)	spread (cm)	min. temp °C	moisture	sun/shade	colour
Nemesia 'Aromatica Deep Blue'		●●●	●●		45	30	-5°			Yellow eye. Part of a series
N. 'Blue Bird'		●●●	●●		30	30	-5°			Yellow eye; semi-trailing habit
N. 'Blue Lagoon'		●●●	●●		38	30	-5°			Larger flowers; upright habit
N. 'Blushing Bride'		●●●	●●		38	45	-5°			Bicolour; vigorous; bushy; scented
N. 'Candy Girl'		●●●	●●		30	30	-5°			Fading flowers give a two-tone effect
N. 'Confetti' syn. *N. denticulata*		●●●	●●		25	38	-5°			Scented
N. 'Fragrant Cloud'		●●●	●●		45	45	-17°			Hardy perennial; domed habit
N. 'Honey Girl'		●●●	●●		30	25	-5°			Maritana Series
N. 'Innocence'		●●●	●●		30	30	-5°			Scented; yellow eye
N. 'Mystic Blue'		●●●	●●		30	30	-5°			Floriferous. Yellow eye
N. 'Ravello'		●●●	●●		38	45	-5°			Good for hanging baskets
N. 'Safari Pink'		●●●	●●		35	30	-5°			Yellow eye; scented
N. 'Sugar Girl'		●●●	●●		30	30	-5°			Yellow eye. Maritana series

☼ *sunny*　☼ *semi-shady*　● *shady*

Nemophila
Baby blue eyes
or Five spot

Nemophila maculata is a somewhat curious hardy annual that forms a mat of spreading succulent branches covered in light green dissected leaves which in summer bear five petalled white blooms.

The common name 'Five spot' comes from the markings at the tip of each petal. Baby blue eyes (*N. menziesii*) is a larger plant, whose long, semi-trailing stems bear pretty sky blue blooms. Neither copes well with wind, especially in more exposed hanging baskets, because the stems are quite brittle. Combine with other plants that enjoy moist compost such as lobelia, fuchsia and the tangerine coloured *Begonia sutherlandii*. Watch for aphids.

Nemophila menziesii 'Snowstorm'

	SPRING	SUMMER	AUTUMN	WINTER	height (cm)	spread (cm)	min. temp °C	moisture	sun/shade	colour	
Nemophila maculata	planting	flower			15	20	-17°	well drained	sun		Purple blue petal tips
N. menziesii	planting	flower			20	30	-17°	well drained	sun		White flower centre
N. m. 'Snowstorm'	planting	flower			20	30	-17°	well drained	sun		Fine dark spots at base of petals

Nicotiana
Tobacco plant

Most of the tobacco plants we grown in our gardens are forms of *Nicotiana* x *sanderae*, a sticky annual or short lived perennial usually treated as a half-hardy annual.

Nicotiana Avalon Series

Nicotiana x *sanderae* Domino Series

Nicotiana plants are compact and very floriferous over a long period and there are many beautiful pastel shades to choose from which can lighten up a shady corner very effectively. The

Merlin series is particularly good for windowboxes and small pots, provided you can keep the compost evenly moist. Deadhead as necessary to maintain flowering. Try mixing with lime green foliage plants like golden feverfew (*Tanacetum parthenium* 'Aureum').

	SPRING	SUMMER	AUTUMN	WINTER	height (cm)	spread (cm)	min. temp °C	moisture	sun/shade	colour	
Nicotiana Avalon Series	planting	flower			30	30	1°	moist	sun		New dwarf with upward facing flowers
N. Domino Series	planting	flower			35	35	1°	moist	sun		Some with a white eye
N. Havana Series	planting	flower			35	30	1°	moist	sun		Very compact; large flowered
N. Merlin Series	planting	flower			25	23	1°	moist	sun		Purple with white eye available
N. Nicki Series	planting	flower			30	30	1°	moist	sun		Light fragrance
N. Starship Series	planting	flower			30	30	1°	moist	sun		Good weather tolerance

planting	flower	well drained	moist	wet

Osteospermum

The range of these sun-loving South African daisies has increased tremendously in recent years, with compact cultivars developed for pot work available in a range of purplish pinks, yellows and white, mostly with a darker, bluish, purplish or bronze satiny reverse.

Added interest comes from the 'eye', which is often deep blue as opposed to yellow. 'Pink Whirls' and the white 'Whirligig' have a fascinating pinwheel flower form, but these plants are not as floriferous as some of the modern cultivars and require more warmth and shelter. A couple of low growing osteospermums are relatively hardy – notably 'White Pim' and *O. jucundum* – and can therefore be used in permanent plantings, provided they have sharp drainage, full sun and the shelter of a warm wall. Allow them to cascade over the edge of a large pot or trough. 'Stardust' is also tougher than most so is worth trying outdoors year-round. All osteospermums form mats or spreading hummocks

Osteospermum
'Weetwood'

of narrow, evergreen leaves. The modern Sunny Series, with male or female names, provides plants that flower continuously for most of the summer and well into autumn. Try them with pelargoniums, trailing verbenas and helichrysums. Representing a big departure from the usual pinks and mauves is Symphony, the latest series to be developed. The colour range is from white through cream and pale yellow to pastel buff and peach tones, yellows and oranges.

The only downside to osteospermums is that they close their flowers in dull weather and towards the evening, and so they should always be grown with an aspect that ensures sun for most of the day. Deadhead frequently. Discard tender perennials at the end of the season or take semi-ripe cuttings in late summer/early autumn to overwinter frost free.

	SPRING	SUMMER	AUTUMN	WINTER	height (cm)	spread (cm)	min. temp °C	moisture	sun/shade	colour	
Osteospermum 'Buttermilk'	✂	●●●●	●●●		40	60	1°	💧	☀	⬜	Delicate shade
O. jucundum	✂	●●●●	●●●		40	60	1°	💧	☀	⬜	Compact, frost hardy cultivar
O. 'Pink Whirls'	✂	●●●●	●●●		30	60	1°	💧	☀	⬜	Pinwheel flower form
O. 'Stardust'	✂	●●●●	●●●		30	60	1°	💧	☀	⬜	Flowers stay open later
O. 'Sunny Alex'	✂	●●●●	●●		35	60	1°	💧	☀	⬜	Strong yellow
O. 'Sunny Boy'	✂	●●●	●●		50	60	1°	💧	☀	⬜	Pinkish purple reverse
O. 'Sunny Girl'	✂	●●●	●●		30	60	1°	💧	☀	⬜	Blue 'eye'
O. 'Sunny Lady'	✂	●●●●	●●		30	90	1°	💧	☀	⬛	Striking dark colour
O. Symphony Series	✂	●●●●	●●●		40	30	1°	💧	☀	⬜	New Series. Very heat tolerant
O. 'Whirligig'	✂	●●●●	●●●		45	60	1°	💧	☀	⬜	Pinwheel flower form
O. 'White Pim'	✂	●●●	●●●		50	60	-4°	💧	☀	⬜	Compact, frost hardy cultivar

☀ *sunny*   ☀ *semi-shady*   ● *shady*

Pelargonium
Geranium

The majority of these drought tolerant tender perennials are very easy to look after and make excellent subjects for planting against a sun-drenched wall or for displaying in pots on the patio. The bushy, upright zonal pelargoniums are the most familiar, with rounded leaves shaded with darker bands of colour and large domed or spherical flower clusters.

There are many excellent named cultivars – including singles and doubles – but you are most likely to find seed raised F1 hybrids at the garden centre, for example Century Series and the early flowering Multibloom and Sensation Series, both of which are noted for their prolific flower production and weather resistance. As their name suggests, Stellar geraniums have star-like flowers with pointed petals and handsome, maple-like leaves often with attractive shading. Look out for the new Fireworks Collection which includes eye-catching bicolours. The pretty Angel cultivars are also becoming popular as patio plants. Their individual blooms are shaped and blotched rather like pansies and the plants are very neat and compact, ideal for planting as specimens. Some geraniums have golden foliage or leaves with bold edgings, colourful zoning and banding. These types were very popular back in the nineteenth

Zonal pelargonium cultivar

century, but you can still buy a reasonable range from garden centres. One of the best known is Mr Henry Cox, with golden yellow, mid-green, dark purple and red leaf shading enhanced by the rose pink blooms. If your patio or terrace is warm and sheltered, you could also try the Regal pelargoniums, which have sumptuous blooms and naturally flower rather earlier than the rest. These plants are historically associated with conservatory and glass house cultivation but breeders have been working to produce more compact, free flowering forms for outdoor use.

Trailing or ivy leaved geraniums have thin stems covered in brittle, ivy-shaped foliage and single, semi-double or fully double flowers. The vigorous 'Amethyst' is an excellent choice for sheltered hanging baskets. 'Rouletta' is one of several trailing cultivars having striped flowers, and L'Elegante is grown as much for its foliage as for its delicate blooms. Kept on the dry side, the leaves develop pinkish-purple tinges and a prominent cream edge. For baskets in windy locations or for large windowboxes and balcony troughs, it is

Pelargonium 'Sensation Scarlet'

P

Flowering Plants

🖐 *planting*   ✺ *flower*   💧 *well drained*   💧 *moist*   💧 *wet* better to choose one of the so-called Continental, Balcon or Balcony geraniums that have been popular in Continental Europe since the 1970s. Examples include members of the Decora Series and the more compact Mini-cascade types. Both produce long branching wiry stems that are much less prone to breakage and the plants have a strongly cascading habit. The loose heads of single flowers are produced in great abundance, but colours tend to be restricted to mainly reds, pinks and lilac.

Pelargonium 'Regal Pink'

Pelargonium 'Regal White'

Deadhead zonal pelargoniums by nipping out spent flowers from within the head. These plants can usually tolerate some shade, provided they are not overwatered. Problems are few but plants may suffer from aphids on flower buds and stem rot due to overwatering. Pelargoniums are also prone to viral infection, which may not have visible symptoms. Check the labels when you buy and look out for plants that are certified virus free. These have improved flowering performance. Overwintered cuttings should be given very little water once rooted, to prevent rotting.

	SPRING	SUMMER	AUTUMN	WINTER	height (cm)	spread (cm)	min. temp °C	moisture	sun/shade	colour	
Amethyst (ivy-leaved pelargonium)		● ● ● ●	● ● ●		30	25	1°	◌◌	☼	■	Semi-double flowered; trailing
Angel Cultivars		● ● ● ●	● ● ●		40	20	1°	◌◌	☼	□	Petite plants
Century Series (zonal pelargonium)		● ● ● ●	● ● ●		45	30	1°	◌	☼	□	Large flowerheads
Decora Series (Continental or Balcony type)		● ● ● ●	● ● ●		60	30	1°	◌◌	☼	■	Excellent trailers for windowboxes
L'Elegante (ivy-leaved pelargonium)		● ● ● ●	● ● ●		25	20	1°	◌◌	☼	□	Variegated foliage, trailing
Lilac Mini Cascade		● ● ● ●	● ● ●		50	20	1°	◌	☼	■	Compact. Good trailer for baskets
Mr Henry Cox		● ● ● ●	● ● ●		30	12	1°	◌◌	☼	□	Bold variegated foliage
Multibloom Series		● ● ● ●	● ● ●		30	30	1°	◌◌	☼	■	Early and abundant flowers
Red Mini-cascade		● ● ● ●	● ● ●		50	20	1°	◌◌	☼	■	Compact. Good trailer for baskets
Regal Cultivars		● ● ● ●	● ● ●		40	30	1°	◌◌	☼	■	Large, ruffled blooms
Rosa Mini-cascade		● ● ● ●	● ● ●		50	20	1°	◌◌	☼	■	Compact. Good trailer for baskets
Rouletta (syn. 'Mexicana')		● ● ● ●	● ● ●		60	20	1°	◌	☼	■	Striped flowers; semi-double; trailing
Sensation Series		● ● ● ●	● ● ●		30	25	1°	◌	☼	□	Some flowers have a white eye
Stellar Cultivars		● ● ● ●	● ● ●		30	20	1°	◌	☼	■	Some speckled, streaked and bicoloured

☼ *sunny*   ☼ *semi-shady*   ● *shady*

Petunia

These sweetly scented half-hardy annuals and tender perennials are one of the mainstays of summer basket and pot displays, the large circular blooms making a bold statement when mixed with smaller flowers such as trailing lobelia, verbena and bidens.

The sticky plants rapidly become smothered in bloom and with regular feeding and deadheading continue long into autumn. The fragrance that builds from a collection of pots and baskets planted with petunias can be quite intoxicating, especially in the early evening.

Petunias do not perform as well in wet summers, but the newer compact growing varieties with smaller single blooms tend to fare better. The double-flowered trailing Tumbelina Series was bred specifically for good weather and disease resistance and the variety 'Priscilla' has been extremely popular, with its purple, mauve-veined flowers that are highly perfumed. Doubloon is another good double flowered series available in a range of colours, but for baskets, the cascading Surfinia petunias continue to dominate. These can only be grown from plugs or plants and occasionally there can be viral problems as a result. It is not unusual for these vigorous plants to survive in pots and baskets over mild winters, but they are best discarded in favour of new stock. One recent addition to look out for is 'Baby Pink Morn', which has petite blooms of sugar pink with a white centre and a compact growth habit – less overpowering in an average sized hanging basket than some Surfinia strains.

From seed, choose from the deservedly popular Wave petunias, which also make good basket plants because the habit is strongly spreading and one well-grown plant can fill an entire container. The Carpet Series produces compact plants in a range of bright clear colours and is ideal for creating colourful displays in patio pots but if you prefer veined

Petunia Million Bells Series 'Cherry'

Flowering Plants

planting   flower   well drained   moist   wet

Petunia Surfinia Series 'Blue Vein'

produce many small flowers and don't require as much deadheading. But for miniature petunia blooms go for the Carillon or Million Bells Series which have a cascading habit. Both of these actually belong to the closely related *Calibrachoa* genus. Try them as single subjects in hanging flower pockets and in hanging baskets in combination with other dainty blooms like *Brachyscome multifida*, Bacopa and *Verbena* 'Blue Cascade'.

Watch for aphids, slugs and snails. Dead head regularly and cut back straggly plants mid-season. Feed and water well to encourage fresh new flowering growth.

flowers, try the subtle pastel mix 'Mirage Reflection'. 'Prism Sunshine' has unusual yellow-fading-to-cream flowers but for something quite dramatic, look for 'Purple Pirouette' – a frilly double with deep purple and white striped blooms. Milliflora petunias like 'Fantasy Mixed'

Petunia 'Prism Sunshine'

	SPRING	SUMMER	AUTUMN	WINTER	height (cm)	spread (cm)	min. temp °C	moisture	sun/shade	colour	
P. Baby Pink Morn (Surfinia)					30	90	1°				Petite flowered trailer
P. Carillon Series (Calibrachoa)					15	30	1°				Ultra small flowers and trailing habit
P. Carpet Series					25	90	1°				Small flowers, compact
P. Doubloon Series					30	90	1°				Double flowered, trailing
P. 'Fantasy Mixed' (Milliflora)					30	45	1°				Very small blooms, some veined
P. Million Bells Series (Calibrachoa)					15	30	1°				Ultra small flowers and trailing habit
P. 'Mirage Reflection'					30	90	1°				Subtle blend of veined blooms
P. 'Prism Sunshine'					25	30	1°				Fades to cream; weather resistant
P. 'Purple Pirouette'					38	30	1°				Frilly striped double blooms
P. Surfinia Series					30	120	1°				Strong trailing plants. Some veined.
P. Tumbelina Series					30	90	1°				Double bloomed trailer
P. Wave Series					45	90	1°				Spreading habit ideal for baskets

☼ *sunny*   ☀ *semi-shady*   ● *shady*

Plumbago
Cape leadwort

This tender evergreen shrub with lax stems bears clusters of soft, sky blue flowers during the summer and well into the autumn.

The Cape leadwort looks best when the main stems are tied onto some kind of support such as a cane wigwam or obelisk. If you have a conservatory or heated greenhouse, you might also try training *Plumbago auriculata* into a standard. For more compact pot plants that need little support, look for 'Escapade Blue' or 'Escapade White'. Check all plants for whitefly before purchase.

Plumbago auriculata

	SPRING	SUMMER	AUTUMN	WINTER	height (cm)	spread (cm)	min. temp °C	moisture	sun/shade	colour	
P. auriculata syn. *P. capensis*	planting	flower flower flower	flower flower		120	120	1°	well drained	sun	■	May be trained as a standard
P. a. alba	planting	flower flower flower	flower flower		120	120	1°	well drained	sun	□	White form of species
P. 'Escapade Blue'	planting	flower flower flower	flower flower		40	50	1°	well drained	sun	■	Slightly deeper blue. Compact
P. 'Escapade White'	planting	flower flower flower	flower flower		35	60	1°	well drained	sun	□	Not as big as 'Escapade Blue'

Portulaca
Sun plant

If you have small pots hung on a sunny wall, especially ones made from terracotta, you need to stick to plants that have high heat and drought tolerance. *Portulaca grandiflora*, the sun plant, is an ideal candidate.

Portulaca grandiflora 'Calypso'

You will find plants in bloom from mid-summer, but several varieties are also available from seed to sow in spring. Plants tend to be low growing with spreading or trailing stems making them ideal for baskets and wall pots, but the hot pink flowered 'Margarita Rosita' is mound forming with good leaf coverage. Typically, this Brazilian sun lover comes in bright mixtures, including shocking pinks, tangerine, canary yellow, carmine red, magenta, lilac and white. 'Peppermint' is an unusual selection with white-flecked-carmine flowers.

The only downside is that the blooms close up in dull weather, though Sundial Series is an improvement, and was bred for better performance in cool, poor conditions as well as earlier flowering from seed.

	SPRING	SUMMER	AUTUMN	WINTER	height (cm)	spread (cm)	min. temp °C	moisture	sun/shade	colour	
Portulaca grandiflora 'Calypso'	planting	flower flower	flower		15	30	1°	well drained	sun	▥	Large double blooms
P. g. 'Double Mixed'	planting	flower flower flower	flower		15	30	1°	well drained	sun	□	Double, earlier flowering
P. g. 'Margarita Rosita'	planting	flower flower	flower		10	35	1°	well drained	sun	■	Large, semi double. Mound forming
P. g. Sundial Mixture	planting	flower flower flower	flower		15	30	1°	well drained	sun	▥	Stays open longer. Earlier flowering
P. g. Sundial Peppermint	planting	flower flower	flower		15	30	1°	well drained	sun	■	Unusual flecked petals
P. g. 'Sunnyside'	planting	flower flower	flower		15	30	1°	well drained	sun	▥	Blooms large double/ semi double

planting   flower   well drained   moist   wet

Primula

In spring, hybrid primroses produce a succession of large, brightly coloured blooms that nestle at the centre of the leaf rosette. Some of these perennials are very hardy and weather resistant – ideal for pots on the patio – whilst others need the protection of a glasshouse or conservatory, so check the label before buying.

Even the tougher strains appreciate some protection from the worst of the winter weather, so find a sheltered spot and either cover plants with fleece if a hard frost is forecast or move pots onto a porch. One of the harbingers of spring, blooming freely alongside snowdrops and aconites, is *Primula* 'Wanda'. This hardy primrose with many small flowers in a glowing purple-red has given rise to the larger flowered Wanda Group, which

Mixed bedding primulas

Primula 'Wanda'

offers mainly jewel-like shades and some pastels, highlighted by bronze-purple tinged foliage. 'Enchantment' is a mix of eye-catching bicolours and for a more subtle display, try 'Springtide'. Try primroses in hanging baskets lined with conifer cuttings, combining them with dwarf cyclaminius daffodils, Dutch Crocus and ivy trails.

Another hybrid group that is extremely useful for container displays is polyanthus. Here the individual blooms are clustered at the top of a stout stem. The leading series Crescendo can begin blooming during mild spells in mid winter though the main show is from mid to late spring. Single colours are available allowing you to colour scheme more effectively. Try the blue with a yellow eye combined with *Euonymus fortunei* 'Emerald 'n' Gold' and *Narcissus* Tête à Tête'.

Hardy primroses and polyanthus are susceptible to attack by slugs and snails, vine weevil grubs and grey mould.

Flowering Plants

	SPRING	SUMMER	AUTUMN	WINTER	height (cm)	spread (cm)	min. temp °C	moisture	sun/shade	colour	
P. Crescendo Series (polyanthus)	● ● ●		⚘ ⚘ ⚘	⚘ ● ●	15	30	-17°	💧💧	☀	▨	Begin flowering winter – in mild spells
P. 'Enchantment' (primrose)	● ● ●		⚘ ⚘ ⚘		10	15	-17°	💧💧	☀	▯	Eye-catching bicoloured blooms
P. 'Husky Mixed' (primrose)	● ● ●		⚘ ⚘ ⚘	●	30	30	-17°	💧💧	☀	▮	Moderately hardy hybrid primrose strain
P. Prima Donna mixed (polyanthus)	● ● ●		⚘ ⚘ ⚘		15	15	-17°	💧💧	☀	▯	Dark foliage
P. Regal Mix (polyanthus)	● ● ●		⚘ ⚘ ⚘	●	25	30	-5°	💧💧	☀	▯	Early flowering
P. 'Spring Fever' (polyanthus)	● ● ●		⚘ ⚘ ⚘	●	15	15	-5°	💧💧	☀	▯	Weather-resistant polyanthus
P. 'Springtide' (primrose)	● ● ●		⚘ ⚘ ⚘		25	30	-17°	💧💧	☀	▮	Early flowers in pastel shades
P. 'Wanda' (primrose)	● ● ●		⚘ ⚘ ⚘	●	15	15	-5°	💧💧	☀	▨	Small flowered bronzy leaves
P. Wanda Group (primrose)	● ● ●		⚘ ⚘ ⚘	●	25	30	-5°	💧💧	☀	▮	Many with dark bronze foliage. Compact

☀ sunny ☀ semi-shady ● shady

Ranunculus
Persian buttercup

The perfectly formed globe-shaped heads of the double Persian buttercup look as though they are made from tissue paper. The leaves are deeply divided, resembling those of wild buttercups.

Ranunculus is a broad genus of annuals, biennials and perennials, with a number of versatile plants that lend themselves well to container gardening.

It is the tender perennials, grown from claw-shaped tubers, that are most suitable for pot work, and these are often available in

Ranunculus asiaticus

garden centres from mid-spring as plants in bud. In a sheltered spot protected from frosts, you can use them to add an air of romance to colour-themed planters and windowboxes.

Try pink or white ranunculus with pastel violas, double daisies and white variegated ivy trails, or for a more vibrant look try orange and red blooms with purple-leaved heuchera.

For Ranunculus blooms in summer, plant corms in early spring. Soak these beforehand to help break the dormancy and prepare the plant for growth.

Watch out for powdery mildew, slugs, snails and aphids. The sap of these plants may irritate if it comes into contact with the skin, so wear gloves when handling them.

Ranunculus asiaticus 'Accolade Mixed'

	SPRING	SUMMER	AUTUMN	WINTER	height (cm)	spread (cm)	min. temp °C	moisture	sun/shade	colour	
R. asiaticus 'Accolade Mixed'	🌱 ● ● ●	● ● ●			30	20	1°	💧	☀️	▨	Showy double flowers
R. a. Turban Group	🌱 ● ● ●	● ● ●			30	20	1°	💧	☀️	▨	Showy double flowers

🌱 *planting*   ● *flower*   💧 *well drained*   💧 *moist*   💧 *wet*

 — handwritten marginal note: I enjoy these flowers they are yellow it would be nice. Pink would be nice.

Flowering Plants

R

Rosa
Miniature *and* Patio roses

You can grow many different kinds of roses in containers, but for patio decoration, the small, cluster-flowered types with a long blooming period and good healthy foliage cover are definitely the best choice.

Ideally, look for miniature cultivars, or those classified as miniature-patio roses, such as the flame orange 'Darling Flame'. The miniature climbing rose 'Warm Welcome' is one of the best of a relatively new line of climbing miniatures and has many small orange-red blooms on long lax stems arising from the base. Roses need a fertile, moisture-retentive compost that's on

Rosa 'Darling Flame'

theAvoid small porous pots as these dry out too quickly and do not keep the roots sufficiently cool. Water evenly and feed with a balanced liquid fertilizer every three weeks in summer. Deadhead regularly and remove disease-affected leaves. Watch for aphids.

	SPRING	SUMMER	AUTUMN	WINTER	height (cm)	spread (cm)	min. temp °C	moisture	sun/shade	colour	
Rosa Angela Rippon (miniature)		●●● ●			45	30	-17°		☀		Double. Some scent
R. 'Anna Ford' (miniature/patio)		●●● ●			45	40	-17°		☀		Semi double. Glossy foliage
R. 'Darling Flame' (miniature/patio)		●●● ●			40	40	-17°		☀		Semi double. Some scent
R. Sweet Magic (miniature/patio)		●●● ●			40	40	-17°		☀		Bright green foliage. Double blooms
R. Warm Welcome (miniature climber)		●●● ●			220	220	-17°		☀		Climber. Semi-double
R. White Pet (polyantha)		●●● ●			45	55	-17°		☀		Double. Good foliage. Some scent

Rudbeckia
Black eyed Susan

Towards the end of summer, the bedding rudbeckias really start to shine, because whilst many other flowers are beginning to look tired, they are bright and fresh with plenty more blooms to come.

Rudbeckia 'Rustic Dwarfs'

The plants are short-lived, hardy, herbaceous perennials that are grown as annuals, derived from *R. hirta*. In recent years these compact floriferous subjects have really been gaining in popularity. 'Toto', 'Becky' and 'Summerlight' are amongst the shortest, though the brown-coned blooms that give the plants their common name of black-eyed

Susan are relatively large. 'Spotlight' has a dark spot at the base of each petal and in 'Becky Mixed', some of the yellow flowers are banded with bronze and gold producing a softer autumnal effect than its taller predecessor, 'Rustic Dwarfs'. Provide constantly moist, but not wet, compost and watch for slug and snail activity.

	SPRING	SUMMER	AUTUMN	WINTER	height (cm)	spread (cm)	min. temp °C	moisture	sun/shade	colour	
R. 'Becky Mixed'		●●●	●		25	30	-17°		●		Single coloured and banded flowers
R. 'Marmalade'		●●●	●		60	30	-17°		●		Pointed petals, black centres
R. 'Rustic Dwarfs'		●●●	●		60	30	-17°		●		A taller species
R. 'Sonora'		●●●	●		38	30	-17°		●		Large blooms
R. 'Spotlight'		●●●	●		20	30	-17°		●		Dark spot at base of each petal
R. 'Summerlight'		●●●	●		20	25	-17°		●		Very compact

☀ *sunny*　☀ *semi-shady*　● *shady*

Salvia

The sage family offers a number of excellent container plants – the brightly coloured, lipped flowers of the half-hardy annuals and tender perennials are the main attraction.

Scarlet sage, *Salvia splendens*, is a familiar bedding plant, but for pots, try the taller, more elegant *S. coccinea* 'Lady in Red', which produces spires of glowing red blooms.

The mealy sage, *S. farinacea*, so called because the stems are covered in a white powder, is quite different in character. This tender perennial, grown as an annual, produces stiffly upright plants with slender spikes of white buds opening to shades of white, blue or purple. The unusual two-toned 'Strata', a combination of silvery green and lavender blue is an excellent newcomer. Try it with silver cineraria, osteospermums and pelargoniums.

Salvia farinacea 'Strata'

	SPRING	SUMMER	AUTUMN	WINTER	height (cm)	spread (cm)	min. temp °C	moisture	sun/shade	colour	
S. coccinea 'Lady in Red'		●●●●	●●		40	30	1°	◖	☼	■	Showy flower spikes
S. farinacea 'Seascape'		●●●●	●●		35	30	1°	◖	☼	■	Blend of three colours
S. f. 'Strata'		●●●●	●●		35	30	1°	◖	☼	☐	Silver and blue bicolour
S. f. 'Victoria'		●●●●	●●		35	30	1°	◖	☼	■	Tender perennial grown as half-hardy annual
S. officinalis		●●			30	30	-5°	◖	☼	☐	Yellow variegated
S. patens 'Cambridge Blue'		●●●●	●●		45	45	-5°	◖	☼	☐	Tender perennial

Scabiosa
Small scabious

These pincushion-flowered plants are hardy perennials derived from the small scabious (*S. columbaria*) and are perfect for adding summer colour to permanent container plantings.

The neat rosettes of grey green divided leaves carry a continuous display of pastel blooms for most of the summer. Like all scabious, the plants prefer a slightly alkaline compost and sharp drainage in winter is critical. Deadhead to keep plants neat.

Scabiosa 'Butterfly Blue'

	SPRING	SUMMER	AUTUMN	WINTER	height (cm)	spread (cm)	min. temp °C	moisture	sun/shade	colour	
Scabiosa 'Butterfly Blue'		●●			40	40	-17°	◖	☼	☐	Grey-green leaves
S. 'Pink Mist'		●●●			40	40	-17°	◖	☼	☐	Grey-green leaves

🌱 *planting*　❋ *flower*　◖ *well drained*　◗ *moist*　◗◗ *wet*

Scaevola

Though a relative newcomer to the hanging basket scene, scaevola has quickly established itself. 'Blue Wonder', often called 'Blue Fan', was once the leading cultivar, a strong growing plant with spreading branches that by the end of the season might reach 1.5m (5ft) across.

Scaevola aemula 'Blue Wonder'

The soft blue fan-shaped blooms that are scattered along the length of the stiff curving stems look well in combination with Surfinia petunias, bidens, ivy-leaved pelargoniums and Tapien verbenas. In 'Blauer Facher' syn. 'Saphira', 'Blue Ice' and 'Brilliant' the flowers are a deeper, more intense blue purple. Pure white or purple cultivars are sometimes available but it is the more showy forms that really catch the attention, such as 'Zig Zag'. Though plants are extremely heat tolerant, it is wise to keep them well watered during hot spells – especially 'Brilliant'. Watch for red spider mite.

	SPRING	SUMMER	AUTUMN	WINTER	height (cm)	spread (cm)	min. temp °C	moisture	sun/shade	colour	
S. aemula 'Blauer Facher' syn. 'Saphira'					20	90	5°				Strong blue, very floriferous
S. a. 'Blue Ice'					20	90	5°				Strong blue, compact, very floriferous
S. a. 'Blue Wonder' syn. 'Blue Fan'					15	120	5°				Vigorous spreading/trailing basket plant
S. a. 'Brilliant'					30	90	5°				Compact, semi trailing, very floriferous
S. a. 'Diamond'					20	60	5°				White petals, edged purple
S. a. 'Zig Zag'					30	60	5°				White petals, central lilac stripe

Scilla
Squill

Most of these hardy dwarf spring bulbs are easy to grow and longlasting.

One of the first to appear is *Scilla mischtschenkoana*, with ice blue flowers. The gentian blue *Scilla siberica* is resilient and can be used to fill in around the base of deciduous pot grown shrubs, but it also makes an ideal companion for dwarf, early flowering daffodils and Wanda hybrid primroses.

Scilla siberica

	SPRING	SUMMER	AUTUMN	WINTER	height (cm)	spread (cm)	min. temp °C	moisture	sun/shade	colour	
S. mischtshenkoana					15	5	-17°				Striped grey-blue and white petals
S. peruviana					30	10	-17°				Large domed heads on a single stalk
S. siberica					15	5	-17°				Excellent for permanent containers
S. s. 'Spring Beauty'					20	5	-17°				Darker and more substantial than species
S. s. 'Alba'					15	5	-17°				White form of species

☼ *sunny*   ☀ *semi-shady*   ● *shady*

Sutera (syn. Bacopa)

Still commonly referred to as bacopa, this trailing tender perennial became a must-have basket plant in the 1990s, with the introduction of *Sutera cordata* 'Snowflake'. Now there is a great deal more choice.

Sutera cordata 'Snowflake'

More recently, plant breeders have been busy introducing a clutch of improved varieties in shades of lilac pink, soft blue and purple as well as the usual white. Most sutera prefer light shade and consistently moist but not wet compost. Ideal companions therefore include busy Lizzies, tuberous begonias, nicotianas and fuchsias. All make excellent compact and free flowering basket plants and with the exception of the mound forming but vigorous 'Candy Floss', have a strongly trailing habit. Members of the Showers Series are strong growing but neat, compact and full of flower. Look out for the pastel 'Lavender' or 'Blue' Showers and the pure white 'Bridal' Showers. 'Olympic Gold' has strong yellow variegation and would add light to a basket of dark coloured blooms. Cut back trailing growth mid-season if necessary to encourage a new flowering flush and watch for aphids.

	SPRING	SUMMER	AUTUMN	WINTER	height (cm)	spread (cm)	min. temp °C	moisture	sun/shade	colour	
S. cordata 'Blizzard'		● ● ●	● ● ●	● ●		7.5	45	3°	●	☼	☐	Improvement on 'Snowflake'
S. c. 'Candy Floss' syn. 'Candy Floss Blue'		● ● ●	● ● ●	● ●		15	45	3°	●	☼	☐	Masses of yellow-eyed blooms
S. c. 'Pink Domino'		● ● ●	● ● ●	● ●		7.5	45	3°	●	☼	☐	Strongly trailing habit. Very floriferous
S. c. 'Sea Mist'		● ● ●	● ● ●	● ●		7.5	35	3°	●	☼	☐	Similar habit to the vigorous 'Blizzard'
S. c. Showers Series		● ● ●	● ● ●	● ●		15	35	3°	●	☼	☐	'Lavender', 'Blue' and 'Bridal Showers'
S. c. 'Snowflake'		● ● ●	● ● ●	● ●		7.5	30	3°	●	☼	☐	Gold variegated leaves

Syringa
Dwarf lilac

For patio gardeners unable to plant directly in the ground, hardy flowering shrubs like the dwarf lilacs provide structure and continuity through the year for very little maintenance.

Syringa

These plants have an old fashioned, cottage garden appeal and look best in wooden half barrels or similarly rustic containers. *Syringa pubescens* subspecies *microphylla* 'Superba' has, like most lilacs, deliciously fragrant blooms. After the initial flowering in late spring and early summer, it often produces blooms on and off until early autumn. Plant in loam based John Innes No 3 compost and mulch to retain moisture.

	SPRING	SUMMER	AUTUMN	WINTER	height (cm)	spread (cm)	min. temp °C	moisture	sun/shade	colour	
Syringa meyeri 'Palibin'	● ●				60	40	-17°	●	☼	☐	Compact, 10cm long flower panicles
S. pubescens subsp. microphylla 'Superba'	● ●		●		90	90	-17°	●	☼	☐	Highly fragrant

🌱 planting   ● flower   💧 well drained   💧 moist   💧 wet

Flowering Plants

Tagetes

French *and* African marigolds

These familiar and easily grown half-hardy annuals are divided into four main groups. Plants commonly referred to as tagetes belong to the signet group and make low spreading domes of fine, feathery foliage smothered in many small yellow, orange or tawny red blooms.

Tagetes mix well with deep or sky blue lobelia in hanging baskets. The French marigolds are more upright with larger individual flowers – single, semi-double or fully double in a range of yellows, oranges and tawny reds as well as bicolours. 'Tiger Eyes' is particularly eye-catching, with red flowers centred with a domed yellow 'crest'. There are many varieties to choose from, available as single colours, and the Safari Series offers a range of long lasting double flowered plants that come into bloom early in the season.

Much larger all round are the showy African marigolds, which are dominated by

Tagetes 'Safari Yellow'

fully double flowered strains in yellows and oranges. The flowers have a tendency to rot with rain and overhead watering,

Tagetes Gem Series

Tagetes 'Safari Tangerine'

so pick a weather resistant series like Inca. As a change from the usual colour range, try the new 'French Vanilla', whose creamy blooms will provide substance in pastel schemes. The Afro-French group of tagetes produces plants of intermediate character which are often easier to mix in containers than the weightier Africans. Try the orange and yellow forms of the early flowering double Zenith with pale blue laurentia or *Brachyscome* 'Purple Splendour'.

Deadhead regularly and watch for slugs and snails, which have a tendency to home in on marigolds.

	SPRING	SUMMER	AUTUMN	WINTER	height (cm)	spread (cm)	min. temp °C	moisture	sun/shade	colour	
T. 'French Vanilla' (African)		● ● ● ● ●	● ●		45	45	1°	◊◊	☼	☐	Less marigold odour
T. Gem Series (Signet)		● ● ● ● ●	● ●		20	30	1°	◊◊	☼	☐	Ferny foliage, masses of tiny blooms
T. Inca Series (African)		● ● ● ● ●	● ●		30	45	1°	◊◊	☼	☐	Very large doubles. Weather resistant
T. Safari Series (French)		● ● ● ●	● ● ●		20	30	1°	◊◊	☼	☐	Long lasting doubles. Early
T. 'Tiger Eyes' (French)		● ● ● ●	● ● ●		20	30	1°	◊◊	☼	■	Blooms with a prominent yellow 'crest'
T. Zenith Series (Afro-French)		● ● ● ● ● ●	● ●		30	30	1°	◊◊	☼	☐	Double. Flowers early. Robust plants

☼ *sunny*   ☀ *semi-shady*   ● *shady*

Flowering Plants

T

85

Thunbergia
Black-eyed Susan

The tender perennial climber, *Thunbergia alata*, can be grown from seed in spring or bought as young plants twined up canes from the houseplant or bedding section of the garden centre.

It makes a first class hanging basket plant, combining well with purple and blue trailers such as Surfinia petunias, Tapien or Temari verbenas. The plant gets its common name from the species' black-throated blooms but in Susie Mix, half the flowers are self-coloured and a creamy white shade. Grow in a warm sheltered spot in sun or light shade.

Thunbergia alata 'Susie Mix'

	SPRING	SUMMER	AUTUMN	WINTER	height (cm)	spread (cm)	min. temp °C	moisture	sun/shade	colour	
T. a. 'African Sunset' syn. 'Blushing Susie'	planting	flower flower flower flower	flower		120	45	7°	well drained	sun		Unusual mixture
Thunbergia alata 'Mixed'	planting	flower flower flower flower	flower		120	45	7°	well drained	sun		Dark eye
T. a. 'Spanish Eyes'	planting	flower flower flower flower	flower		120	45	7°	well drained	sun		Unusual mixture
T. a. 'Susie Mix'	planting	flower flower flower flower	flower		120	45	7°	well drained	sun		Some with a dark eye and some without
T. a. 'Susie Orange'	planting	flower flower flower flower	flower		120	45	7°	well drained	sun		Dark eye
T. a. 'Susie White'	planting	flower flower flower flower	flower		120	45	7°	well drained	sun		Greenish eye

Tropaeolum
Nasturtium

The half-hardy annual nasturtiums have a cottage garden appeal and are easily grown. Some are too vigorous for container work and when well fed tend to produce an abundance of large rounded leaves at the expense of flower.

Tropaeolum majus mixed

Breeders have introduced several more compact strains that are ideal for pots and baskets. A good example is the Whirlybird Series which has a wide colour range and the single or semi double blooms that are upward facing and sit well above the leaves. 'Gleam Hybrids' are semi-cascading and work well in baskets with trailing lobelia. Most nasturtiums are grown from seed – try putting a few into a hanging basket in early summer and watch the plants develop through the season. Watch for black aphids, slug and snail damage and caterpillars, which can skeletonize foliage with alarming speed.

	SPRING	SUMMER	AUTUMN	WINTER	height (cm)	spread (cm)	min. temp °C	moisture	sun/shade	colour	
Tropaeolum majus 'Alaska'	planting	flower flower flower	flower flower		30	50	1°	well drained	sun		White marbled leaves
T. m. 'Empress of India'	planting	flower flower flower	flower flower		30	50	1°	well drained	sun		Dark, purple tinged foliage
T. m. 'Gleam Hybrids'	planting	flower flower flower	flower flower		38	60	1°	well drained	sun		Doubles. Semi-trailing
T. m. 'Hermine Grashoff'	planting	flower flower flower	flower		20	20	1°	well drained	sun		Double
T. m. 'Jewel Mixture'	planting	flower flower flower	flower flower		45	45	1°	well drained	sun		Semi-double, early, compact
T. m. Whirlybird Series	planting	flower flower flower	flower flower		30	35	1°	well drained	sun		Single, or semi-double, upward facing

planting   flower   well drained   moist   wet

Tulipa
Tulip

Although tulips in general make superb container plants including the beautifully sculpted Lily-flowered group and Single Late varieties like the dramatic maroon-black 'Queen of Night', short growing types are particularly useful.

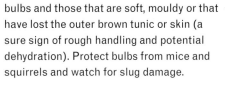

Greigii tulips are particularly resilient and usually have handsome maroon striped foliage that develops well before the blooms open. One of the brightest is 'Red Riding Hood'. These plants are often best planted on their own to give the foliage room to develop. Slightly later flowering is the coral coloured 'Toronto', which is unusual in having several flowers per stem. Try it with pots of creamy violas. For a cool, ivory white tulip with excellent weather resistance, grow the Fosteriana tulip 'Purissima' and for a pretty romantic touch try the Double Late flowered Angélique. Discard bruised bulbs and those that are soft, mouldy or that have lost the outer brown tunic or skin (a sure sign of rough handling and potential dehydration). Protect bulbs from mice and squirrels and watch for slug damage.

	SPRING	SUMMER	AUTUMN	WINTER	height (cm)	spread (cm)	min. temp °C	moisture	sun/shade	colour	
T. 'Angélique' (Double Late)	●				30	13	-17°	💧💧	☀		Large double blooms
T. 'Johann Strauss' (Kaufmanniana)	●				20	15	-17°	💧💧	☀		Maroon striped leaves
T. praestans 'Fusilier'	●				30	13	-17°	💧💧	☀		Several flowers per stem
T. 'Purissima' (Fosteriana)	●				20	13	-17°	💧💧	☀		Very weather resistant
T. 'Queen of Night' (Single Late)	●				30	13	-17°	💧💧	☀		Dramatic maroon-black colour
T. 'Red Riding Hood' (Greigii)	●				20	13	-17°	💧💧	☀		Bold maroon leaf markings

Verbena

These tender perennials, forms of *Verbena* x *hybrida* divide into roughly two groups, the upright and mound forming types such as the excellent Romance Series and the spreading or trailing types that are so valuable in baskets.

The best of the latter used to be the Cascade Series, which produced much smaller bloom clusters in shades of blue, purple, pink, red and white. The Tapien series is newer, and a marked improvement on the Cascade Series. There is also the Temari Series, which has larger flowers in each individual cluster and broader foliage. Breeders have worked hard to come up with even more alternatives, seeking to increase the range of colours and flower size and to improve on flowering performance. Several new strains are becoming available now, including the Tukana and Babylon Series. Watch for aphids, slugs and snails.

	SPRING	SUMMER	AUTUMN	WINTER	height (cm)	spread (cm)	min. temp °C	moisture	sun/shade	colour	
Verbena Aztec Series		● ● ●	● ●		20	45	1°	💧💧	☀		Semi trailing, or low, spreading
T. Babylon Series		● ● ●	● ●		20	45	1°	💧💧	☀		Larger rounded heads of flower
V. Romance Series		● ● ●	● ●		25	30	1°	💧💧	☀		Finely divided foliage, small blooms
V. Temari Series		● ● ●	● ●		20	45	1°	💧💧	☀		Compact, spreading. Early flowering
V. Tapien Series		● ● ●	● ●		20	45	1°	💧💧	☀		Large, rounded flower clusters
T. Tukana Series		● ● ●	● ●		20	45	1°	💧💧	☀		Very large, rounded flowerheads

☀ *sunny*   ☀ *semi-shady*   ● *shady*

Viola

Baskit Spring sowing (handwritten note)

The bedding violas, derived from *Viola* x *wittrockiana*, are short-lived hardy perennials that are grown as annuals or biennials. Spring sowings produce summer flowering plants whilst summer sowings – setting the young plants out in pots and baskets in autumn – produce winter or spring blooms depending on the variety and time of sowing. Growers now supply garden centres with plants in flower virtually year round.

Viola 'Sorbet Orange Duet'

Flowering Plants

Pansies have large, rounded blooms, often with a 'face' or central black blotch. Plants commonly referred to as violas have smaller blooms with the dainty violet shape and may be plain, blotched or strongly bicoloured. They are ideal for planting in windowboxes and hanging baskets, where the sweet fragrance can be better appreciated. A mass of viola flowers can be very striking once plants have settled in, as the blooms all line up to face the same direction. Try one of the new cascading violas for summer baskets, such as the softly shaded 'Four Seasons Mixture'.

Some pansies and violas are very hardy and weather resistant. For large blooms in a wide range of colours, plant members of the improved Universal Series or Ultima Series. The latter remains more compact through the season. The Forerunner series and especially the Floral Dance Series also have excellent winter flowering performance. Although not as hardy, members of the Imperial Series provide pretty alternatives for spring displays. As a change from a bright mix of colours, try the aptly named 'Antique Shades', a blend of tawny reds, velvet browns blended with gold, dusky pinks and creamy yellows. Amongst violas, the leading winter and spring flowering series is the floriferous and very weather resistant Sorbet Series, which includes

Viola Penny Series

🌱 *planting*   ☀ *flower*   💧 *well drained*   💧 *moist*   💧 *wet*

many delightful bicolours. If you plant hanging baskets with pansies or violas, take them under cover during periods of hard frost as otherwise plants may die due to dehydration when their roots freeze.

Pansies and violas are prone to fungal diseases and should always be planted in fresh compost to avoid 'pansy sickness'. In winter and spring it is particularly important to clear away debris promptly to lessen the risk of grey mould. Pansies have long, tough flower stalks that look unsightly if left in place after deadheading. Rather than just nipping off the developing seedpod only, use nail scissors to cut the stalk at the base. Watch for slugs, snails and aphids and keep plants well watered to lessen the risk of powdery mildew.

	SPRING	SUMMER	AUTUMN	WINTER	height (cm)	spread (cm)	min. temp °C	moisture	sun/shade	colour	
V. Clear Crystals (pansy)					20	25	-17°				Clear coloured pansies without blotches
V. Floral Dance Series (pansy)					20	25	-17°				Hardy, early flowering pansy
V. Forerunner Series (pansy)					20	25	-17°				Winter and spring flowering
V. Four Seasons Mixed (viola)					15	30	-17°				Long trails; good in baskets
V. Gemini Series (viola)					20	30	-17°				Larger than normal 'viola' flowers
V. 'Imperial Antique Shades' (pansy)					15	25	-17°				Old-fashioned looking pansy
V. Padparadja (pansy)					15	25	-17°				Striking colour
V. Penny Series (viola)					15	20	-17°				Clear colours
V. Princess Series (viola)					15	20	-17°				Some flowers bicoloured
V. Rippling Waters (pansy)					20	25	-17°				Bold white edge
V. Sorbet Series (viola)					15	15	-17°				Viola with prolific winter and spring blooms
V. Ultima Series (pansy)					20	25	-17°				More compact version of Universal
V. Universal Series (pansy)					20	25	-17°				Classic winter flowering pansy

☼ sunny   ☀ semi-shady   ● shady

Foliage Plants

Some plants, including types of tender perennial, certain herbs, houseplants, ornamental grasses and ground cover, have leaves that are almost as colourful as flowers. The great advantage of using foliage varieties in container plantings is that their display is usually much longer lasting and requires less intensive upkeep than that of flowers.

Watering is an important factor, though, since moisture-loving types like mint are susceptible to scorching and powdery mildew if allowed to dry out. Some houseplants, such as tradescantia, tolmiea and coleus, are easily raised from cuttings but take care to harden off plants that have been grown indoors as they won't be used to the higher light levels and cooler temperatures and so may scorch or bleach with sudden exposure. Plain green foliage can add greatly to the success of the overall composition, providing a cooling backdrop for certain shades and adding so many more interesting shapes and textures in addition to those offered by blooms. Many white-variegated, gold- or lime green- leaved plants thrive in shade, a situation in which most flowers tend to manage less well. However, Lamium cultivars are particularly good in cool, shady situations, combining beautiful silvery leaves with abundant blooms. In soaring heat, drought-resistant foliage plants, including succulents, come into their own. Those with blue-grey or felted leaves, sparkling and intricately cut silver foliage, continue their display despite the odd missed watering and keep arrangements looking fresh.

Many herbs come into this section. They are invariably heat tolerant, though not all thrive in drought and most release a delicious aroma when the foliage is disturbed or crushed. Why not add to the sensual appeal of your containers and baskets by mixing colourful aromatic and edible plants with fragrant flowers?

Acaena
New Zealand bur

The evergreen ground cover plant, acaena, makes a low carpet of finely cut foliage covered from late summer through autumn and winter with attractive red seed burs that follow the insignificant flowers.

This is a useful hardy plant that combines particularly well with tussock forming grasses and sedges. Several cultivars have a metallic quality, especially the richly coloured 'Kupferteppich' syn. 'Copper Carpet' and 'Blue Haze', otherwise known as 'Pewter'. Grow in full sun and ensure good winter drainage.

Acaena novae-zelandiae

	SPRING	SUMMER	AUTUMN	WINTER	height (cm)	spread (cm)	min. temp °C	moisture	sun/shade	flower colour	
Acaena microphylla	planting		flower	flower	5	15	-17	well drained	sunny	▨	Bronze tinted foliage
A. m. 'Kupferteppich' (syn. 'Copper Carpet')	planting		flower	flower	5	60	-17	well drained	sunny	▨	Dark copper brown leaves
A. novae-zelandiae	planting		flower	flower	15	90	-17	well drained	sunny	▨	Small, ovoid to spherical flowerheads
A. saccaticupula 'Blue Haze' (syn. *A.* 'Pewter')	planting	flower	flower	flower	15	75	-17	well drained	sunny	▨	Blue-grey ferny leaves

Adiantum
Maidenhair fern

Looking far too exotic for outdoor cultivation, the hardy maidenhair ferns provide filigree foliage to contrast with the broad solid leaves of shade lovers, such as hostas.

The plants have many small leaflets arranged on wiry branched stems and are either deciduous or evergreen. In *Adiantum aleuticum* these branchlets form attractive whorls. The new fronds of *A. a.* 'Japonicum' are red tinted and in *A. venustum*, which looks much more like the classic maidenhair fern, the new foliage in early spring is a lustrous bronze-pink. *Adiantum pedatum* has mahogany black stems that branch to form foliage-covered fans.

Grow in humus-rich compost, mulch with bark to conserve moisture and water frequently in dry spells. Shelter from wind.

	SPRING	SUMMER	AUTUMN	WINTER	height (cm)	spread (cm)	min. temp °C	moisture	sun/shade	foliage colour	
Adiantum aleuticum	planting				75	75	-17	moist	semi-shady	▨	Deciduous/semi evergreen
A. a. 'Japonicum'	planting				75	75	-17	moist	semi-shady	▨	New fronds red tinted
A. pedatum	planting				40	40	-17	moist	semi-shady	▨	Deciduous fan-shaped fronds
A. venustum	planting				15	100+	-17	moist	semi-shady	▨	Evergreen. New fronds bronze-pink

planting   flower   well drained   moist   sunny   semi-shady

Ajuga
Bugle

Though occasionally invasive in open ground, the carpeting bugles are invaluable for seasonal baskets and permanent planters alike.

These hardy perennials are mainly grown for their foliage, but short, upright blue flower spikes appear in late spring, which is when plants generate fresh leaf rosettes. In mild areas leaves can be almost evergreen, but if you want good winter cover use the deep purple-black *A. reptans* 'Braunherz'. The pink and cream splashed 'Burgundy Glow' makes a lovely foil for pink, white and mauve flowers in a hanging basket and can be used to cover the sides of a moss-lined basket filled with soft coloured herbs. Susceptible to powdery mildew, as well as aphids on new growth.

Ajuga reptans 'Burgundy Glow'

	SPRING	SUMMER	AUTUMN	WINTER	height (cm)	spread (cm)	min. temp °C	moisture	sun/shade	flower colour	
Ajuga pyramidalis 'Metallica Crispa'	planting				15	40	-17	well drained/moist	part sun	■	Crinkled, metallic purple leaves
A. reptans 'Atropurpurea'	planting				15	90	-17	well drained/moist	sun	■	Maroon-purple leaves
A. r. 'Braunherz'	planting				15	90	-17	well drained/moist	sun	■	Glossy maroon-purple leaves. Evergreen
A. r. 'Burgundy Glow'	planting				15	60	-17	well drained	sun	■	Leaves pink, cream and grey-green
A. r. 'Catlin's Giant'	planting flower				20	90	-17	well drained/moist	part sun	■	Large, bronzed leaves; tall flower spikes
A. r. 'Variegata'	planting				15	60	-17	well drained/moist	part sun	■	Cream and grey-green variegated leaves

Alchemilla
Lady's mantle

Alchemilla mollis

The grey-green leaves of *Alchemilla mollis* are pleated with scalloped edges and glisten enchantingly with rain drops.

Grow Alchemilla in large containers to contrast with taller ornamental grasses and plants with strap-shaped or sword-shaped leaves, such as *Iris foetidissima* 'Variegata'. If foliage looks tired later in the season, cut back hard, water and feed to generate fresh new growth. Quite different in character are the alpine species whose leaves are deeply lobed.

	SPRING	SUMMER	AUTUMN	WINTER	height (cm)	spread (cm)	min. temp °C	moisture	sun/shade	flower colour	
Alchemilla alpina	planting	flower flower flower			12	50	-17	well drained/moist	sun	□	Mat of 5–7 lobed leaves
A. conjuncta	planting	flower flower flower flower			40	30	-17	well drained/moist	part sun	□	Blue-green 7–9 lobed leaves
A. erythropoda	planting	flower flower flower flower			30	20	-17	well drained/moist	sun	□	7–9 lobed toothed leaves
A. mollis	planting	flower flower flower flower			60	75	-17	well drained/moist	part sun	□	Soft, hairy, light-green 'scalloped' leaves

planting   flower   well drained   moist   wet

Artemesia
Wormwood

Some of the more compact growing, evergreen artemisias make excellent permanent container plants, thriving in sheltered patio locations as opposed to the open garden, where the combination of exposure and poor winter drainage can prove fatal.

Artemisia schmidtiana and the miniature version 'Nana' make dense mounds of silken filigree foliage in metallic silver-green. 'Powis Castle' also has finely cut leaves, silver-white in colour but is larger all round and more open in habit. Use it to cascade over the edge of a large permanent container or combine it with white, pink or mauve osteospermums and *Scaevola aemula* cultivars. Cut back tall shoots as needed.

Artemesia 'Powis castle'

Artemesia schmidtianta

	SPRING	SUMMER	AUTUMN	WINTER	height (cm)	spread (cm)	min. temp °C	moisture	sun/shade	flower colour	
Artemisia 'Powis Castle'					90	120	-5	💧💧	☀		Silver filigree foliage
A. schmidtiana					30	45	-17	💧💧	☀		Finely cut silky silver folige
A .s. 'Nana'					10	30	-17	💧💧	☀		Compact form
A. stelleriana 'Boughton Silver'					15	50	-17	💧💧	☀		Felted, silver white dissected leaves
A. vulgaris 'Oriental Limelight'					90	90	-17	💧💧	◐		Jagged, creamy yellow splashed leaves

Asparagus
Asparagus fern
or Emerald feather

More familiar as a houseplant, asparagus ferns will happily spend summers in pots or hanging baskets outdoors, but only in moist compost.

The long, feathery, bright green trails of emerald feather (*Asparagus densiflorus* Sprengeri group) look wonderful in a basket filled with other shade loving plants, including New Guinea Hybrid impatiens, pendulous begonias and fuchsias. Blend with variegated trailers such as ground ivy or Chlorophytum (spider plant). The asparagus fern, *A. setaceus*, is actually a climber but initially the plant is arching, with wiry stems covered in fern-shaped fronds.

Asparagus

	SPRING	SUMMER	AUTUMN	WINTER	height (cm)	spread (cm)	min. temp °C	moisture	sun/shade	foliage colour	
Asparagus densiflorus Sprengeri Group					90	50	7	💧💧	◐		Long arching stems
A. setaceus (syn. *A. plumosus*)					120	50	1	💧💧	◐		Frond-like foliage

☀ *sunny* ◑ *semi-shady* ● *shady*

Dichondra micrantha 'Silver Falls'

An exciting new addition to the range of hanging basket plants is *Dichondra micrantha* 'Silver Falls'.

This tender perennial is strongly cascading with trails up to 1.2m (4ft) long, carrying slightly cupped, circular leaves in metallic silver grey. The effect is similar to strings of little silver bells. Although this looks like a plant that would thrive in dry conditions, it enjoys moist compost during the summer growing period. It is very heat and drought tolerant, though. Mix it with ivy leaved geraniums, trailing verbenas, pink and lilac nemesias and diascias or small flowered

Dichondra micrantha 'Silver Falls'

Surfinia petunias like 'Baby Pink Morn'. Alternatively, use it to add sparkle to a basket planted with mixed herbs.

Glechoma

The variegated ground ivy (*Glechoma hederacea* 'Variegata'), sometimes erroneously called trailing nepeta because of its tiny lilac flowers, is a hanging basket and windowbox staple.

This hardy semi-evergreen ground cover plant can trail to 1.8m (6ft) in a season if kept 'untethered' and planted in the ground, where it spreads freely.

It can be kept better under control when planted in a container, windowbox or hanging basket. To keep a tub or container in balance, however, you may need to cut Glechoma back now and then. The benefit is that the occasional trimming also encourages side shoots to grow.

The rounded, kidney shaped leaves are arranged in pairs along the stem. They have toothed edges and are marbled white with a bold, creamy white margin. When thinking about suitable companion plants to site in a container, use variegated ground ivy to make a bright contrast with the dark blue trailing lobelia 'Sapphire' and red balcony geraniums.

This vigorous plant is happy in full sun or shade but does need to be kept moist, as it is prone to powdery mildew. If it succumbs midway through the summer, cut the growth back hard and provide it with a liquid feed to promote fresh new shoots. At the end of the season, salvage the plants and pot them up to keep for next year – an unheated cold frame or cold greenhouse should suffice.

Ground ivy is also extremely easy to propagate from cuttings taken in spring or autumn, since plants root readily at the leaf nodes.

Glechoma hederacea

🖎 planting   ❂ flower | 💧 well drained   💧 moist   💧 wet

Helichrysum

The extremely vigorous *Helichrysum petiolare* is a tender perennial with felted silver-grey leaves and horizontally spreading, branched shoots that rise towards the tips. Its value as a plant for large containers and baskets cannot be overstated since it withstands all kinds of neglect including underfeeding and drought.

Helichrysum petiolare 'Variegatum'

The only downside is that it can swamp less vigorous plants unless you trim it back every now and then. But teamed with suitable partners – bidens, trailing petunias, trailing verbena and ivy leaved geraniums – it performs beautifully.

For a slightly less vigorous foliage foil, try the pale apple green leaved 'Limelight', perfect for accenting cerise pink, magenta and deep purple blooms. 'Variegatum' is the most compact with very attractive cream variegation, ideal for pastel or white and silver arrangements.

These plants are trouble free. They can be cut back and overwintered frost free as stock plants – provided they are kept quite dry – and root easily from cuttings taken in late summer.

	SPRING	SUMMER	AUTUMN	WINTER	height (cm)	spread (cm)	min. temp °C	moisture	sun/shade	flower colour	
Helichrysum italicum subsp. *serotinum*	🌱	● ● ● ●	●		40	75	5	💧💧	☀	▓	Curry plant
H. petiolare	🌱		● ● ●		50	120	1	💧💧	☀	☐	Vigorous spreading. Grey foliage
H. p. 'Limelight'	🌱		● ● ●		50	120	1	💧💧	☀	☐	Soft yellow-green leaves
H. p. 'Variegatum'	🌱		● ● ●		50	90	1	💧💧	☀	☐	Subtle cream and grey leaves

Houttuynia

The aptly named *Houttuynia cordata* 'Chameleon' is a hardy herbaceous ground cover plant with brightly variegated heart shaped leaves that are most colourful in full sun.

The combination of red, cream and green makes this plant as eye-catching as a flowering specimen. 'Chameleon' prefers constantly moist compost and can either be planted singly to fill a pot with its creeping underground stems or combined with plants having similar requirements. Try bringing out the red tones with a Fan Series lobelia, carmine impatiens or the Japanese blood grass, *Imperata cylindrica* 'Rubra', or contrast it with blue leaved hostas.

Houttuynia cordata 'Chameleon'

Foliage Plants

H

☼ *sunny*   ☀ *semi-shady*   ● *shady*

Imperata
Japanese blood grass

Imperata cylindrica 'Rubra'

Imperata cylindrica 'Rubra' (syn. *Imperata cylindrica* 'Red Baron') is a moisture-loving grass whose upright shoots are suffused deep red towards the tips – a colour that becomes more pronounced in autumn.

Imperata cylindrica 'Rubra' reaches 30–35cm (12–14in) in height and makes clumps about 20–30cm (8–12in) wide. Grow it in humus-rich, moisture retentive compost with light shade. It will withstand a minimum temperature of -10°C (50°F) and in cold areas should be moved under protection for the winter.

After an exceptionally good summer, plants may produce fluffy silver plumes. Try planting Japanese blood grass with contrasting foliage plants like purple ajuga or the black grass, *Ophiopogon planiscapus* 'Nigrescens'.

Lamium
Spotted dead nettle *or* Variegated archangel

Lamium maculatum 'White Nancy'

If you want to lighten a shady corner with a pretty container, the silvery-white or gold-leaved spotted dead nettles are an obvious choice. These hardy herbaceous ground cover plants make a dense carpet of small, beautifully marked leaves.

Forms of *Lamium maculatum* flower from mid to late spring, and on and off through the growing season, with hooded blooms in white, pink or purple, but the evergreen foliage is the main attraction. The aptly named 'White Nancy' works wonderfully in shady hanging baskets with impatiens, fuchsias and lobelias and the foliage also adds sparkle to winter containers. The leaves of 'Beacon Silver' are as bright but frequently develop purple-pink spotting. For butter yellow leaves try 'Aureum' or the all-yellow 'Cannon's Gold'. Light shade is best to avoid scorching. One intriguing lamium is the variegated yellow archangel, *L. galeobdolon* 'Hermann's Pride' whose leaves are silver-white with green veining. It is a vigorous spreader but could be used in hanging baskets or to combine with a sturdy white-variegated or blue-leaved hosta. Lamiums can be divided but they also take easily from cuttings, rooting at the leaf nodes. Watch for slug and snail damage and the occasional aphid problem. Keep moist to avoid problems with leaf scorch and powdery mildew.

	SPRING	SUMMER	AUTUMN	WINTER	height (cm)	spread (cm)	min. temp °C	moisture	sun/shade	flower colour	
Lamium galeobdolon 'Hermann's Pride'	🌱 🌿 🌿 ✹	✹			60	90+	-17	💧💧	☀️◐		Silver leaves with unusual net veining
L. maculatum 'Aureum'	🌱 ✹ ✹ ✹				20	60	-17	💧💧	☀️◐		Yellow leaves with central white stripe
L. m. 'Beacon Silver'	🌱 ✹ ✹ ✹				20	90	-17	💧💧	☀️◐		Silvery leaves becoming purple spotted
L. m. 'Cannon's Gold'	🌱 ✹ ✹				20	45	-17	💧💧	☀️◐		All-yellow leaves
L. m. 'Pink Pewter'	🌱 ✹ ✹				20	90	-17	💧💧	☀️◐		Silvery foliage
L. m. 'White Nancy'	🌱 ✹ ✹				20	90	-17	💧💧	☀️◐		Silver leaves narrow green edge

🌱 planting   ✹ flower   💧 well drained   💧💧 moist   💧💧💧 wet

Lotus
Parrot's beak

Lotus berthelotii is a tender, evergreen, trailing sub shrub with clusters of soft, needle-like silver-blue or silver-green leaves on long, unbranched stems.

The cascades can reach about 90–120cm (3–4ft) in length in a season. It is not by any means guaranteed, but in spring and early summer, the plants may produce glossy orange-red to scarlet curving blooms (hence the common names of parrot's beak or lobster claw). This plant is useful in hanging baskets – try mixing it with *Dichondra micrantha* 'Silver Falls', or use it to tumble down the side of a tall, slender planter or an urn set on a plinth. It adds a sub-tropical flavour to container plantings and mixes

Lotus berthelotii

well planted with hot reds and oranges. Overwinter frost free under glass, keeping plants very dry.

Lysimachia
Creeping Jenny *or* Congested loosestrife

Whether you choose the plain green or acid green leaved version of creeping Jenny (*Lysimachia nummularia* 'Aurea'), you'll have an abundance of vertical trails clothed in pairs of circular leaves.

This hardy evergreen, ground cover perennial can be invasive in moist borders but its vigour is appreciated in hanging baskets. Small buttercup-like blooms open from the leaf axils in early summer, but the display doesn't last long. A semi-shaded position is preferred for 'Aurea', whose

Lysimachia nummularia

delicate leaves can scorch in a hot sunny spot. Creeping Jenny makes an ideal companion for busy lizzies, pendulous begonias and trailing lobelia. It is easy to propagate from cuttings, rooting at the leaf nodes.

The variegated form of congested

Lysimachia nummularia 'Aurea'

loosestrife (*Lysimachia congestiflora*) is a tender evergreen perennial with fleshy, pointed leaves. The foliage of 'Outback Sunset' has a broad, irregular, yellow margin and clusters of golden yellow trumpet shaped flowers are produced from the shoot tips all summer.

Watch for slugs and snails.

	SPRING	SUMMER	AUTUMN	WINTER	height (cm)	spread (cm)	min. temp °C	moisture	sun/shade	flower colour	
Lysimachia congestiflora 'Outback Sunset'	🌱	❋ ❋ ❋ ❋	❋		15	50	1	💧💧	☼		Yellow variegated fleshy leaves
L. nummularia 'Aurea'	🌱 🌱	❋			5	90	-17	💧💧	☼		Butter yellow foliage
L. punctata	🌱 🌱	❋			90	60	-17	💧💧	☼		Cup-shaped yellow flowers

☼ sunny　☼ semi-shady　● shady

Melissa
Variegated lemon balm

The variegated and gold leaved forms of lemon balm are particularly brightly coloured in spring when the new shoots emerge. The leaves may be used in pot-pourri or as a herbal tea infusion.

This hardy herbaceous plant is a herb whose leaves smell strongly of lemon sherbet when disturbed. Although the upright shoots will eventually grow to 60cm (2ft) plus, the height can be controlled by cutting back, which promotes bushy, fresh leafy growth. Left to its own devices, it develops tall, slender, flowering shoots in late summer with insignificant white-tinged-lilac blooms; the intensity of the leaf colour diminishes. Grow in moisture-retentive compost in light shade to prevent scorching and team up with other moisture-loving plants, such as purple and blue violas.

Melissa officinalis

	SPRING	SUMMER	AUTUMN	WINTER	height (cm)	spread (cm)	min. temp °C	moisture	sun/shade	flower colour	
Melissa officinalis 'All Gold'	🌱🌱🌱	✱	✱		60	45	-17	◐	☀	⬜	Golden yellow leaves
M. o. 'Aurea'	🌱🌱🌱	✱	✱		60	45	-17	◐	◑	⬜	Yellow splashed leaves

Mentha
Ginger mint *or* Pineapple mint

Mints have a reputation for being invasive in a border setting, but these hardy herbs are easily controlled when planted in pots. *Mentha* x *gracillis* 'Variegata' and *M. suaveolens* 'Variegata' are excellent for containers.

Mentha x gracillis 'Variegata'

Two variegated forms, the yellow splashed ginger mint (*Mentha* x *gracillis* 'Variegata') with smooth leaves tasting of ginger and the white-margined pineapple mint (*M. suaveolens* 'Variegata'), which has a fruity aroma, are particularly useful. The spreading underground stems weave in between other plants and in hanging baskets, especially, the coloured shoots intermingle nicely with flowers. The white variegated leaves of pineapple mint look lovely in pastel and white flowered schemes, and ginger mint's yellow foliage complements purples, reds and cerise pinks. Keep well watered to avoid powdery mildew and watch out for rust.

	SPRING	SUMMER	AUTUMN	WINTER	height (cm)	spread (cm)	min. temp °C	moisture	sun/shade	flower colour	
Mentha x gracillis 'Variegata'	🌱🌱🌱	✱			30	60	-17	◐	☀	⬜	Golden yellow splashed glossy leaves
M. suaveolens 'Variegata'	🌱🌱🌱	✱			45	90	-17	◐	◑	⬜	Bold white variegated leaves

🌱 *planting*　✱ *flower*　◐ *well drained*　◐ *moist*　◐◐ *wet*

Ocimum
Purple basil

This half-hardy annual has a number of decorative leaf varieties, but the purple foliage of 'Dark Opal and 'Purple Ruffles', with its wavy leaf margins, are ideal for summer container plantings.

Contrast them with pink blooms. To maintain a good supply of rich foliage, pinch out the flowers regularly and harvest the leafy shoots for cooking. Grow in light compost in a sheltered, sunny spot and water freely during dry spells to deter powdery mildew. Basil will thrive with flowering annuals and tender perennials when treated to regular foliar feeds.

Ocimum basilicum purpurascens 'Purple Ruffles'

Foliage Plants

	SPRING	SUMMER	AUTUMN	WINTER	height (cm)	spread (cm)	min. temp °C	moisture	sun/shade	flower colour	
Ocimum basilicum var. *purpurascens* 'Dark Opal'					45	15	1	💧	☀		Red purple leaves
O. b. var. *purpurascens* 'Purple Ruffles'					45	15	1	💧	☀		Dark purple leaves with ruffled edges

Origanum
Oregano *or* Wild marjoram

The gold leaf and variegated forms of oregano are useful in seasonal hanging baskets, as well as permanent container schemes and for brightening up herb collections.

These low spreading, woody based plants have a dense coverage of very small leaves, which are evergreen to semi-evergreen in mild winters. All are aromatic and edible, though the value in cooking varies. Oregano is drought tolerant, preferring a sunny, well-drained situation in loam based compost. It dislikes winter wet and benefits from a mulch of grit. The tiny clustered flowers of *Origanum vulgare* 'Aureum' and *O. v.* 'Gold Tip' give the best display. Clip over after flowering to keep growth bushy; you may also need to cut plants back to basal growth in spring. For easy mixing with blue and mauve flowers or blue-leaved grasses such as *Festuca glauca*, pick the yellow-green 'Aureum Crispum', whose colour intensifies towards autumn, or the two-tone 'Gold Tip'. 'Country Cream' is sometimes available in the herb section at garden centres.

Origanum vulgare 'Country Cream'

	SPRING	SUMMER	AUTUMN	WINTER	height (cm)	spread (cm)	min. temp °C	moisture	sun/shade	flower colour	
Origanum vulgare 'Aureum'					30	45	-17	💧	☀		Golden tinted foliage
O. v. 'Country Cream'					30	40	-17	💧	☀		White variegated
O. v. 'Gold Tip' syn. 'Variegatum'					40	45	-17	💧	☀		Gold shot tips. Good flowers
O. v. 'Aureum Crispum' syn. 'Curly Gold'					30	45	-17	💧	☀		Curly golden foliage

☀ *sunny*   ☀ *semi-shady*   ● *shady*

Perilla
Beefsteak plant

Once commonly grown as a dot plant in formal bedding displays, the annual beefsteak plant, *Perilla frutescens*, still has lots to offer patio gardeners, providing foliage interest well into the autumn.

Perilla frutescens var. crispa

These bushy, upright plants have large, glossy, purple-black leaves – in the variety *crispa*, the foliage has frilly edges – and make dramatic focal points for mixed plantings of flowering annuals and tender perennials. Try mixing Perilla with the vivid pink daisies of *Brachyscome* 'Strawberry Mousse'.

Perilla needs full sun, shelter from wind, and moisture-retentive but well-drained compost. The leaves are aromatic and edible. Insignificant white flowers appear in summer. Watch for aphids on shoot tips.

	SPRING	SUMMER	AUTUMN	WINTER	height (cm)	spread (cm)	min. temp °C	moisture	sun/shade	flower colour	
Perilla frutescens var. *crispa*	planting	flower flower			50	30	-5	well drained	sun		Dark purple-bronze frilly edged leaves
P. f. var. *purpurascens*	planting	flower flower			50	30	-5	well drained	sun		Dark purple leaves

Petroselinum
Moss-curled parsley

This hardy, biennial herb is normally grown as an annual because gardeners and cooks alike are only interested in the ornamental and very tasty foliage, and not in the yellow-green umbrella-shaped heads that appear the following year.

Two varieties of moss-curled parsley, 'Afro' and 'Envy', are readily available and can be grown from seed if you can't find them in the herb section of your garden centre. Use either one to provide foliage interest in seasonal plantings, including hanging baskets, where you can harvest the curly foliage as long as it doesn't harm the display. The bright green combines well with white, pink, apricot or scarlet blooms. Grow in moisture-retentive but well-drained compost in sun or part shade, and pick off yellowing leaves regularly.

Petroselinum 'Envy'

	SPRING	SUMMER	AUTUMN	WINTER	height (cm)	spread (cm)	min. temp °C	moisture	sun/shade	foliage colour	
Petroselinum 'Afro'	planting planting				30	45	-17	well drained	sun/part shade		Tightly curled, dark-green leaves
P. 'Envy'	planting planting				30	45	-17	well drained	sun/part shade		Upright growth, long stems

planting   flower   well drained   moist   wet

Plechostachys

For a long time this plant was known as *Helichrysum microphyllum* because of its resemblance to the silver grey, felted *Helichrysum petiolare*.

Plechostachys serpyllifolia, as it is now correctly named, is a tender perennial that thrives in similar conditions – full sun and well-drained compost – but the drought tolerant foliage is tiny, giving a filigree effect as the stems weave through the flowers. Growing 30cm (12in) high and spreading to a little over 60cm (24in), this plant is much more delicate than *H. microphyllum* and less likely to take over a hanging basket, especially one planted with dainty pink or mauve nemesias or diascias, and soft blue or mauve pink *Brachycome multifida*.

Plechostachys serpyllifolia

Plectranthus

Variegated mintleaf *or* Swedish ivy

The variegated, evergreen Swedish ivy, *Plectranthus forsteri* 'Marginatus', is most commonly grown as a houseplant but can spend the summer outdoors in sheltered pots, baskets and window troughs.

The shoots grow upright at first, then trail and are clothed in light grey-green oval shaped leaves with toothed edges and a white margin. The variegated mintleaf, *Plectranthus madagascariensis*, is becoming more popular as a patio plant now that people appreciate its remarkable drought tolerance. It is also extremely useful grown trailing over a hanging basket, where its aromatic leaves can be appreciated by those walking past or under the suspended arrangement.

This white-variegated plant, with bristle covered stems, spreads through the compost and sends up vertical shoots clothed in firm, fleshy leaves that give off a minty aroma when disturbed.

Plectranthus are best placed in a position out of the midday heat and sun, which can cause the foliage to scorch. Water freely during the growing season and feed monthly.

Plectranthus ciliatus 'Easy Gold'

	SPRING	SUMMER	AUTUMN	WINTER	height (cm)	spread (cm)	min. temp °C	moisture	sun/shade	flower colour	
Plectranthus ciliatus 'Easy Gold'	🌱	●			45	45	10	◌◌	◐	☐	Australian; attractive, golden foliage
P. forsteri 'Marginatus'	🌱	●			45	45	10	◌◌	◐	☐	White variegated, aromatic
P. madagascariensis	🌱	●			25	60	10	◌◌	◐	☐	White variegated, strongly aromatic

☼ *sunny*　　◐ *semi-shady*　　● *shady*

Salvia
Common sage

One of the most useful foliage plants for baskets and sunny patio containers is the yellow splashed form of the herb sage, *Salvia officinalis* 'Icterina'. This plant also produces flowers of a blue hue in early to mid summer.

This soft coloured evergreen combines beautifully with purple pinks, soft blues and pale yellow or cream flowers, for example, *Brachsycome multifida* Mist Series, bacopa, ageratum and *Tagetes* 'French Vanilla'. Try combining it as well with the intense blue-purple blooms of *Salvia farinacea* 'Victoria'.

The foliage of the purple-tinted *S. o.* Purpurascens Group works well with red and magenta flowers, such as pelargoniums and verbenas, and also with the soft oranges and yellows of *Osteospermum* 'Symphony Series'. 'Tricolor', with its pretty pink and cream splashed leaves, is the least vigorous of the three, and is best grown with plants that won't swamp it, such as heliotrope or

nemesia. Provide full sun and well-drained compost, preferably loam based. Keep plants from summer containers to use in autumn and winter displays. Cut stems back by about half in spring to promote bushy regrowth.

Salvia officinalis 'Tricolor'

	SPRING			SUMMER			AUTUMN			WINTER			height (cm)	spread (cm)	min. temp °C	moisture	sun/shade	colour	
Salvia officinalis 'Icterina'		🌱		❋	❋									30	30	-5	💧	☼		Variegated yellow and grey-green
S. o. Purpurascens Group		🌱		❋	❋									30	45	-5	💧	☼		Purple tinted
S. o. 'Tricolor'		🌱		❋	❋									20	30	-5	💧	☼		Pink, cream splashed leaves

Sedum
Stonecrop

Many of the drought tolerant ground covering sedums work well in pots, even the more invasive types, and are particularly useful for small containers that tend to dry out quickly.

Sedum spathulifolium 'Cape Blanco'

Sedum spathulifolium 'Cape Blanco' makes a carpet of fleshy, evergreen rosettes covered in a white bloom. It grows in little soil and tends to rot in deep, moist compost. Grow as a small potted specimen or as a foreground to upright or mound-forming alpines in a stone trough. *S. lineare* 'Varietatum' is a tender perennial with long vertical trailing stems clothed in pointed succulent, grey-white variegated leaves. Use it in summer hanging baskets with ivy-leaved geraniums.

	SPRING			SUMMER			AUTUMN			WINTER			height (cm)	spread (cm)	min. temp °C	moisture	sun/shade	colour	
Sedum lineare 'Variegatum'			🌱	❋										10	60	1	💧	☼		Narrow, pointed, white-variegated leaves
S. spathulifolium 'Cape Blanco'	🌱	🌱		❋										5	45	-17	💧	☀		Tight, grey-white rosettes form carpet

🌱 *planting*   ❋ *flower*   💧 *well drained*   💧 *moist*   💧 *wet*

Solenostemon

Flame nettle *or* Coleus

The flame coloured, beautifully variegated forms of *Solenostemon scutellarioides* (syn. *Coleus blumei*) are available from late spring to early autumn as individually potted plants. When growing from seed, choose Rainbow Series or the more compact Wizard Series both of which have a stunning range of warm, bright colours.

The semi-trailing, red leaved 'Scarlet Poncho' works well in hanging baskets. The frilly 'Black Dragon', whose dark purple leaves have crimson red centres, looks good outdoors combined with crimson red busy Lizzies.

These tender perennials are easy to propagate from cuttings and will root from shoot tips pushed into moist compost. A single plant bought early on could generate scores of plants by the season end. Pinch out shoot tips to promote bushiness and remove the blue flower spikes as soon as possible, otherwise the leaf colour fades. Water well in dry weather and grow in fertile, moisture-retentive compost in sun or part shade.

Solenostemon scutellarioides 'Black Dragon'

	SPRING	SUMMER	AUTUMN	WINTER	height (cm)	spread (cm)	min. temp °C	moisture	sun/shade	flower colour	
Solenostemon scutellarioides 'Black Dragon'		●●●●	●●●		45	60	5	◐◐	☀		Frilly edged purple-black leaves, red centres
S. s. 'Palisandra'		●●●●	●●●		30	60	5	◐◐	☀		Large leaves, purple with narrow, lime edge
S. s. Rainbow Series		●●●●	●●●		45	60	5	◐◐	☀		Wide range of bicolours
S. s. 'Scarlet Poncho'		●●●●	●●●		30	60	5	◐◐	☀		Semi-trailing, red with narrow gold edge
S. s. Wizard Series		●●●●	●●●		20	45	5	◐◐	☀		Wide range of bicolours

Stachys

Lamb's ears *or* Lamb's lugs *or* Lamb's tongue

The name of lamb's ears comes from the soft felting of the foliage. *Stachys byzantina* 'Silver Carpet' is good for ground cover.

The grey-green leaves of 'Big Ears' are twice the size and even more tactile. 'Primrose Heron' has yellowy-green leaves the same size as 'Silver Carpet' that are bright in spring and in autumn. Grow in well-drained, loam-based compost and protect from too much winter wet. Mulch with grit or gravel to keep moisture away from the leaves.

Stachys byzantina 'Big Ears'

	SPRING	SUMMER	AUTUMN	WINTER	height (cm)	spread (cm)	min. temp °C	moisture	sun/shade	colour	
Stachys byzantina 'Big Ears'	●●●●	●●			38	60	-17	◐◐	☼		Extra large, grey-green felted leaves
S. b. 'Primrose Heron'	●●●				15	60	-17	◐◐	☼		Yellowish green leaves
S. b. 'Silver Carpet'	●●●				15	60	-17	◐◐	☼		Silver felted leaves

☼ *sunny*   ☀ *semi-shady*   ● *shady*

Foliage Plants

Tanacetum

Golden feverfew
or Silver lace
bush

Tanacetum parthenium 'Aureum' is a bushy, short-lived perennial with white flowerheads, a woody base and is often best as a young plant.

It has been classified under Chrysanthemum and Pyrethrum in the past and you may know it better by these names. If you want to grow your own supply, the little white daisy flowers produce a mass of seed that germinates where it falls, but trays of golden feverfew are also readily available from the bedding plant sections of garden centres in spring. Use the bright, heavily dissected foliage as a highlight among vivid purple, magenta and cerise pink blooms such as petunias and busy lizzies. Golden feverfew can also be used in hanging baskets year round.

The silver lace bush (*Tanacetum ptarmiciflorum* 'Silver Feather') is a short-lived tender perennial with silver white

Tanacetum parthenium 'Aureum'

feathery foliage making delicate fans. It is particularly good for romantic white or pastel coloured arrangements. Overwinter young plants raised from cuttings taken in early summer in a frost free greenhouse.

	SPRING	SUMMER	AUTUMN	WINTER		height (cm)	spread (cm)	min. temp °C	moisture	sun/shade	colour	
Tanacetum parthenium 'Aureum'	🌱	✹ ✹ ✹			🌱	45	30	-17	💧💧	☀	☐	Dissected leaves, golden, evergreen
T. ptarmiciflorum 'Silver Feather'	🌱	✹			🌱	60	40	1	💧💧	☀	☐	Silver feathery leaves

Tolmiea

Pick-a-back
plant

Tolmiea menziesii

Tolmiea menziesii 'Taff's Gold' is a semi-evergreen hardy perennial that makes a mound of maple shaped, yellow speckled leaves.

It gets its common name of pick-a-back plant from the fact that new plants arise at the base of the leaf. These root when they make contact with the ground.

Tolmiea thrives in full or part shade and so is particularly useful planted in pots decorating shady corners. Try combining it with busy lizzies, fuchsias, lobelia and the apricot coloured *Begonia sutherlandii*.

Dull greenish to purple-brown flowers appear in late spring and early summer, but these can be cut off to allow the plant to put in more strength to the foliage. Grow in humus-rich, moisture-retentive compost. It can reach 30cm (12in) in height and spreads roughly 45cm (18in).

🌱 *planting*	✹ *flower*	💧 *well drained*	💧💧 *moist*	💧💧💧 *wet*

Tradescantia
Inch plant

One way to add variety to summer baskets is to use trailing houseplants like Tradescantia. The common, white striped *Tradescantia fluminensis* 'Quicksilver' is lovely in baskets with white or pastel busy Lizzies, trailing fuchsias, pendulous begonias and trailing lobelias.

Bulking up quantities from a single plant is easy, as shoot tip cuttings root in water. *Tradescantia zebrina* has purple, silver and green striped leaves and can be used to complement purple and cerise trailing petunias. There are also pink and purple tinted cultivars. Somewhat different in character is *T. pallida* 'Purpurea' with fleshy purple foliage. Try it with sugar pink or cerise ivy-leaved geraniums and *Dichondra micrantha* 'Silver Falls'. All the Tradescantia described have intermittent flushes of small, three-petalled flowers.

Pinch out shoot tips to promote bushiness and keep moist during the summer growing season. Watch for aphids, vine weevil and slugs.

	SPRING	SUMMER	AUTUMN	WINTER	height (cm)	spread (cm)	min. temp °C	moisture	sun/shade	flower colour	
T. fluminensis 'Quicksilver'					15	20	10	💧💧	◐		Green and white striped leaves
T. pallida 'Purpurea' (syn. Setcreasea purpurea)					20	40	10	💧	☀		Purple felted leaves
T. zebrina 'Purpusii' (syn. Zebrina purpusii)					15	20	10	💧💧	☀		Purple silver and green striped leaves

Trifolium
Ornamental clover

The hardy creeping ornamental clovers make unusual but easy to grow subjects for pots and baskets.

Trifolium repens 'Purpurascens' with its purple-maroon trefoil foliage, edged lime green, creates a dramatic effect when teamed up with other foliage plants such as coleus (Solenostemon) and golden feverfew. The leaves of *T. pratense* 'Susan Smith' are a real curiosity, with bright yellow veining. From early to mid-summer, pinkish clover flowers appear. Divide to increase numbers in spring.

	SPRING	SUMMER	AUTUMN	WINTER	height (cm)	spread (cm)	min. temp °C	moisture	sun/shade	colour	
T. pratense 'Susan Smith' (syn. 'Goldnet')					30	60	-17	💧	☀		Clover-like leaf with yellow net veining
T. repens 'Purpurascens'					15	90	-17	💧💧	☀		Deep maroon purple clover leaves

☀ sunny   ◐ semi-shady   ● shady

Architectural Plants

This section contains plants with a strong sculptural character. Large architectural plants often work best planted singly in pots where their structure can be appreciated without distraction.

This applies particularly to those with a symmetrical construction such as Agave, Yucca, Phormium, Cordyline and many ferns. Big leaved species including palms, *Fatsia japonica* and the hardy Japanese banana, *Musa basjoo*, instantly add a tropical feel to a patio. Mature specimens are often quite expensive to buy but luckily you only need a small collection of these striking subjects mixed in among other plants to create the atmosphere of exotica.

As well as helping to create the illusion of far off places, this group of plants can also be used to enhance modern buildings and features such as decks or swimming pools: the smooth, bold lines of the plants mirror the architectural simplicity of the hard landscaping. Many tussock forming grasses, sedges and grass-like plants have been placed in this section. The narrow leaves contrast beautifully with plants having broad, rounded foliage such as elephant's ears (Bergenia) or hostas, but collections of grasses in pots of different shapes and sizes also look striking, especially against a plain backdrop.

With plants like Japanese maple and the columnar bamboos, the individual leaflets as well as the overall shape and gracefulness of the plant give it a special presence. Again, these are best planted singly to maximise their impact. Some flowering plants combine sculpted blooms with architectural foliage, such as Agapanthus and Indian shot (Canna). Plants such as lilies are grown exclusively for their exotic blooms and can be mingled with other plants while in flower. Although small by comparison to most plants in this section, rosette-forming succulents like houseleek (Sempervivum), Echeveria and Aeonium have a beautiful form that merits close inspection.

A

Acer palmatum

Japanese maple

If you have a shaded area sheltered from wind, such as a space under trees or a small courtyard enclosed by buildings, you could introduce Japanese maples.

These hardy shrubs or small trees look good in wooden barrels or glazed ceramic pots. These need to be wide as well as deep. There are scores of elegant *Acer palmatum* cultivars, but the best of these slow-growing plants for containers have arching branches that become twisted and gnarled, such as 'Crimson Queen' and 'Garnet'. *A shirasawanum* 'Aureum' prefers deep shade to prevent its green leaves from scorching. Mulch the roots with bark to keep plants moist. If temperatures drop below about -10°C (14°F), insulate with straw or bubble wrap plastic. Protect against wind scorch.

Acer palmatum 'Garnet'

	SPRING	SUMMER	AUTUMN	WINTER	height (cm)	spread (cm)	min. temp °C	moisture	sun/shade	foliage colour	
A. p. var. dissectum	planting	flower			120	180	-15	moist	semi-shady		Finely cut fingered leaves
A. p. var. dissectum 'Crimson Queen'	planting	flower			150	180	-15	moist	semi-shady		Red-purple leaves
A. p. var. dissectum 'Garnet'	planting	flower			120	180	-15	moist	semi-shady		Similar habit to A. p. var. dissectum
A. shirasawanum 'Aureum'	planting	flower			150	100	-15	moist	semi-shady		Bright lime-green leaves

Acorus

Japanese rush

Variegated forms of the semi-evergreen, grass-like perennial *Acorus gramineus* can add a splash of colour and contrasting leaf texture to container plantings.

Although a waterside plant, forms such as 'Ogon' will grow happily in moisture-retentive, soilless compost. The arching fans of narrow, grassy foliage form eye-catching clumps and are useful in sheltered autumn and winter displays. Contrast 'Ogon' with the maroon leaves of *Heuchera micrantha* var. *diversifolia* 'Palace Purple'. 'Hakuro-nishiki' is a compact gold-leaved plant.

Acorus gramineus 'Variegatus'

	SPRING	SUMMER	AUTUMN	WINTER	height (cm)	spread (cm)	min. temp °C	moisture	sun/shade	foliage colour	
Acorus gramineus 'Hakuro-nishiki'	planting		planting		15	20	-5	wet	semi-shady		Neat, golden foliage
A. g. 'Ogon'	planting		planting		30	30	-5	wet	semi-shady		Glossy, yellow striped foliage
A. g. 'Variegatus'	planting		planting		30	25	-5	wet	semi-shady		Cream and yellow striped

planting · flower · moist · wet · semi-shady

Architectural Plants

Aeonium

These tender succulent sub-shrubs, originating from Morocco, are highly architectural and older plants make stunning pot specimens that add a touch of exotica to patio displays.

During the colder months, grow aeoniums in a cool or temperate greenhouse or keep inside as houseplants. Move them outside in summer when the night temperatures have risen to 10°C (50°F) and over.

The thick, leafless, upright stems bear sculpted leaf rosettes at the ends of the branches and, in the purple forms especially, these look like large flowers. The rosettes of the species, *Aeonium arboreum*, are pale green, but in the most dramatic form,

'Zwartkop', the foliage is almost black and glossy.

Aeoniums associate well with silver-grey and blue-leaved foliage plants, especially those with spiky or sword-shaped leaves reminiscent of desert landscapes, for example, agave, yucca and astelia. In hot climates, grow in light shade.

Plant aeoniums in free-draining, loam-based, gritty compost and in summer, water thoroughly and then allow plants to almost completely dry out. Keep very dry in winter to prevent rotting.

Aeonium arboreum 'Zwartkop'

	SPRING	SUMMER	AUTUMN	WINTER	height (cm)	spread (cm)	min. temp °C	moisture	sun/shade	flower colour	
A. arboreum	planting	flower			90	60	10	well drained/moist	sun/shade		Pale green rosettes
A. a. 'Atropurpureum'	planting	flower			90	60	10	well drained/moist	sun/shade		Bronze-purple with green centres
A. a. 'Zwartkop'	planting	flower			90	60	10	well drained/moist	sun/shade		Purple-black rosettes

Agapanthus

African *or* Nile lily

The African lily, *A. africanus*, is a statuesque perennial with strap-shaped evergreen leaves and tall flower stems bearing large spherical heads of blue, trumpet-shaped blooms. Its effect on the patio is distinctly sub tropical. 'Albus' is striking in twilight.

Agapanthus africanus

These plants and derivatives, such as the dwarf, white-variegated 'Tinkerbell', are tender and must be moved to a conservatory or frost-free greenhouse over winter. Robust hardy hybrids include 'Loch Hope' and the white-flowered cultivar 'Bressingham White'. Grow in loam-based compost and provide good drainage, but water freely during summer. Liquid feed regularly up to flowering time.

	SPRING	SUMMER	AUTUMN	WINTER	height (cm)	spread (cm)	min. temp °C	moisture	sun/shade	flower colour	
Agapanthus africanus 'Albus'		planting	flower		90+	45	1	well drained	sun		Tender but exotic looking
A. 'Bressingham White'	planting	flower			90	60	-15	well drained	sun		Superior, white flowered hybrid
A. campanulatus 'Isis'	planting	flower			75	30	-15	well drained	sun		Borderline hardy. Good deep colour
A. 'Lilliput'	planting	flower			40	40	-15	well drained	sun		Dwarf form
A. 'Loch Hope'	planting	flower			120+	60	-15	well drained	sun		Hardy, large flowered
A. 'Tinkerbell'	planting	flower			50	40	1	well drained	sun		Tender dwarf, white margined foliage

planting · flower · well drained · moist · wet

Agave
Century plant

Making a bold rosette of succulent, blue-grey leaves, the tender perennial *Agave americana* eventually grows into a magnificent specimen plant. But beware – leaf tips are fashioned into vicious spines!

This sun loving and extremely drought tolerant plant gets its common name from the fact that it can take many years for the tall flower spikes to appear. The species must be overwintered dry at a temperature above 5–7°C. Variegated cultivars are less hardy than the species. Grow Agave in loam-based compost with sharp drainage, such as John Innes No 2. with added grit, and in autumn, prepare for winter by reducing the watering steadily. Watch for slugs and scale insects.

Agave americana

	SPRING	SUMMER	AUTUMN	WINTER	height (cm)	spread (cm)	min. temp °C	moisture	sun/shade	foliage colour	
A. americana	🌱 🌱				90+	1.2+	5	◊◊	☼		Blue-grey leaves
A. a. 'Mediopicta'	🌱 🌱				90+	1.2+	10	◊◊	☼		Central yellow stripe
A.a. 'Variegata'	🌱 🌱				90+	1.2+	10	◆◊	☼		Cream edged leaves

Arctotis
African daisies

The most common types of African daisy are the showy Harlequin Hybrids, which used to go under the name *Arctotis* x *hybrida* or x *Venidioarctotis*. These make handsome rosettes of wavy edged, silver green leaves.

Arctotis hybrids

The unbranched flower stems arise from the rosettes bearing large, vividly coloured daisies in shades of pink, white, orange, apricot, rich red and yellow. Blooms often have dark centres or contrasting zoning around the eye. A number of named cultivars produced from cuttings are available, including the excellent 'Flame' whose orange-red blooms add a sub-tropical note. Enhance the colouring by planting in terracotta and surrounding with blue-grey foliage plants. These short-lived tender perennials are normally discarded at the end of the season.

Grow in a warm sunny spot on the patio, planting in well-drained but moisture-retentive compost. Aphids, leaf minor, and slugs and snails may cause problems.

	SPRING	SUMMER	AUTUMN	WINTER	height (cm)	spread (cm)	min. temp °C	moisture	sun/shade	flower colour	
Arctotis Harlequin Hybrid 'Apricot'		🌱 ● ● ●	●		45	30	5	◊◊	☼		Flowers close in shade
A. Harlequin Hybrid 'China Rose'		🌱 ● ● ●	●		45	30	5	◆◊	☼		Dusky pink blooms
A. Harlequin Hybrid 'Flame'		🌱 ● ● ●	●		45	30	5	◊◊	☼		Attractive orange blooms
A. Harlequin Hybrid 'Mahogany'		🌱 ● ● ●	●		45	30	5	◊◊	☼		Dramatically dark

☼ *sunny*   ☀ *semi-shady*   ● *shady*

Aspidistra
Cast iron plant

Once a popular parlour plant in the 19th century, the aspidistra or cast iron plant lives up to its reputation for toughness when it is moved outdoors.

Hardy to -4°C, it thrives in pots set in sheltered shady corners, and depending on the microclimate could be left outside all year round provided the plants have been properly hardened off. The long, paddle-shaped leaves are dark green and leathery with a strong architectural presence, and in *Aspidistra elatior* 'Variegata' they are striped with cream. Strange mauve flowers sometimes appear at soil level in summer. Watch for slug damage.

Aspidistra elatior

	SPRING	SUMMER	AUTUMN	WINTER	height (cm)	spread (cm)	min. temp °C	moisture	sun/shade	flower colour	
Aspidistra elatior	🌱	✹			90	30	-4	◊◊	☀	▢	Insignificant flowers at soil level
A. e. 'Variegata'	🌱	✹			90	30	-4	◊◊	☀	▢	Cream striped foliage

Asplenium scolopendrium
Hart's tongue fern

Asplenium scolopendrium

Unlike many ferns, the hart's tongue is tolerant of occasional drought and thrives in alkaline, loam-based compost mixed with organic matter like leaf mould.

This shade-loving evergreen usually has simple, glossy, rich green leaves arranged in a shuttlecock formation. Remove last year's dead or damaged foliage as necessary in the spring when the new fronds have unfurled.

Try contrasting the strap-shaped leaves with those of the hardy maidenhair ferns. The hart's tongue is a very variable plant in the wild and produces many different leaf forms, including curiosities like the cristate types with heavily dissected and wavy shoot tips.

	SPRING	SUMMER	AUTUMN	WINTER	height (cm)	spread (cm)	min. temp °C	moisture	sun/shade	foliage colour	
Asplenium scolopendrium					60	60	-30	◊◊	☼	▢	syn. *Phyllitis scolopendrium*
A. s. Cristatum Group					60	80	-30	◊◊	☼	▢	Crested shoot tips

| 🌱 planting | ✹ flower | 🌰 harvest | ◊ well drained | ◊◊ moist | ◊◊◊ wet |

Astelia

Plants from New Zealand have become very popular in recent years and the metallic-looking *Astelia chathamica*, often referred to as Silver spear, has just the right look for a contemporary outdoor room.

Astelia chathamica

This highly architectural plant, making a clump of arching, sword-shaped leaves, is easily grown in pots filled with moisture-retentive soilless compost, but do not overwater. When brought under cover for winter, the plants need to be kept on the dry side.

Insignificant yellow-green flowers appear in spring and are followed by orange berries on female plants, but the main attraction is the silver-green foliage. New on the scene is the subtly cream and bronzy pink striped *A. nervosa* 'Westland', which is a little shorter. Only buy plants that are firmly rooted in their pots.

	SPRING	SUMMER	AUTUMN	WINTER	height (cm)	spread (cm)	min. temp °C	moisture	sun/shade	flower colour	
Astelia chathamica					120	180	-5				Metallic foliage
A. nervosa 'Westland'					60	150	-5				New variegated cultivar

Ballota

Hailing from the Mediterranean, these drought tolerant sub-shrubs look good in simple stone troughs mulched with slate or pebbles. The felted leaves are almost spherical and are arranged in opposite pairs along the strongly upright stems.

In the somewhat tender *Ballota acetabulosa*, the white woolly coating makes the plants silver green while *B. pseudodictamnus* is overall grey-green. In contrast, the cultivar 'All Hallows Green' has lime-tinted, slightly crinkled leaves. These last two plants are borderline hardy. Flowers are insignificant but they open in the leaf axils from decorative, shell shaped calyces that remain for some time.

Use ballotas as a foil for bright flowers such as pelargoniums or make a more

Ballota 'All Hallows Green'

subtle blend by mixing with herbs like thyme and lavender. Cut plants back in spring to generate fresh growth.

	SPRING	SUMMER	AUTUMN	WINTER	height (cm)	spread (cm)	min. temp °C	moisture	sun/shade	flower colour	
Ballota acetabulosa					60	75	-5				White felted shoots and leaves
B. 'All Hallows Green'					60	60	-15				Lime-green foliage
B. pseudodictamnus					45	60	-15				Yellowy grey-green leaves, white stems

☼ sunny   ☼ semi-shady   ☼ shady

Bergenia
Elephant's ears

Evergreen perennials that get better looking in winter are rare, but the hardy elephant's ears is noted for how its clumps of large oval leaves take on rich hues when the temperature drops – *B. purpurscens* and 'Abendglut' are classic examples.

Any bergenia can be grown in pots, but the compact 'Wintermärchen' is ideal with its weather resistant flowers and red tinted leaves that have a dark maroon red reverse.

This plant is frequently neglected and though it will tolerate poor soil and dry shade, you'll be rewarded by providing moisture-retentive humus-rich compost and by feeding and watering regularly during the summer.

Bergenia 'Bressingham White'

	SPRING	SUMMER	AUTUMN	WINTER	height (cm)	spread (cm)	min. temp °C	moisture	sun/shade	flower colour	
Bergenia 'Abendglut' ('Evening Glow')	● ●		✂ ✂ ✂		30	60	-15	◖	☀	▨	Semi-double. Leaves red tinted
B. 'Bressingham White'	● ●		✂ ✂ ✂		45	60	-15	◖	☀	☐	Large flowers
B. cordifolia 'Purpurea'	●		✂ ✂ ✂		60	75	-15	◖	☀	▨	Thick, red tinted foliage
B. purpurascens	● ●		✂ ✂ ✂		45	30	-15	◖	☀	▨	Leaves beetroot red in winter
B. 'Silberlicht' ('Silver Light')	● ●		✂ ✂ ✂		45	60	-15	◖	☀	☐	Early flowering
B. 'Wintermärchen' ('Winter Fairy Tale')	● ●		✂ ✂ ✂		45	60	-15	◖	☀	▨	Small glossy leaves, red tinted in winter

Brassica
Ornamental kale
or Ornamental cabbage

Some of the best plants for brightening up the autumn and winter patio are the ornamental cabbages (*Brassica oleracea* var. *capitata*) and kales (*B. o.* var. *acephala*). Kales have deeply dissected leaves and no heart, giving a feathery appearance.

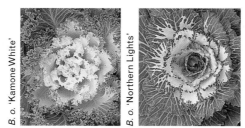

B. o. 'Kamone White'

B. o. 'Northern Lights'

Use the plants to colour scheme autumn and winter pots, for example blend white variegated types with white-berried *Gaultheria mucronata*, white mini cyclamen and white heathers. Plant in a row in troughs and windowboxes or tightly packed in a large barrel. Slugs and wood pigeons may attack and plants often bolt (start to flower) in spring.

	SPRING	SUMMER	AUTUMN	WINTER	height (cm)	spread (cm)	min. temp °C	moisture	sun/shade	foliage colour	
Brassica oleracea var. *acephala* 'Feather'		✂ ✂ ✂			30	30	-15	◖	☀	▯	Feathered white leaves
B. oleracea var. *acephala* 'Kamone White'		✂ ✂ ✂			30	30	-15	◖	☀	▯	Feathered red/white inner leaves; veining
B. oleracea var. *acephala* 'Peacock'		✂ ✂ ✂			35	30	-15	◖	☀	▯	Feathery leaves
B. oleracea var. *capitata* 'Northern Lights'		✂ ✂ ✂			25	50	-15	◖	☀	▯	Frilled, pink, white or purple-red centres
B. oleracea var. *capitata* 'Osaka'		✂ ✂ ✂			25	50	-15	◖	☀	▯	Frilled, purple pink or white centres
B. oleracea var. *capitata* 'Tokyo'		✂ ✂ ✂			25	30	-15	◖	☀	▯	Frilled pink, red or white centres

✂ *planting*   ● *flower*   ◖ *well drained*   ◗ *moist*   ◗◗ *wet*

Brugmansia
Angel's trumpets

There can be few flowers more exotic looking than those of Brugmansia or Datura as this group of tender shrubs was formerly known. The pendant, trumpet-shaped blooms have an intoxicating evening fragrance – *Brugmansia aurea* being one of the most powerfully scented at night.

Brugmansia x candida 'Variegata'

Brugmansias grow quickly during the summer and plants should be placed in a sheltered corner, at the back of lower growing pot plants to give room for the huge flowers of cultivars like the double white 'Knightii' or pale peach 'Grand Marnier' to be displayed properly. 'Variegata' has delightful variegated foliage. Grow in John Innes No. 3 with good drainage. Water freely in summer and very sparingly while plants are being overwintered indoors – an unheated bedroom will suffice. Cut plants back to a framework of branches in spring and begin hardening them ready to move outdoors in late spring and early summer. All parts are highly poisonous. Watch for greenfly, whitefly and red spider mite.

	SPRING	SUMMER	AUTUMN	WINTER	height (cm)	spread (cm)	min. temp °C	moisture	sun/shade	flower colour	
Brugmansia arborea 'Knightii'		● ● ● ●	●		180	150	7	◐	☼	☐	Double flowers
B. aurea		● ● ● ●	●		250	100	7	◐	☼	▨	Not widely available; best for evening scent
B. x candida 'Grand Marnier'		● ● ● ●	●		250	150	7	◐	☼	▨	'Variegata' has white-edged leaves
B. suaveolens		● ●			200	150	7	◐	☼	☐	Different colour forms available

Canna
Indian shot

The tropical looking cannas are half-hardy rhizomatous perennials that are grown for their large, banana like leaves and flamboyant blooms.

'Tropicana' is one of the best of the variegated cultivars and is stunning with or without the orange flowers. The green leaved 'Lucifer' is quite compact and has red flowers highlighted with a yellow petal margin. Grow cannas in moisture-retentive compost and water freely during the summer. Before the first frosts, cut plants to ground level and dig up rhizomes to store frost free in moist peat substitute. Divide and pot up in spring.

Canna indica

	SPRING	SUMMER	AUTUMN	WINTER	height (cm)	spread (cm)	min. temp °C	moisture	sun/shade	flower colour	
Canna 'Black Knight'		● ● ● ●	●		180	60	1	◐	☼	▨	Brown leaves
Canna indica		● ● ● ●	●		200	50	1	◐	☼	▨	Bright red or soft orange flowers
C. 'Lucifer'		● ● ●			80	50	1	◐	☼	▨	Green foliage. Compact
C. 'Striata'		● ● ●			150	60	1	◐	☼	▨	Leaves light green with yellow veins
C. 'Tropicana'		● ● ● ●	●		180	60	1	◐	☼	▨	Bronze-purple leaves veined orange
C. 'Wyoming'		● ● ● ●	●		180	60	1	◐	☼	▨	Brown foliage

☼ sunny   ☼ semi-shady   ● shady

C

Carex
Ornamental sedge

In recent years more and more gardeners have realised the decorative value of growing ornamental sedges and grasses in containers. The fine foliage looks good contrasted against smooth, solid paving stones. Raising plants up above ground level helps to display the beautiful arching shape of the tussock-forming types.

Bronze and red-brown leaved sedges add a contemporary flavour when planted in metallic finish containers and work particularly well surrounded by pots of blue and silver grasses. For example, you could combine the upright, but arching *Carex buchananii* with blue oat grass (*Helictotrichon sempervirens*) and blue or silver festucas. Add textural variety to collections of sedges and grasses with rounded cobbles and pebbles, as well as glossy broad-leaved plants like elephant's ears (Bergenia). Purple and silver marbled heucheras, silver filigree artemisias, red tinted houseleeks, purple ajugas and metallic blue or bronze acaenas (New Zealand bur) also associate well.

Carex oshimensis 'Evergold'

Carex conica 'Snowline'

Carex buchananii

The leaf colour of ornamental sedges varies from the pale silvery green of 'Frosted Curls', through greens and browns to white or yellow variegated types. 'Snowline' has a subtle cream leaf margin, while 'Fisher's Form' is more showy. Try with blue-leaved hostas.

Perhaps the best known of all the ornamental sedges is *Carex oshimensis* 'Evergold', which forms low arching tussocks of bright gold-striped glossy leaves, lovely in blue glazed pots and a real winter sparkler. *C. siderostica* 'Variegata' has green and white striped leaves and pink flushed leaf bases. This creeping sedge will fill a pot with handsome foliage and is useful for brightening up dull, shady corners with hostas and ferns.

Although sedges mostly prefer moisture-retentive to moist compost, they are usually pretty tough, with a certain amount of drought tolerance.

	SPRING	SUMMER	AUTUMN	WINTER	height (cm)	spread (cm)	min. temp °C	moisture	sun/shade	flower colour	
Carex buchananii	planting	flower			75	75	-5	moist	sun		Bronze. Vase shape, good vertical accent
C. comans bronze	planting	flower			45	90	-15	moist	sun		Pale silvery green. Curled ends
C. comans 'Frosted Curls'	planting	flower	planting		60	45	-5	moist	part shade		White leaf margin
C. conica 'Snowline'	planting/flower				15	25	-5	moist	part shade		Bronze-brown leaves. Borderline hardy
C. flagillifera	planting	flower	planting		45	90	-15	moist	sun		Warm red-brown foliage. Borderline hardy
C. morrowii 'Fishers Form'	planting/flower				40	30	-5	moist	part shade		Bright cream leaf margins
C. oshimensis 'Evergold'	planting/flower		planting		25	38	-15	moist	part shade		Bright yellow stripes
C. siderosticta 'Variegata'	planting/flower		planting		30	40	-15	moist	part shade		Broad leaves, white margins, pink flushed

planting   flower   well drained   moist   wet

Chamaerops
Dwarf fan palm

Looking rather similar to the Chusan fan palm (*Trachycarpos fortunei*), the dwarf fan palm, *Chamaerops humilis*, can be distinguished by its multi-stemmed habit and spiny leaf stems.

The architectural foliage varies in colour and can be silvery green or blue tinted. Grown in a pot this half-hardy palm will only reach about 2m (6ft) in height, with a spread of roughly 1m (3ft). Plant in John Innes No 3 with good drainage and stand in full sun or preferably very light shade. In spring, top dress with fish, blood and bone or apply regular high nitrogen liquid feeds in spring and early summer to encourage leaf growth.

During a warm summer, orange berries may appear. In mid to late autumn, move to a sheltered spot outdoors and particularly for young plants, wrap up both pot and top growth with insulating material (see page 33) or move to a conservatory. Water sparingly in winter.

Chamaerops humilis

Chlorophytum
Spider plant

Everyone knows the spider plant, with its green and white striped leaves and long trailing stems bearing baby plants. This evergreen houseplant is able to tolerate neglect, largely due to the fleshy, moisture-storing roots but it does so much better given a little care and attention.

Chlorophytum comosum 'Vittatum'

You can use chlorophytum in summer hanging baskets, once the plants have been hardened off. The variegated foliage looks particularly good in all white schemes or combined with tropical reds, oranges or hot pinks and lush greens, for example, orange pendulous begonias, trailing asparagus fern, white marbled *Nasturtium* 'Alaska' and orange-red busy Lizzies.

Use plants that have already started to flower to ensure that you get the cascade effect of the spidery plantlets. Feed regularly with liquid fertilizer and for best results, protect from wind and strong sunlight.

	SPRING	SUMMER	AUTUMN	WINTER	height (cm)	spread (cm)	min. temp °C	moisture	sun/shade	flower colour	
Chlorophytum comosum 'Variegatum'	● ●	✂ ● ●	● ●		60	90	5	◊◊	☀		White leaf margins
C. c. 'Vittatum'	● ●	✂ ● ●	● ●		60	90	5	◊◊	☀		Central white stripe

☀ *sunny*   ☀ *semi-shady*   ● *shady*

Cordyline
Cabbage palm

A striking architectural plant for the sunny terrace, *Cordyline australis* and its coloured leaf forms are widely grown as accent plants.

Young specimens with a starburst of sword-shaped leaves can be planted in the middle of a large pot or vase on a pedestal, surrounded by lower growing and trailing plants. The green leaved species and cultivars such as 'Sundance' are the hardiest. Sharp drainage and a warm wall may be enough to see plants through the winter in mild areas. Others can be wrapped up for the winter or moved inside to give larger specimen plants the following year. Grow in John Innes No 3 with extra grit. Plants often become multi-stemmed, but pot grown ones are unlikely to flower.

Cordyline australis

Cordyline australis 'Sundance'

	SPRING	SUMMER	AUTUMN	WINTER	height (cm)	spread (cm)	min. temp °C	moisture	sun/shade	foliage colour	
Cordyline australis	planting				150	100	-5	well drained	sun/part		Green sword-shaped leaves
C. a. 'Albertii'		planting			120	90	5	well drained	sun		Bold cream variegation. Pink midribs
C. a. Purpurea Group		planting			150	100	5	well drained	sun		Purple/bronze foliage
C. a. 'Sundance'	planting				150	100	-5	well drained	sun/part		Red midrib and base of leaves
C. a. 'Torbay Dazzler'		planting			120	90	10	well drained	sun		Bold cream stripes
C. a. 'Torbay Red'		planting			150	100	10	well drained	sun		Deep wine-red leaves

Deschampsia
Tufted hair grass
or Tussock grass
or Wavy hair grass

The shimmering flowers of the tufted hair grass, *Deschampsia caespitosa*, are enchanting through summer and autumn – the slightest breeze sending waves of movement through the gauzy flowers.

This hardy, tussock-forming grass sends up slender but rigid flower stems in summer up to 1.2m (4ft). The flowers change colour subtly, developing a silvery sheen as they mature. Wavy hair grass, *Deschampsia flexuosa*, is also evergreen and the form 'Tatra Gold' is grown for its bright yellow tussocks of thread like leaves. Grow deschampsias in moisture-retentive, humus-rich compost and water freely during dry spells.

Deschampsia caespitosa

	SPRING	SUMMER	AUTUMN	WINTER	height (cm)	spread (cm)	min. temp °C	moisture	sun/shade	flower colour	
Deschampsia caespitosa 'Bronzeschleier'	planting			flower				120	120	-15	moist	sun/part		Earliest to flower (syn. 'Bronze Veil')
D. c. 'Goldschleier' (syn. 'Golden Veil')	planting			flower				120	120	-15	moist	sun/part		Pale, shimmering flowers
D. c. 'Goldtau' (syn. 'Golden Dew')	planting			flower				75	75	-15	moist	sun/part		Compact cultivar
D. flexuosa 'Tatra Gold'	planting			flower				50	50	-15	moist	sun		Bright yellow-green tussocks

planting · flower · well drained · moist · wet

Dryopteris

Male fern *or*
Copper shield
fern

Several ferns will take to being grown in pots but the male fern, *Dryopteris filix-mas*, with its bold shuttlecock habit, is one of the easiest and most architectural.

Once established, this woodlander is tolerant of dry shade and will also cope with full sun, though it does better in partial shade. The crested male fern, *D. filix-mas* 'Cristata' is a fine example of the many decorative forms that arise in nature. The ends of the fronds and frond segments have tassel-like extensions. In the evergreen, copper shield fern, when the new fronds unfurl in spring they are coppery pink gradually darkening with age. Remove the old leaves to tidy the plant ready for this display. Grow in humus-rich compost and water freely during the growing season.

Dryopteris filix-mas 'Cristata'

Dryopteris filix-mas

	SPRING	SUMMER	AUTUMN	WINTER	height (cm)	spread (cm)	min. temp °C	moisture	sun/shade	foliage colour	
Dryopteris erythrosora	🌱 🌱				60	38	-15	💧💧	☀	▦	New fronds coppery pink to red
D. filix-mas	🌱 🌱				100	60	-15	💧💧	☀	▦	Shuttlecock habit
D. filix-mas 'Cristata'	🌱 🌱				90	50	-15	💧💧	☀	▦	Tassel-like ends of fronds, frond segments

Echeveria

The sculpted rosettes of *Echeveria secunda* var. *glauca* (syn. *E. glauca*) measure 15cm (6in) across and have a beautiful blue-grey bloom – the perfect foil for the coral red, yellow tipped blooms. These appear in summer on 30cm (12in) long stems.

This succulent needs maximum light and very sharp drainage, as it can be prone to rotting, and is best planted singly in small terracotta pots or grouped in shallow bowls or small troughs. For a rivièra feel on a sunny patio, try displaying it with a collection of other succulents, for example, Agave, Aeonium, Sempervivum and potted red-flowered pelargoniums.

Plant in John Innes No 2 with extra grit and mulch the surface of the compost to keep the moisture from the stem and its lower leaves. Overwinter in a frost-free place, such as a conservatory. In mild gardens, this variety may survive outdoors all year round, especially in a spot that does not receive much direct rainfall.

Echeveria glauca

☼ *sunny*   ☀ *semi-shady*   ☀ *shady*

Eryobotrya
Loquat

Although the loquat or Japanese medlar, *Eriobotrya japonica*, produces edible fruits, the chief reason for growing this tender shrub on the patio is for its tropical looking foliage.

Eriobotrya japonica

The large leaves are up to 30cm (12in) in length with toothed margins and have a corrugated appearance due to the deep venation. The upper surface is glossy green, while the reverse is rusty brown due to a felted covering of hairs. Fragrant white flowers may appear through autumn and winter, followed in spring by spherical to pear shaped orange-yellow fruits. These are quite likely to be damaged by frosts without protection. Plants may reach 1.5m (5ft) by 1m (3ft) in around five years and at this size will need a substantial container, such as a Versailles planter to make the plant stable.

Grow against a warm wall for extra winter protection, although they are hardy to -5°C.

Eucomis
Pineapple flower
or Pineapple lily

It is not difficult to see how *Eucomis bicolor* got its common name. The stout, maroon-blotched stem that emerges from a basal rosette of strap-like leaves carries a pineapple-shaped head of tightly packed stary flowers, topped with a tuft of leaves.

The individual blooms are greenish white and on close inspection, the petals are prominently edged with maroon and the centres are also marked with the same colour. This exotic looking, borderline hardy bulbous perennial is best planted in pots under glass in early spring and started into growth, then hardened off and put in a sheltered spot outdoors after the risk of frost has passed. There are other less well-known species, including the white pineapple lily, *E. autumnalis*. In *E. comosa*, the flowerheads are longer and more cylindrical, though still with the same top-knot of leaves. The hardy cultivar *E. c.* 'Sparkling Burgundy' is outstanding with leaves and flower stems coloured rich purple. Grow in well-drained, gritty but humus-rich compost. Feed and water well during the growing season, leaving the compost to dry out a little between waterings. As a precaution, store the bulbs in their pots under cover over winter.

Eucomis comosa

	SPRING	SUMMER	AUTUMN	WINTER	height (cm)	spread (cm)	min. temp °C	moisture	sun/shade	flower colour	
Eucomis autumnalis		● ●			50	50	-15	▲▲	☼◗		Borderline hardy; pale, wavy-edged leaves
E. bicolor		● ●			50	30	-15	▲▲	☼◗		Maroon flecked flower stems
E. comosa		● ●			75	30	-15	▲	☼◗		Longer slimmer flower spikes than *E. bicolor*
E. comosa 'Sparkling Burgundy'		● ●			90	50	15	▲▲	☼◗		Burgundy coloured foliage

⚘ planting   ● flower   ⬭ harvest   ▲ well drained   ▲▲ moist   ▲▲▲ wet

Fargesia
Bamboo

Some bamboos are too vigorous to grow in pots but there are a number of suitable species. Two of the best are *Fargesia murieliae* and the dark stemmed *Fargesia nitida*, both of which would make wonderfully tall but lightweight specimen plants for a shady, sheltered courtyard.

Fargesia nitida

They steadily increase to produce light green columns of foliage that arch out elegantly at the top. The individual leaves are small, pointed and flutter in the slightest breeze. The variety *Fargesia murieliae* 'Simba' is particularly suitable for pot cultivation since the stems only reach about 1.8m (6ft) in height and the plant is altogether more compact.

Bamboos thrive in moisture-retentive, humus-rich, loam-based compost and enjoy regular liquid feeds through the growing season. Plant in large wooden half barrels or glazed ceramic pots. Water generously and mulch to retain moisture. Prevent congestion and enhance the shape of plants by occasionally thinning out some of the oldest culms, cutting them at soil level.

	SPRING	SUMMER	AUTUMN	WINTER	height (cm)	spread (cm)	min. temp °C	moisture	sun/shade	foliage colour	
Fargesia murieliae					300	100	-15	●●	●		Airy foliage plant
F. m. 'Simba'					180	90	-15	●●	●		Compact
F. nitida					300	100	-15	●●	●		New culms are bare till their second year

Fatsia
False castor oil plant

Glossy leaved plants work well in shade because they reflect the light. The tropical looking false castor oil plant, *Fatsia japonica*, is happiest given a sheltered shady spot where the large, lobed leaves grow lush and green.

Older plants may produce branched flower stems in autumn with spherical flower clusters followed by black, berry like fruits. Although garden centres occasionally stock this plant in the outdoor trees and shrubs section, you'll certainly find it in houseplants. But you will need to harden the plants off gradually and only put them out after the last likely frosts. Plain, green-leaved fatsias are moderately hardy, though they fare best in city or coastal gardens that are relatively frost free. Some of the young leaves and shoots may be frost damaged in spring but established plants often recover well. Remove old leaves that have died to keep plants tidy.

Fatsia japonica 'Variegata'

	SPRING	SUMMER	AUTUMN	WINTER	height (cm)	spread (cm)	min. temp °C	moisture	sun/shade	flower colour	
F. japonica					150	150	-5	●●	◐		Large glossy palmate leaves
F. j. 'Variegata'					120	120	0	●●	◐		Broad cream leaf margins

☼ *sunny*   ◐ *semi-shady*   ● *shady*

Festuca
Fescue

These hardy, evergreen grasses make dense rounded tussocks of very fine leaves that are perfectly symmetrical. Selected forms of *Festuca glauca* can be almost artificially blue.

This is a rare colour for foliage and stands out all the more for that reason. The blue is intensified when combined with yellow or bronzy-purple foliage. *Festuca amethystina* has grey-green leaves and tall, elegant flower stems that bear green, purple or violet flowers. Provide full sun and well-drained, gritty compost. In late winter or early spring, either shear plants back to allow for the colourful new growth or 'groom' the foliage by combing through with your fingers to remove the dead leaves.

Festuca glauca 'Blaufuchs'

	SPRING	SUMMER	AUTUMN	WINTER	height (cm)	spread (cm)	min. temp °C	moisture	sun/shade	flower colour	
F. amethystina	✹ ●	●			25	30	-15	◊	☀	▨	Grey green leaves. Flowers to 45cm
F. glauca	✹ ✹	● ●			25	20	-15	◊	☀	▨	Grey-blue leaves. Flowers to 35cm
F. g. 'Blaufuchs' (syn. 'Blue Fox')	✹ ✹	● ●			20	25	-15	◊	☀	▨	More pronounced blue
F. g. 'Elijah Blue'	✹ ✹	● ●			25	25	-15	◊	☀	▨	More pronounced blue
F. g. 'Golden Toupee'	✹ ✹	● ●			23	23	-15	◊	☀	▨	Bright yellow spring foliage turning glaucous
F. valesiaca 'Silbersee'	✹ ✹	● ●			12	15	-15	◊	☀	▨	Light silvery blue. Compact

Hakonechloa
Japanese hakone grass

Two very similar varieties of the hardy deciduous grass *Hakonechloa macra* are now fairly widely available. Both make low clumps of arching, ribbon like foliage that is pale golden-yellow streaked with green.

Hakonechloa macra 'Aureola'

The shape of the plant is enhanced when grown to fill a pot completely, since the leaves cascade to oriental effect over the rim. Flowers are produced but these are hardly noticeable. Try growing specimens alongside blue leaved hostas for maximum contrast of colour and form.

Hakone grass is a woodlander and prefers moisture-retentive, humus-rich compost. *Hakonechloa macra* 'Alboaurea' will take full sun given sufficient moisture but develops red tints if left exposed for too long. 'Aureola' becomes bronze-tinted in autumn.

	SPRING	SUMMER	AUTUMN	WINTER	height (cm)	spread (cm)	min. temp °C	moisture	sun/shade	flower colour	
Hakonechloa macra 'Alboaurea'	✹ ✹		● ● ●		35	40	-15	◊	◐	▨	Yellow leaves with narrow green stripes
H. m. 'Aureola'	✹ ✹		● ●		35	40	-15	◊	◐	▨	Yellow leaves, green stripes; autumnal bronze

✹ planting　　● flower　　◊ well drained　　◊ moist　　◊ wet

Helictotrichon
Blue oat grass

Helictotrichon sempervirens

Looking rather like a giant blue fescue, *Helictotrichon sempervirens* makes a robust specimen plant for a container.

The evergreen tussock of fine, blue-grey blades grows to 45cm (18in) in height and spreads to 75cm (30in), but the flower stems that appear in late spring and early summer grow to 1.2m (4ft). These arch out gracefully and the tips bear nodding, oat-like heads, hence the common name.

Grow in full sun in any good, free draining compost that does not get too wet in winter.

Hemerocallis
Daylily

These hardy perennial plants have an architectural quality that extends from the strap like foliage to the strong upright stems that bear the sculpted blooms. Many varieties flower repeatedly from late spring to late summer.

Although the common name refers to the fact that individual blooms in each cluster usually last for a day, some open late afternoon and stay open till later the following day. New daylily cultivars appear every year, recently concentrating on producing dwarf, compact, repeat blooming types in a wide range of colours. The yellow 'Stella de Oro' is typical of these, growing to only 28cm (11in) and flowering early to mid summer, then on and off until autumn. Although the compact types are ideal for pots, you can grow just about any of these tough, moderately drought resistant plants in pots where they may escape the ravages of slugs and snails. The taller, large flowered daylilies with a more open habit tend to be more elegant and

Hemerocallis 'Golden Chimes'

their bold flowers make a strong statement in a grouping on the terrace. Plants rarely need staking and are good in windy gardens. Grow in soil-based, humus-rich compost and water freely during summer.

	SPRING	SUMMER	AUTUMN	WINTER	height (cm)	spread (cm)	min. temp °C	moisture	sun/shade	flowers colour	
Hemerocallis 'Cherry Cheeks'					70	90	-15				Black anthers, greenish throat. Evergreen
H. 'Corky'					80	40	-15				Floriferous. Blooms open 2 days. Evergreen
H. 'Golden Chimes'					65	75	-15				Ruffled petals, yellow throat. Semi-evergreen
H. 'Stafford'					70	90	-15				Yellow-green throat. Evergreen
H. 'Stella de Oro'					30	45	-15				Rounded petals, light fragrance. Evergreen

☼ *sunny*   ☼ *semi-shady*   ☀ *shady*

Hosta
Plantain lily

Variegated hostas such as 'Shade Fanfare' and *Hosta undulata* var. *albomarginata* are ideal plants for enhancing sunless courtyards and terraces. Blue-green and blue-grey hostas such as 'Halcyon' and *H. sieboldiana* var. *elegans* also seem to glow in shade.

Hosta sieboldiana
var. *elegans*

Unlike some classic waterside plants, even the large leaved cultivars adapt well to being grown in pots. In fact this may be the only way to prevent new growth from being shredded by slugs and snails. Although small foliage types exist, the rosettes of large, heart-shaped leaves belonging to cultivars like 'Frances Williams' and the pale yellow-green 'Sum and Substance' create more drama and make a bold statement against a backdrop of solid walls and paving. For textural variety, combine with grassy plants or strap-like leaved plants such as ornamental sedges and grasses, variegated *Iris foetidissima* and shade tolerant daylilies. Grow in moisture-retentive loam-based compost and mulch with grit to conserve moisture and deter slugs.

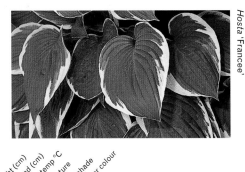

Hosta 'Francee'

	SPRING	SUMMER	AUTUMN	WINTER	height (cm)	spread (cm)	min. temp °C	moisture	sun/shade	flower colour	
Hosta 'Francee'	planting	flower			55	100	-15	moist	sun/shade		Olive-green leaves, edged cream
H. 'Frances Williams'	planting				60	90	-15	moist	sun/shade		Leaves puckered, blue-green, yellow margin
H. 'Halcyon'	planting	flower			40	70	-15	moist	sun/shade		Relatively small, grey-blue leaves
H. sieboldiana var. *elegans*	planting	flower			90	120	-15	moist	sun/shade		Large, heavily crinkled, blue-grey leaves
H. 'Sum and Substance'	planting	flower			75	120	-15	moist	sun/shade		Light acid green puckered leaves
H. undulata var. *albomarginata*	planting	flower			55	60	-15	moist	sun/shade		Green, cream margin (syn. 'Thomas Hogg')

Hydrangea

There are scores of common *Hydrangea macrophylla* cultivars, most of which have the mop-head or Hortensia flower type where showy sterile flowers are arranged in rounded heads. Their leaves are large and broad.

H.m. 'Mme E. Mouillère'

H.p. 'Grandiflora'

The beautiful white 'Mme Emile Mouillère' is one of the easiest and most free flowering for pot cultivation and it is luminous in a shady corner. Forms of *H. paniculata* flower on the new season's wood so can be pruned hard in spring to control the size and encourage extra large blooms. Watch for nutrient deficiency symptoms – hydrangeas prefer humus-rich, slightly acidic compost. Fungal infections can be problematic in autumn. Protect from wind.

	SPRING	SUMMER	AUTUMN	WINTER	height (cm)	spread (cm)	min. temp °C	moisture	sun/shade	flower colour	
Hydrangea macrophylla 'Mme Emile Mouillère'		flower flower flower			120	120	-15	moist	sun/shade		Hortensia. White flowers, pinkish with age
H. m. 'Pia' (syn. 'Pink Elf')		flower flower flower			60	90	-15	moist	sun/shade		Compact cultivar. Hortensia
H. paniculata 'Grandiflora'		flower	flower flower		150	120	-15	moist	sun/shade		Large showy blooms
H. paniculata 'Pink Diamond'		flower	flower flower		150	120	-15	moist	sun/shade		Develops unusual deep rose-pink colour
H. paniculata 'Unique'		flower	flower flower		150	120	-15	moist	sun/shade		Very large, showy blooms
H. serrata 'Blue Bird'		flower flower	flower flower		120	120	-5	moist	sun/shade		Lacecap. Red autumn colour

planting   flower   harvest   well drained   moist   wet

Lilium
Lily

Many hardy hybrid lilies and a few of the sun-loving species can be grown in pots.

Although the compact cultivars are easier to maintain, it is well worth growing the taller, large flowered types like the headily perfumed regal lily, *Lilium regale*, and the groups African Queen and Pink Perfection, because the drooping, trumpet-shaped blooms create an exotic ambience when mixed with sub-tropical foliage plants. Grow in John Innes No 2 with extra grit and leaf mould. Feed with a high potash fertilizer every two to four weeks in the growing season and water freely. Plant autumn or spring. Repot in autumn and store the bulbs in their pots under cover, keeping the compost just moist.

Lilium regale

	SPRING	SUMMER	AUTUMN	WINTER	height (cm)	spread (cm)	min. temp °C	moisture	sun/shade	flower colour	
Lilium African Queen Group					150	15	-5		☼		Highly fragrant trumpets. Needs support
L. 'Connecticut King'					90	15	-15		☼		Long lasting blooms
L. 'Enchantment'					90	15	-15		☼		Easy to grow. Speckled centres
L. Pink Perfection Group					150	15	-15		☼		Brown specked. Slight fragrance
L. regale					150	15	-15		☼		Large, highly fragrant trumpets. Give support
L. 'Sterling Star'					120	15	-15		☼		Highly fragrant trumpets. Needs support

Liriope muscari
Lily turf *or* Giant lily turf

Liriope muscari 'John Burch'

The tough evergreen ground cover plant *Liriope muscari* makes solid clumps of strap-like leaves and is invaluable for bringing late flower colour to permanent containers.

The poker like blooms of the species and associated cultivars come in shades of purple or white and are reminiscent of giant grape hyacinths. Of the variegated types, 'John Burch' makes a particularly good choice, having larger than normal flowers and gold-banded leaves. Several kinds have persistent blue-black berry like fruits after flowering.

	SPRING	SUMMER	AUTUMN	WINTER	height (cm)	spread (cm)	min. temp °C	moisture	sun/shade	colour	
Liriope muscari					30	40	-15		☀		Tough evergreen
L. m. 'Big Blue'					45	38	-5		☽		Purple black winter berries
L. m. 'John Burch'					50	40	-15		☽		Gold variegated, large flowers
L. m. 'Monroe White'					30	30	-15		☀		White form of species
L. m. 'Variegata'					45	30	-15		☽		Cream margins. Blue-black fruits

☼ *sunny*   ☽ *semi-shady*   ☀ *shady*

Magnolia

The large blooms of magnolias look almost hand crafted. Some of the deciduous spring flowering shrubby types can be grown in large pots such as wooden half barrels, where they slowly produce rounded to spreading specimens of pleasing habit.

Plant in autumn or at flowering time when you can select plants that are already in

Magnolia stellata 'Royal Star'

bloom. Some strains take years to come into flower and this way you can guarantee that the plant has reached maturity. Use humus-rich compost designed for long-term planting. Most prefer slightly acidic soil but the star magnolia (*M. stellata*) and the hybrid 'Leonard Messel' tolerate a little lime. Mulch with bark to conserve moisture and water freely in dry spells. Place in full sun to part shade and shelter from wind. Buds and young foliage exposed to early morning sun after frost will suffer damage, so avoid such a location.

	SPRING	SUMMER	AUTUMN	WINTER	height (cm)	spread (cm)	min. temp °C	moisture	sun/shade	colour	
Magnolia x loebneri 'Leonard Messel'	●		planting		180	180	-15	●●	☼	▨	Star-shaped blooms. Light fragrance
M. x soulangiana	● ●		planting		180	180	-15	●●	☼	☐	Goblet-shaped, whitish blooms
M. x soulangiana 'Lennei'	● ●		planting		180	180	-15	●●	☼	☐	Goblet-shaped, pink blooms
M. stellata 'Royal Star'	● ●		planting		150	180	-15	●●	☼	☐	Star-shaped blooms, light fragrance

Miscanthus
Chinese silver grass

The deciduous *Miscanthus sinensis* has given rise to many fine cultivars which have a strong presence in the garden with their upright cane-like stems and cascading ribbons of foliage.

Some of the less vigorous types make handsome container specimens. For variegated foliage choose the cool green and white striped eulalia grass *M. s.* 'Variegatus' or for an oriental note try the zebra grass, *M. s.* 'Zebrinus' which has horizontal gold banding. It works well contrasted with broad leaved foliage plants like cannas and hostas.

Miscanthus sinensis 'Silberfeder'

	SPRING	SUMMER	AUTUMN	WINTER	height (cm)	spread (cm)	min. temp °C	moisture	sun/shade	colour	
Miscanthus sinensis 'Kleine Fontäne'	planting planting	● ●			110	60	-15	●●	☼	☐	Early flowering
M. sinensis 'Silberfeder'	planting planting		● ●		180	90	-15	●●	☼	☐	Excellent silvery to brown-pink flowers
M. sinensis 'Variegatus'	planting planting		● ●		150	75	-15	●●	☼	☐	Flowers not reliable. White-striped foliage
M. sinensis 'Zebrinus'	planting planting		● ●		120	60	-15	●●	☼	▨	Zebra grass. Horizontal yellow banding

🌱 planting   ✹ flower   ● well drained   ●● moist   ●●● wet

Musa
Japanese banana

If you want to give your patio or terrace a lush sub-tropical feel, include a potted banana in your collection of large-leaved foliage plants. The Japanese banana, *Musa basjoo*, is the hardiest, surviving temperatures as low as -5°C (23°F).

Musa basjoo

The plant has a prodigious summer growth rate, producing giant paddle-shaped leaves that telescope out of the central stem. It needs plentiful supplies of water and liquid plant food.

Most plants eventually sucker from the base, forming a mini banana grove, and more mature stems may also flower and produce small inedible fruits, adding to the exotic character.

Although frost kills off the leaves, you can insulate the stem and roots so that the following year, the plant is even taller and more impressive looking. In colder gardens plants may die back to the roots but provided these have been protected or the plant brought under cover for the winter, new shoots will sprout from the base, as *Musa basjoo* is surprisingly resilient. The Japanese banana is quite likely to reach 1.8–2m (6ft–6ft 6in) in a pot.

Nerium oleander
Oleander

A familiar sight in the Mediterranean, oleanders make wonderful patio plants with an abundance of summer colour. Plants become quite large so it's a good idea to grow in mobile pots to make transferring them back to the conservatory an easier proposition.

These tender evergreen shrubs have long, leathery lance-shaped leaves and clusters of swirling five-petalled flowers. There are scores of named cultivars, and the flowers come as singles or doubles in shades of white, pale yellow, pink, peach, purple and red. 'Petite Pink' is a dwarf cultivar but most make large plants up to 2m (6ft 6in) in height. You may find plants in garden centres in early summer in the houseplants or patio plants area, but you can find a much wider range through specialist nurseries.

Prune lightly in late spring to keep plants nicely shaped. Grow in John Innes No 3, and liquid feed monthly during the growing season. All parts are highly poisonous and contact may exacerbate skin allergies. Toxicity even extends to the water that drains out of pots into saucers.

Nerium oleander 'Petite Pink'

	SPRING	SUMMER	AUTUMN	WINTER	height (cm)	spread (cm)	min. temp °C	moisture	sun/shade	colour	
Nerium oleander 'Album Plenum'	🌱	● ● ● ● ●			200+	100+	2	💧	☀	☐	Double
N. o. 'Isle of Capri'	🌱	● ● ● ● ●			200+	100+	2	💧	☀	☐	Pale yellow
N. o. 'Petite Pink'	🌱	● ● ● ● ●			100	60	2	💧	☀	☐	Compact growing
N. o. 'Provence'	🌱	● ● ● ● ●			200+	100+	2	💧	☀	☐	Salmon pink
N. o. 'Roseum Plenum'	🌱	● ● ● ● ●			200+	100+	2	💧	☀	☐	Double
N. o. 'Variegatum'	🌱	● ● ● ● ●			200+	100+	2	💧	☀	☐	Double. Leaves creamy-yellow variegated

☀ *sunny*   ☀ *semi-shady*   ● *shady*

Ophiopogon
Black grass *or* Lilyturf

Although ophiopogon looks like a grass, it is actually a member of the lily family which is grown for its handsome evergreen foliage. The spidery plants with narrow arching leaves spread by runners and can fill a pot by themselves.

The most familiar is the striking maroon-black *Ophiopogon planiscapus* 'Nigrescens', or black grass. This has a very contemporary look and is particularly effective next to metallic blue and silver foliage plants such as *Astelia chathamica*, *Heuchera* 'Pewter Moon' and *Acaena microphylla* 'Kupferteppich'. Or, for a touch of the Orient, try it with lacquer red impatiens. The tenderer Japanese *O. jaburan* 'Vittatus' has brightly variegated white or creamy yellow-edged leaves and is a taller growing plant. It would make a good companion for a blue-leaved hosta and could also provide interesting foliage detail in a summer hanging basket. Grow in moisture-retentive, slightly acidic peat based or peat-substitute compost. *Ophiopogon planiscapus* 'Nigrescens' tolerates periods of drought.

Ophiopogon planiscapus 'Nigrescens'

	SPRING	SUMMER	AUTUMN	WINTER	height (cm)	spread (cm)	min. temp °C	moisture	sun/shade	flower colour	
Ophiopogon planiscapus 'Nigrescens'					20	30+	-15				Almost black leaves and blue-black fruits
O. jaburan 'Vittatus'					60	30	-5				Blue berries. White edged leaves
O. japonicus					30	30	-15				Green leaves, blue-black berries

Phoenix
Canary Island date palm

Phoenix canariensis is a graceful palm with long spreading to arching rich green fronds.

It can be grown in a pot for a few years whilst still a young plant but it is not hardy and needs a minimum of 10–15°C (50–59°F), so must be taken under heated glass for the winter in most areas. Alternatively, in mild coastal plots and in frost-free inner city gardens, you could keep this exotic looking plant outside all year, protecting the delicate inner fronds in winter by drawing the outer leaves up and tying them round. Use insulating material to protect top growth and roots (see page 33).

Plant *Phoenix canariensis* in gritty, free-draining compost and place plants in full sun close to a warm wall that will offer protection by radiating back some heat at night.

Phoenix canariensis

planting   flower   harvest | well drained   moist   wet

Phormium
Mountain Flax *or* New Zealand Flax

In recent years, scores of colourful phormiums have been introduced by breeders in New Zealand. Some derive from the upright *Phormium tenax* (New Zealand flax) while others are more like the arching *P. cookinanum* or mountain flax.

These evergreens make a striking architectural statement with their broad, strap-shaped leaves and pole-like flower stems that shoot up in the height of summer. But it is the foliage that is the chief attraction, and in pot grown specimens, the flower stems are best removed. Phormiums are ideal in frost-free coastal gardens being tolerant of salt and wind, but can be used on sunny or lightly shaded patios that are protected by the house from really hard frosts.

Phormium 'Sundowner'

	SPRING	SUMMER	AUTUMN	WINTER	height (cm)	spread (cm)	min. temp °C	moisture	sun/shade	flower colour	
Phormium 'Bronze Baby'	✿	●			120	120	-12	◊◊	☼	▣	Dark maroon bronze narrow arching leaves
P. cookianum subsp. hookeri 'Cream Delight'	✿	●			120	150	-12	◊◊	◐	□	Arching. Broad central cream leaf stripe
P. 'Jester'	✿	●			120	120	-12	◊◊	☼	□	Pinky orange, lime green variegated leaves
P. 'Pink Panther'	✿	●			100	100	-12	◊◊	☼	□	Deep salmon pink with brown margins
P. 'Sundowner'	✿	●			150	120	-12	◊◊	☼	□	Erect, bronzy brown leaves with pink margins
P. 'Yellow Wave'	✿	●			150	120	-12	◊◊	☼	▣	Arching yellow-green leaves

Phyllostachys
Fishpole *or* Golden bamboo *or* Black bamboo

Bamboos have a reputation for being rampant spreaders but the genus Phyllostachys contains some well-behaved plants that only gradually spread and which can be controlled by pruning.

Phyllostachys nigra

Phyllostachys aurea

The heights and spreads given here are a guide only. These tall, graceful evergreens will need a very large container to satisfy their needs. Pick something like a wooden half-barrel to begin with. The black bamboo, *P. nigra*, is prized for its glossy black culms but they only develop after two to three years. It is slightly taller than *P. aurea*. Needs a sheltered spot to prevent wind scorch.

	SPRING	SUMMER	AUTUMN	WINTER	height (cm)	spread (cm)	min. temp °C	moisture	sun/shade	culm colour	
Phyllostachys aurea	✿ ✿				300	150	-15	◊◊	◐	▨	Yellow-green culms
P. nigra	✿ ✿				300	150	-15	◊◊	◐	■	Black culms in third year
P. n. f. henonis	✿ ✿				300	150	-15	◊◊	◐	□	Bright yellowish green culms
P. n. 'Boryana'	✿ ✿				300	150	-15	◊◊	◐	□	Yellowish-green, blotched brown culms

☼ sunny   ◐ semi-shady   ● shady

P

Architectural Plants

Pinus
Dwarf mountain pine *or* Scots pine

There are several very similar forms of the dwarf mountain pine, *Pinus mugo*, all of which make rounded plants with tightly packed upright stems clothed in needles.

These are true dwarfs, taking many years to increase in size appreciably so the heights and spreads given are a guide only. Try planting them in glazed ceramic pots as part of a Chinese or Japanese style grouping. *Pinus sylvestris*, the Scots pine, perhaps surprisingly also has dwarf and slow growing cultivars. The foliage of 'Gold Coin' is bright golden yellow and 'Watereri' may be trained and pruned to make the oriental style of topiary known as cloud pruning. Grow in well-drained loam based compost.

Pinus mugo 'Humpy'

	SPRING	SUMMER	AUTUMN	WINTER	height (cm)	spread (cm)	min. temp °C	moisture	sun/shade	foliage colour	
Pinus mugo 'Gnom'	🌱🌱		🌱🌱🌱		45	45	-15	💧	☀		Flatter growing initially
P. mugo 'Humpy'	🌱🌱		🌱🌱🌱		45	45	-15	💧	☀		Purplish-brown winter buds
P. mugo 'Mops'	🌱🌱		🌱🌱🌱		45	45	-15	💧	☀		Almost round in shape
P. sylvestris 'Gold Coin'	🌱🌱		🌱🌱🌱		90	90	-15	💧	☀		Trim in spring to keep compact
P. sylvestris 'Watereri'	🌱🌱		🌱🌱🌱		120	120	-15	💧	☀		Good for cloud pruning

Pleioblastus

This genus includes two excellent variegated bamboos that are rhizomatous or creeping but never problematical and which take happily to being grown in a surprisingly wide variety of containers.

The leaves of *Pleioblastus viridistriatus* are butter-yellow streaked with green and the upright culms have an open habit. In *P.*

Pleioblastus viridistriatus

variegatus, the leaves clothing the dense upright culms have bold creamy white stripes. Both thrive in moist compost with a good depth of organic mulch and like all bamboos, appreciate regular liquid feeds during the growing season. Best in a sheltered spot out of strong, hot sunlight and planted in broad containers to accommodate the spreading rhizomes. Cut all growth back to soil level in late winter before new shoots start to appear. These bamboos associate well with blue leaved hostas.

	SPRING	SUMMER	AUTUMN	WINTER	height (cm)	spread (cm)	min. temp °C	moisture	sun/shade	foliage colour	
Pleioblastus variegatus	🌱🌱				90	120	-15	💧💧	◑		Creamy white stripes
P. viridistriatus (syn. *P. auricomus*)	🌱🌱				120	60	-15	💧💧	◑		Bright butter-yellow striped green

🌱 *planting*   ✹ *flower*   💧 *well drained*   💧💧 *moist*   💧💧💧 *wet*

Polystichum
Shield fern

The evergreen shield ferns make handsome specimens for pots in a shaded sheltered courtyard or on a paved terrace. In the soft shield fern, *Polystichum setiferum*, the fronds are elegantly pointed and finely divided – even more so in the Divisilobum Group.

Polystichum setiferum

Meanwhile the texture of the hard shield fern *P. aculeatum* is more leathery and there is a distinct sheen to the dark evergreen leaves. To appreciate the newly opening fronds in spring, it is best to tidy away last year's leaves. Grow in humus rich but well drained compost and keep moist during the summer months. Like all ferns, polysticums associate well with grassy leaved plants such as carex, broad leaved perennials including hostas and bergenias and woodland ground cover species like *Lamium maculatum* 'White Nancy'.

	SPRING	SUMMER	AUTUMN	WINTER	height (cm)	spread (cm)	min. temp °C	moisture	sun/shade	colour	
Polystichum aculeatum	🌿🌿🌿	🌿🌿🌿	🌿		60	90	-15	💧💧	shady	◻	Glossy and leathery textured fronds
P. setiferum	🌿🌿🌿	🌿🌿🌿	🌿		120	100	0	💧💧	shady	◻	Dark-green, highly dissected fronds
P. s. Divisilobum Group	🌿🌿🌿	🌿🌿🌿	🌿		70	70	0	💧💧	shady	◻	Fronds more finely divided

Ricinus
Castor oil plant
or Castor bean

Once chiefly grown as a dot plant to add sub-tropical flavour to bedding schemes, varieties of the castor oil plant (*Ricinus communis*) continue to bring an exotic note to sunny sheltered patios and courtyards.

This fast growing half-hardy annual produces very large palmate leaves that in some varieties such as 'Gibsonii' have a metallic sheen with either rich bronzy or maroon-red colouring. Flowers appear through summer and are followed by branched heads of showy spiky seed pods. In the new 'Carmencita Pink', these are a deep but vivid pink as opposed to the more usual red. Please note that this is a poisonous plant. The seeds in particular are highly toxic. Grow in moisture retentive compost in full sun and shelter from wind.

Ricinus communis

	SPRING	SUMMER	AUTUMN	WINTER	height (cm)	spread (cm)	min. temp °C	moisture	sun/shade	colour	
Ricinus communis 'Carmencita Pink'	🌿	●●●●	●●●		150	120	1	💧💧	sunny	◻	A green variant of 'Carmencita'
R .c. 'Carmencita'	🌿	●●●●	●●●		150	120	1	💧💧	sunny	◼	Deep bronzy red foliage
R. c. 'Gibsonii'	🌿	●●●●	●●●		150	100	1	💧💧	sunny	◼	Dark metallic red leaves
R. c. 'Impala'	🌿	●●●●	●●●		120	90	1	💧💧	sunny	◻	Bronze green leaves. New foliage bronzy red

☀ *sunny*   ☀ *semi-shady*   ☀ *shady*

Sempervivum
Houseleek

If you enjoy making potted collections, then you might like to try growing houseleeks. There are scores of subtly different Sempervivum species and varieties to choose from, and garden centres offer quite a selection, though alpine specialists are worth a visit if you really get hooked.

Sempervivum 'Hester'

Sempervivum 'Reinhard'

These hardy succulents produce circular leaf rosettes, in shades of green, grey, purple or red tinting, for example 'Commander Hay'. Some appear silvery due to a hairy coating, such as the cobweb houseleek, *S. arachnoideum*. Seemingly able to survive on virtually nothing, houseleeks slowly expand to form ground-encrusting colonies as one individual rosette sends out runners. Stary pinkish-red or yellow flowers appear infrequently on stout scaly stems. Grow in John Innes No2 with plenty of extra grit for sharp drainage. Shallow containers such as alpine pans are ideal and look good when a range of different kinds is displayed together, for example down a flight of steps. Alternatively, plant up a small stone trough with a contrasting group of houseleeks and mulch with slate shards or gravel.

	SPRING	SUMMER	AUTUMN	WINTER	height (cm)	spread (cm)	min. temp °C	moisture	sun/shade	flower colour	
Sempervivum 'Alpha'	planting	flower			5	20	-15	well drained	sun		Green. Slight fur. Pink tinting
S. arachnoideum (cobweb houseleek)	planting	flower			2.5	20	-15	well drained	sun		Place under glass in winter
S. 'Commander Hay'	planting	flower			5	25	-15	well drained	sun		Red-purple with green tips
S. 'Hester'	planting	flower			5	20	-15	well drained	sun		Low-growing, easy plant
S. 'Reinhard'	planting	flower			5	20	-15	well drained	sun		Great for pots, troughs and sinks
S. tectorum (common houseleek)	planting	flower			7.5	30	-15	well drained	sun		Attractive flowers

Trachycarpus
Chusan fan palm

Few plants create an aura of the sub-tropics like palms.

Fortunately, the exotic looking Chusan fan palm (*Trachycarpus fortunei*) with its spectacular leaves is relatively hardy, especially once plants are a few years old. Though not ideally suited to pot cultivation, it will be happy initially given copious water in dry spells and regular feeds from the start of the growing season to midway through summer. Grow in a sheltered site, protected from wind and strong sunlight. Plant using loam-based compost with plenty of additional humus. In colder areas, move pots under glass for the winter or wrap up with insulating material.

Trachycarpus fortunei

planting · flower · well drained · moist · wet

Uncinia
Hook sedge

Uncinia unciniata rubra

The New Zealand hook sedges resemble some of the brown carex, but the leaves of this hardy evergreen are slightly broader and quite lustrous, making upright tussocks or arching hummocks.

Provided the compost is kept moist, these plants thrive in pots and being somewhat tender will relish the protection of the patio in winter. Try combining with matt blue and silver foliage plants or mix potted specimens with pots of dwarf red or maroon black phormiums, black leaved aeoniums, red and green houseleeks and black grass (*Ophiopogon planiscapus* 'Nigrescens').

	SPRING	SUMMER	AUTUMN	WINTER	height (cm)	spread (cm)	min. temp °C	moisture	sun/shade	flower colour	
Uncinia rubra					30	35	-10				Glossy, mahogany red leaves
U. unciniata					35	30	-10				Upright growth, bright red-brown foliage
U. unciniata rubra					25	30	-10				Tussocks of deep reddish brown leaves

Yucca
Adam's needle *or* Spanish dagger

It is not hard to see how the yuccas got their common names. These highly architectural evergreen foliage plants make rosettes of stiff, sword shaped leaves that come to a sharp point – dangerously so in *Yucca gloriosa*.

However, if you don't have young children and want to create an atmosphere of desert heat or the Mediterranean on your patio, one or two yuccas may be worth the risk! Yuccas may take a few years to reach flowering size, especially in *Y. gloriosa*, and if you want to see the spectacular heads of creamy-white bells, its wise to choose a free-flowering cultivar such as *Yucca flaccida* 'Ivory'.

Yucca gloriosa 'Variegata'

	SPRING	SUMMER	AUTUMN	WINTER	height (cm)	spread (cm)	min. temp °C	moisture	sun/shade	flower colour	
Yucca filamentosa (Adam's needle)					60	75	-15				Flower spikes up to 1.8m
Y. f. 'Variegata'					60	75	-15				Cream variegated with pink tinting
Y. flaccida 'Golden Sword'					60	75	-15				Broad, creamy yellow banding
Y. f. 'Ivory'					60	75	-15				Flowers to 1.5m
Y. gloriosa (Spanish dagger)					60	60	-5				Blue-green leaves. Flowers to 2.1m
Y. gloriosa 'Variegata'					60	60	-5				Yellow-edged leaves

U
Y

Architectural Plants

☼ *sunny*   ☽ *semi-shady*   ● *shady*

Evergreen Plants

Plants that are hardy and retain their leaves throughout the winter months are invaluable for permanent containers, and there is a surprisingly large number of them to choose from. Evergreen plants add good contrast and instant variety to containers of all kinds.

Many plants in this section have Japanese or Chinese origins and are shade tolerant. If you want to create an oriental atmosphere on a patio that does not receive strong sunlight, you could for example choose from Skimmia, Rhododendron, Pieris, Camellia, Aucuba and *Osmanthus heterophyllus*.

Small-leaved evergreens with a dense habit can often be clipped into simple geometric forms (see pages 34–5). Candidates include box (Buxus), Osmanthus, myrtle, *Ligustrum delavayanum* and *Ilex crenata*. Holly, bay and *Viburnum tinus* can also be trained to make more substantial round-headed standards and cones that are useful for adding a touch of formality in period or strongly architectural and minimalist settings.

Many evergreen plants such as spotted laurel, Euonymus, small-leaved hebes and silver-leaved herbs including Santolina are available in autumn as small 'liners' or rooted cuttings, and these are perfect for making up winter baskets and seasonal arrangements that include autumn and winter bedding and heathers.

Although much of the emphasis of evergreens in this section is on autumn, winter and spring, (due to variegated foliage, berries and winter blooms), some evergreens reach a highpoint in summer. Mediterranean plants like the dwarf lavenders, rosemary, thyme and Santolina draw in bees and butterflies with their fragrant, nectar-rich flowers and *Choisya ternata* – the Mexican orange blossom – also has perfumed blooms in early summer, though this plant is chiefly grown for its glossy foliage. If you have a conservatory, you might also like to try growing citrus fruits outdoors during summer.

Aucuba
Spotted laurel

Certain hardy shrubs make colourful short-term pot plants and hardy evergreens like the variegated varieties of *Aucuba japonica*, really help to brighten up all sorts of autumn, winter and spring containers.

Aucuba japonica 'Crotonifolia'

In autumn, use the glossy, yellow splashed foliage as a foil for red or deep pink mini cyclamen or make a tangy combination with flame or lime-green coloured *Calluna vulgaris* and orange berried winter cherry (*Solanum capsicastrum*). In winter try it as a

Aucuba japonica 'Variegata'

foil for the dark red budded *Skimmia japonica* 'Rubella' or scarlet berried *Skimmia* x *reevesiana*. And for spring, why not try growing it with blue flowered polyanthus and dwarf yellow or cream flowered daffodils.

	SPRING	SUMMER	AUTUMN	WINTER	height (cm)	spread (cm)	min. temp °C	moisture	sun/shade	flower colour	
Aucuba japonica 'Crotonifolia'			🌸🌸🌸🌸🌸		150	150	-15	◐	◑	▦	Bright gold variegation. Female plant
A. j. 'Golden King'			🌸🌸🌸🌸🌸		150	150	-15	◐	◑	☐	Bright gold variegation. Male plant
A. j. 'Rozannis'			🌸🌸🌸🌸🌸		150	150	-15	◐	◑	▦	Male or female plants available
A. j. 'Variegata'			🌸🌸🌸🌸🌸		100	100	-15	◐	●	▦	Compact, plain-leaved. Male or female

Buxus
Box *or* Boxwood

The fine foliage and dense habit of this slow-growing, hardy evergreen shrub makes it an ideal candidate for clipping and *Buxus sempervirens* is a favourite for creating topiary shapes.

Buxus sempervirens

Other forms of box can also be clipped, including the pretty cream variegated 'Elegantissima'. Dwarf box or English box, *B. s.* 'Suffruticosa' may be trained to form miniature round-headed standards. The sentinel-like 'Graham Blandy', makes a fine accent for a shady patio. Several cultivars of *B. microphylla* also form pleasing natural shapes, including the aptly named 'Green Pillow'.

	SPRING	SUMMER	AUTUMN	WINTER	height (cm)	spread (cm)	min. temp °C	moisture	sun/shade	foliage colour	
Buxus microphylla 'Green Pillow'			🖑🖑🖑		45	90	-15	◐	◑	▦	Makes a natural spreading dome
B. sempervirens			🖑🖑🖑		120+	120+	-15	◐	◑	▦	Dense rounded green leaves
B. s. 'Elegantissima'			🖑🖑🖑		120	120	-15	◐	◑	▥	Cream variegation
B. s. 'Graham Blandy' (syn. 'Greenpeace')			🖑🖑🖑		180	30	-15	◐	◑	▦	Natural slim column
B. s. 'Latifolia Marginata'			🖑🖑🖑		120	150	-15	◐	◑	▥	Gold leaf margins
B. s. 'Suffruticosa'			🖑🖑🖑		30	45	-15	◐	◑	▦	Dwarf box

🖑 *planting*   🌸 *flower*   💧 *well drained*   ◑ *semi-shady*   ● *shady*

Calluna
Scottish heather
or Ling

The dwarf shrubby Scottish heathers, forms of *Calluna vulgaris*, are grown for their late flowers and also sometimes for colourful foliage that can be particularly bright in autumn and winter.

Calluna vulgaris 'Spring Cream'

Two of the best examples are the carpeting 'Robert Chapman' and 'Wickwar Flame', both of which make a transformation from gold through orange to red in the cold months of the year. 'Silver Queen' has a downy coating making the leaves appear silver-grey – a perfect foil for the light mauve flowers – and 'Spring Cream', as the name suggests, has cream-tipped new growth. Clip over plants lightly in spring to remove old flowering stems. This keeps them neat and compact. Grow in ericaceous or lime-free compost and use rainwater if you live in a hard water area. Plants with coloured foliage are particularly useful for adding a vibrant note to seasonal autumn and winter plantings.

	SPRING	SUMMER	AUTUMN	WINTER	height (cm)	spread (cm)	min. temp °C	moisture	sun/shade	flower colour	
Calluna vulgaris 'County Wicklow'	planting	flower	flower		25	35	-15	well drained	sun		Double blooms. Compact
C. v. 'Gold Haze'	planting	flower	flower		45	45	-15	well drained	sun		Pale yellowish green
C. v. 'Robert Chapman'	planting	flower	flower		25	65	-15	well drained	sun		Gold foliage, turning orange then red
C. v. 'Silver Queen'	planting	flower	flower		40	55	-15	well drained	sun		Silvery grey leaves
C. v. 'Spring Cream' (syn. 'Spring Torch')	planting	flower	flower		35	45	-15	well drained	sun		Cream tips to shoots in spring. Compact
C. v. 'Wickwar Flame'	planting	flower	flower		50	65	-15	well drained	sun		Golden foliage, turning orange then red

Camellia

A collection of camellias with their large sculpted winter and spring blooms might seem like an impossible dream for the patio gardener, but many of these choice evergreen shrubs are suitable for pot cultivation.

In fact, if you have alkaline or lime-rich soil, it may be your only solution, since camellias require acidic or ericaceous conditions. Some of the compact, less vigorous, free-flowering cultivars are particularly suited. Varieties like 'Freedom Bell' and *Camellia* x *williamsii* 'Anticipation' should be reasonably easy to find in garden centres in autumn and at flowering time but the others listed here may have to be sourced from specialist nurseries.

Camellia

	SPRING	SUMMER	AUTUMN	WINTER	height (cm)	spread (cm)	min. temp °C	moisture	sun/shade	flower colour	
Camellia 'Freedom Bell'	flower		planting	flower	220	18-	-15	moist	part		Semi-double flowers
C. japonica 'Bob's Tinsie'	flower		planting		180	100	-15	moist	part		Small, anemone-centred blooms. Compact
C. j. 'Bokuhan' (syn. 'Tinsie')	flower		planting	flower	90	60	-15	moist	sun		Miniature. Anemone form
C. j. 'Commander Mulroy'	flower		planting	flower	200	100	-15	moist	part		Double blooms, pink in bud
C. x *williamsii* 'Anticipation'	flower		planting		300	200	-15	moist	part		Peony form

planting · flower · well drained · moist · wet

Chamaecyparis
False cypress

Dwarf and slow growing conifers are invaluable for winter and year round container displays.

If planted in the ground, these conifers could eventually grow very big, but they will remain compact in their container for years before they get too big and have to be discarded or planted in open ground. Two of the most popular for giving height and structure to evergreen displays from autumn through till spring are the flame-shaped *Chamaecyparis lawsoniana* 'Elwoodii' and 'Elwood's Gold'. *C. pisifera* 'Boulevard' is best as a young plant with very attractive fluffy blue and silver foliage. It likes to be kept moist and will tolerate light shade. Mix them with *Euonymus fortunei* cultivars, trailing ivy, heathers, violas and dwarf bulbs.

Chamaecyparis pisifera 'Squarrosa Sulphurea'

	SPRING	SUMMER	AUTUMN	WINTER	height (cm)	spread (cm)	min. temp °C	moisture	sun/shade	foliage colour	
Chamaecyparis lawsoniana 'Chilworth Silver'					45	15	-15				Narrowly conical. Silver blue
C. lawsoniana 'Elwood's Gold'					45	15	-15				Columnar, blue in winter
C. lawsoniana 'Elwoodii'					45	15	-15				Column with gold tipped shoots
C. pisifera 'Boulevard'					45	30	-15				Silvery blue foliage
C. pisifera 'Squarrosa Sulphurea'					45	60	-15				Cascading, thread like golden foliage

Choisya ternata
Mexican orange blossom

Choisya ternata

The glossy leaved Mexican orange blossom (*Choisya ternata*) is actually a hardy relative of citrus with similarly aromatic leaves and sweetly fragrant, waxy-textured flowers.

It is quite happy as a pot specimen. In full sun, surrounded by plants of Mediterranean character, Choisya helps to create a Riviera-like atmosphere on the terrace. But this shrub will also tolerate a good deal of shade. For a cool scheme, try contrasting the foliage with the large leaved, white flowered hydrangea 'Mme Emile Mouillère', and white variegated hostas and grasses such as the fountain like *Miscanthus sinensis* 'Variegatus'.

Choisya ternata 'Sundance'

	SPRING	SUMMER	AUTUMN	WINTER	height (cm)	spread (cm)	min. temp °C	moisture	sun/shade	flower colour	
Choisya ternata					150	150	-15				Glossy foliage of three leaflets
C.t. 'Aztec Pearl'					150	150	-15				Narrow leaflets
C. t. 'Sundance'					120	120	-15				Bright yellow-green foliage

☼ *sunny*   ☼ *semi-shady*   ● *shady*

Citrus

If you have a conservatory for overwintering plants, you might like to try growing pots of tender orange and lemon trees on a sunny sheltered terrace during the summer months.

Citrus limon

Citrus have glossy aromatic foliage and headily fragrant blossom and are attractive and fun to grow. The bitter or Seville orange and the sweet orange cultivar 'Washington' are among the easiest for fruiting, along with the hardier hybrid citrus, Meyer's lemon (*Citrus x meyeri* 'Meyer'), an everbearing type, which means that it produces fruits and flowers together all year round. Its oval, smooth-skinned fruits are an excellent lemon substitute. The lemon, 'Garey's Eureka', more commonly known as 'Quatre Saisons' is also everbearing. Buy grafted plants from a reputable supplier. Avoid sudden changes in temperature or light which can cause plants to lose leaves. Water freely in spring and summer but less in winter. Feed with specialist fertilizer. Watch for scale insect, mealy bug, spider mite and whitefly.

	SPRING	SUMMER	AUTUMN	WINTER	height (cm)	spread (cm)	min. temp °C	moisture	sun/shade	foliage colour	
Citrus aurantium (Seville orange)		● ● ● ●	🌰🌰🌰		180	150	3	💧	☀	■	Dark orange bitter fruits
C. limon 'Garey's Eureka'	🌰●🌰●🌰●	🌰●🌰●🌰●	🌰●🌰●🌰●	🌰●🌰●🌰●	180	150	3	💧	☀	■	Everbearing (syn. 'Quatre Saisons')
Citrus x meyeri 'Meyer'	🌰●🌰●🌰●	🌰●🌰●🌰●	🌰●🌰●🌰●	🌰●🌰●🌰●	180	150	3	💧	☀	■	Everbearing. Small, round 'lemons'
C. sinensis 'Washington' (sweet orange)	● ● ●			🌰🌰🌰	180	150	3	💧	☀	■	Navel type oranges ripen in winter/spring

Cotoneaster

Most of these hardy deciduous or evergreen shrubs are grown for their autumn and winter berries.

Some small-leaved evergreens are compact with a prostrate habit and arching branches and look well cascading over the rim of large containers. 'Gnom' has narrow leaves that are tinged bronze in winter and profuse red berries. *C.* 'Hybridus Pendulous' is a small weeping tree suitable for growing in a half barrel.

Cotoneaster 'Hybridus Pendulous'

	SPRING	SUMMER	AUTUMN	WINTER	height (cm)	spread (cm)	min. temp °C	moisture	sun/shade	berry colour	
Cotoneaster 'Hybridus Pendulous'	🌱 🌱	●	🌱 🌱	🌰🌰🌰	150	120	-15	💧	☀	■	Small weeping tree
C. salicifolius 'Gnom'	🌱 🌱	●	🌱 🌱	🌰🌰🌰	20	85	-15	💧	☀	■	Red berries
C. x suecicus 'Coral Beauty'	🌱 🌱	●	🌱 🌱	🌰🌰🌰	25	120	-15	💧	☀	■	Orange fruits

🌱 planting   ● flower   🌰 harvest | 💧 well drained   💧 moist   💧 wet

Cryptomeria
Japanese cedar

Some of the slow growing cultivars of this moisture-loving conifer have beautiful foliage and make good pot specimens for year-round colour and interest.

Cryptomeria japonica 'Elegans Compacta'

After several years, plants can either be discarded or transferred to the garden. In the oriental looking *Cryptomeria japonica* 'Sekkan-sugi' the arching shoot tips are creamy yellow when new, ageing to almost white in winter. The growth of *C.j.* 'Spiralis' is very dense, the narrow leaves curving and twisting round the shoots to give an effect similar to ringlets. 'Elegans Compacta' has a dwarf conical habit and the soft, fluffy juvenile foliage turns deep bronze-purple in winter. *C.j.* 'Vilmoriniana' makes a small rounded plant with light green foliage becoming red-brown in winter – beautiful with gold or lime-green coloured callunas. Cryptomerias prefer slightly acidic compost and should be watered freely in the growing season.

	SPRING	SUMMER	AUTUMN	WINTER	height (cm)	spread (cm)	min. temp °C	moisture	sun/shade	foliage colour	
Cryptomeria japonica 'Elegans Compacta'			🌿🌿🌿		200	150	-15	💧	☀		Fluffy winter-bronzed foliage
C. j. 'Sekkan-sugi'			🌿🌿🌿		200+	150+	-15	💧	☀		Cream variegated
C. j. 'Spiralis'			🌿🌿🌿		200	150	-15	💧	☀		Twisted shoots
C. j. 'Vilmoriniana'			🌿🌿🌿		100	100	-15	💧	☀		Very slow growing

Erica

For winter flowers in pots and hanging baskets, the honey-scented *Erica carnea* cultivars are hard to beat. These hardy, low-growing evergreen shrubs are available from garden centres as inexpensive one year old plants but it is better to go for the two and three year old specimens which have instant impact and more flower power.

Erica x darleyensis 'Kramer's Rote'

Some cultivars like 'Myretoun Ruby' and 'Springwood White' have an exceptionally long blooming period, the latter being an excellent choice for winter baskets. Try it with white violas, white variegated ivies and *Euonymus fortunei* 'Emerald Gaiety'. The spreading 'Ice Princess' carries long upright spikes over bright green foliage and is considered the best white flowered cultivar. For foliage effect try *E. x darleyensis* 'Kramer's Rote', whose spring shoot tips are red and cream variegated or the tree heather, *E. arborea* 'Albert's Gold'.

	SPRING	SUMMER	AUTUMN	WINTER	height (cm)	spread (cm)	min. temp °C	moisture	sun/shade	flower colour	
Erica arborea 'Albert's Gold'			🌿🌿🌿		180	80	-15	💧	☀		Tree heather. Bright lime foliage
E. carnea 'Ice Princess'	● ●		🌿🌿	●	15	60	-15	💧	☀		The best white
E. c. 'Myretoun Ruby'	● ● ●		🌿🌿	● ●	22.5	45	-15	💧	☀		Flowers darken with age
E. c. 'Pink Spangles'	●		🌿	● ●	22.5	30	-15	💧	☀		Compact mound
E. c. 'Springwood White'	● ● ●		🌿🌿	● ● ●	15	60	-15	💧	☀		Carpeting habit
E. x darleyensis 'Kramer's Rote'	● ● ●		🌿🌿	● ●	30	40	-15	💧	☀		Magenta flowers and bronze-green leaves

☼ *sunny*   ☀ *semi-shady*   ● *shady*

Eucalyptus
Tasmanian blue gum

Young plants of the tender gum tree *Eucalyptus globulus* have rounded, blue green leaves with a white bloom.

These are arranged in pairs whose bases wrap around the stem and the effect is quite sculptural. The colour is particularly striking when used as a foil for exotic orange and red flowered patio plants such as canna. One year old seedlings are usually available for a short period in late spring – you will find them in the patio plants section of the garden centre. Plant in free draining loam-based compost and stand in full sun. Pinch out shoot tips to encourage bushiness. This plant grows to a height of 100cm (3ft) and spreads to 50cm (18in).

Eucalyptus globulus

Euonymus
Wintercreeper

Two of the most robust variegated evergreens for pot work are the shrubby groundcover plants *Euonymus fortunei* 'Emerald Gaiety' which is white-variegated and its gold-variegated counterpart 'Emerald 'n' Gold'.

The flexible stems are covered in small, leathery leaves that become pink tinged over winter. When set against a wall both are capable of turning into self-clinging climbers. Young plants, little more than rooted cuttings, are available in autumn for making up winter hanging baskets, but wintercreepers have year-round appeal because of their colourful foliage. Relatively new on the scene is 'Blondy', whose pale yellow leaves have a fine green margin.

Euonymus fortunei 'Blondy'

Euonymus 'Emerald 'n' Gold'

'Sunspot' with its golden yellow central blotch surrounded by deep green is also showy and makes a good foil for the dwarf, golden yellow flowered day lily 'Stella de Oro'. 'Silver Queen' is more shrubby than the small leaved wintercreepers with bright cream variegation – excellent for large, permanent containers.

	SPRING	SUMMER	AUTUMN	WINTER	height (cm)	spread (cm)	min. temp °C	moisture	sun/shade	foliage colour	
Euonymus fortunei 'Blondy'	🌱🌱🌱		🌱🌱🌱		60	90	-15	◐	☀	▢	Yellow leaves narrow green margin
E. fortunei 'Emerald 'n' Gold'	🌱🌱🌱		🌱🌱🌱		60	120	-15	◐	☀	▢	Gold and green variegated
E. fortunei 'Emerald Gaiety'	🌱🌱🌱		🌱🌱🌱		60	120	-15	◐	☀	▢	White and green variegated
E. fortunei 'Silver Queen'	🌱🌱🌱		🌱🌱🌱		120	120	-15	◐	☀	▢	Cream and green variegated
E. fortunei 'Sunspot'	🌱🌱🌱		🌱🌱🌱		60	90	-15	◐	☀	▢	Leaves with large central yellow blotch
E. japonicus 'Microphyllus Albovariegatus'	🌱🌱🌱		🌱🌱🌱		60	60	-5	◐	☀	▢	Green and white. Upright habit

🌱 planting   ✹ flower   🌰 harvest   ◐ well drained   ◑ moist   ◆ wet

Gaultheria

The prickly dark evergreen foliage of the hardy acid-loving shrub, *Gaultheria mucronata* (syn. *Pernettya*) comes to life in late summer and autumn when the large spherical white, pink or red berries ripen. These are great for colour-schemed autumn and winter pots.

Gaultheria mucronata

Though you will often buy plants at this time and can expect to enjoy the display well into winter, if you want berries in subsequent years there must be a male plant in the vicinity to facilitate pollination of the female flowers. Grow one in the border provided the soil is lime free. *G. m.* 'Bell's Seedling' is self fertile, bearing crops of deep red berries. Tiny white bell shaped blooms appear in late spring and early summer, but for the interim period, these shrubs are best placed in the background. The low creeping wintergreen, *Gaultheria procumbens*, makes a matt of small deep glossy green leaves that bear clusters of dark scarlet-red berries through autumn and winter.

	SPRING	SUMMER	AUTUMN	WINTER	height (cm)	spread (cm)	min. temp °C	moisture	sun/shade	flower colour	
Gaultheria mucronata 'Bell's Seedling' (m/f)					120	120	-15				Self fertile. Deep red
G. m. 'Mulberry Wine'					120	120	-15				Magenta ageing to dark purple
G. m. 'Parelmoer' (syn. 'Mother of Pearl')					120	120	-15				Light pink
G. m. 'Signaal'					120	120	-15				Scarlet red
G. m. 'Sneeuwwitje' (syn. 'Snow White')					120	120	-15				White
G. procumbens (wintergreen)					15	90	-15				Deep scarlet red

Hebe

These evergreen shrubs offer some of the most beautiful late flowering plants in the garden, but the large-leaved, large flowered kinds are only borderline hardy.

One tender variety regularly used for pot work is *Hebe* x *franciscana* 'Variegata'. It makes a fine show on the summer patio with its large, glossy, cream-edged leaves and scattered purple-pink blooms. *H. cupressoides* 'Boughton Dome' has tiny bright green leaves and a very tight habit; *H.* 'Red Edge' with grey, pink-margined leaves is also compact though it benefits from being sheared over mid-spring.

Hebe 'Red Edge'

	SPRING	SUMMER	AUTUMN	WINTER	height (cm)	spread (cm)	min. temp °C	moisture	sun/shade	flower colour	
Hebe cupressoides 'Boughton Dome'					60	90	-15				Compact. Bright green leaves
H. x *franciscana* 'Variegata'					90	90	-5				Large waxy leaves, cream edged
H. pinguifolia 'Pagei'					30	90	-15				Silvery grey foliage
H. 'Red Edge'					60	60	-5				Grey leaves, pink margin. Pink in winter
H. topiaria					60	90	-15				Rounded compact habit
H. 'Wiri Dawn'					40	50	-5				Long, narrow leaves. Tapered blooms

☼ *sunny*   ☼ *semi-shady*   ● *shady*

Hedera
English ivy

The foliage of *Hedera helix* or English ivy is extremely variable with leaves ranging from diamond shapes, for example 'Little Diamond', to the classic-lobed outline – some like 'Tres Coupe' being finely cut and elegantly pointed.

Hedera helix cultivar

Cultivars can be gold or cream-edged, silver-grey, marbled, or speckled – whatever plants you are using in your arrangement, there is sure to be a perfect ivy to complement them.

They trail over the rims of pots and baskets, softening the hard lines of containers and providing a counterbalance for top-heavy arrangements. But ivies are also climbers and can be used to cover wire topiary frames. Because they root at the leaf joints, you can also use ivies to cover the base of moss filled baskets and wall planters. These plants are available year round as pots of rooted cuttings. Ivies are extremely drought tolerant.

	SPRING	SUMMER	AUTUMN	WINTER	height (cm)	spread (cm)	min. temp °C	moisture	sun/shade	foliage colour	
Hedera helix 'Adam'					15	120	-10				Pale green with silver edge
H. h. 'Eva'					15	120	-15				Grey-green, broad cream margin
H. h. 'Kolibri'					15	90	-15				White spots and speckles
H. h. 'Goldchild'					15	120	-10				Green with gold edge to blue-grey and cream
H. h. 'Little Diamond'					25	60	-15				Small, diamond shaped. White and grey
H. h. 'Très Coupé'					15	90	-15				Finely cut green foliage

Heuchera

Whereas once the dark, glossy leaved *H. micrantha* 'Palace Purple' was the only foliage heuchera available, this evergreen perennial now comes in an array of subtly varying forms.

There are numerous deep purple red variants and some pale greens like the aptly named 'Mint Frost'. The latter is typical of many, having distinct veining and a marbling of metallic silver. Some like 'Palace Purple' have leaves that are jagged and deeply indented, whilst others, including the beautifully marked 'Pewter Moon', have rounded leaves with gentle scalloping. Try heucheras with grasses and sedges.

Heuchera micrantha 'Palace Purple'

	SPRING	SUMMER	AUTUMN	WINTER	height (cm)	spread (cm)	min. temp °C	moisture	sun/shade	foliage colour	
Heuchera 'Chocolate Ruffles'					40	60	-15				Wavy-edged purple leaves, red reverse
H. micrantha var. *diversifolia* 'Palace Purple'					60	60	-15				Dark metallic, maroon-purple
H. 'Mint Frost'					40	30	-15				Rounded purple leaves with pale marbling
H. 'Pewter Moon'					40	30	-15				Pale green overlaid silver. Darker veins

planting   flower   harvest   well drained   moist   wet

Ilex
Holly *or* Japanese holly

Many of the large leaved variegated hollies have sparkling winter hardy foliage and berries and make excellent, round-headed standards – you could try a pair on either side of your front door. Alternatively, following their natural habit, clip these plants with secateurs to make a cone shape between 1.5 and 1.8m (5–6ft) tall.

The new shoots of 'Handsworth New Silver' are purple and the white variegated leaves show pink tints when young. In 'Silver Queen' the new shoots are shrimp pink. The Japanese *Ilex crenata* and 'Golden Gem' have small leathery leaves and are naturally compact. These respond well to clipping and can be shaped into domes or rounded organic forms. Plant larger hollies in wooden half barrels or similar sized containers to accommodate the root system, planting in loam based, well-drained but moisture retentive compost.

Ilex crenata 'Golden Gem'

	SPRING	SUMMER	AUTUMN	WINTER	height (cm)	spread (cm)	min. temp °C	moisture	sun/shade	foliage colour	
Ilex x altaclarensis 'Golden King' (F)					180	100	-15				Glossy gold-edged leaves. Red berries
I. aquifolium 'Silver Queen' (M)					180	100	-15				White margin. New growth salmon pink
I. aquifolium 'Handsworth New Silver' (F)					180	100	-15				Spiny white edge. New shoots purple
Ilex crenata					90	90	-15				Small dark leathery rounded leaves. Slow
I. c. 'Golden Gem'					90	90	-15				Yellow-green foliage. Slow

Juniperus

Juniperus communis

Compact growing forms of the drought tolerant junipers are ideal for permanent container plantings situated in full sun.

These evergreen conifers feature narrow columnar specimens like *Juniperus communis* 'Hibernica'; mound forming types such as the steely 'Blue Star'; and spreading, semi-prostrate varieties like the very pale green 'Sulphur Spray'. Unlike many conifers, most can be lightly pruned to control their size and shape.

	SPRING	SUMMER	AUTUMN	WINTER	height (cm)	spread (cm)	min. temp °C	moisture	sun/shade	foliage colour	
Juniperus communis 'Green Carpet'					30	100	-15				Carpet of deep green
J. c. 'Hibernica' (Irish juniper)					180	30	-15				Narrow column. Very slow
J. horizontalis 'Blue Chip'					30	120	-15				Bright blue carpet. Slow
J. x media 'Gold Sovereign' (syn. 'Blound')					60	150	-15				Semi prostrate, bright golden yellow
J. squamata 'Blue Star'					30	50	-15				Silver-blue mound
J. virginiana 'Sulphur Spray'					100	100	-15				Spreading fans of pale sulphur

☼ *sunny*   ☼ *semi-shady*   ● *shady*

Lavandula
Lavender

Dwarf English lavenders, forms of _Lavandula angustifolia_, make wonderful pot plants with their aromatic evergreen foliage and mid- to late summer blooms that are a magnet for bees and butterflies.

Lots of varieties of these hardy, drought tolerant Mediterranean herbs exist, but for classic lavender coloured flowers it is hard to beat _L. a._ 'Munstead', or the more uniform 'Hidcote'. Try either of these in windowboxes or planted singly in terracotta pots ranged along the edge of the terrace. Somewhat less hardy but with greater flower power are the French lavenders. A form commonly known as 'Papillon' has a tuft of long violet purple petals topping each head and it flowers for months from late spring to late summer. Grow lavenders in loam-based, free-draining compost.

Lavandula angustifolia 'Hidcote'

	SPRING	SUMMER	AUTUMN	WINTER	height (cm)	spread (cm)	min. temp °C	moisture	sun/shade	flower colour	
Lavandula angustifolia 'Hidcote'	🌱	🌱 ● ●			60	75	-15	💧	☀	■	Silvery grey-green leaves
_L. a._ 'Loddon Pink'	🌱	🌱 ● ●			45	45	-15	💧	☀	▢	Grey green leaves. Unusual flower colour
_L. a._ 'Munstead'	🌱	🌱 ● ●			45	60	-15	💧	☀	▢	Variable habit as often seed raised
_L. a._ 'Nana Alba'	🌱	🌱 ● ●			30	30	-15	💧	☀	□	Petite, white flowered form
L. stoechas subsp. _pedunculata_ (syn. _L. s._ 'Papillon')	🌱	● ● ● ●	●		75	75	-10	💧	☀	■	Flowerheads topped with showy 'tufts'

Laurus nobilis
Sweet bay

Laurus nobilis angustifolia

These aromatic shrubs from the Mediterranean region have leathery, wavy-edged, dark green leaves. They can be purchased as small flame-shaped plants in the herb section of the garden centre, or as more mature specimens clipped into balls, cones, spirals or lollipop headed standards typically around 1.5m tall.

Clipping is best done with secateurs to avoid unsightly brown edges. Grow bay (_Laurus nobilis_) in full sun or light shade, out of strong, cold, drying winds which could scorch the foliage, and insulate stems of standards in winter using foam pipe insulation. Sweet bay eventually grows into a substantial shrub or topiary specimen so provide a sufficiently large container – a thick wooden half barrel would be ideal, as wood helps to insulate the roots from frost.

🌱 _planting_   ● _flower_   💧 _well drained_   💧 _moist_   💧 _wet_

Leucothoe

Switch ivy,
Drooping
leucothoe *or*
Fetterbush

This North American native plant is useful for large permanent containers in shade. *Leucothoe fontanesiana* ultimately makes quite a large shrub and would work well in a wooden half barrel planted with other acid loving plants of an upright habit to contrast with its arching stems.

The new growth is red-tinted and in late spring the plant bears clusters of many tiny white flask shaped blooms. For year round

Leucothoe 'Scarletta'

interest, try the cream marbled cultivar 'Rainbow', whose young leaves are flushed pink, or for a more elegant, compact version of the species go for 'Rollissonii' which has small narrow leaves – not so easy to track down but worth the hunt. In recent years 'Scarletta' has become a popular plant for making seasonal arrangements for autumn and winter. This bushy little plant is quite different to the rest, with small pointed leaves flushed red and maroon. It needs good light to colour up well. Try it with the red-berried *Skimmia* x *reevesiana* and white heathers. Warning – Leocothoe are highly toxic if ingested.

	SPRING	SUMMER	AUTUMN	WINTER	height (cm)	spread (cm)	min. temp °C	moisture	sun/shade	flower colour
Leucothoe fontanesiana	🌱 ● ●	●		🌱 🌱		120	180	-15	💧	☀	New growth red tinted
L. f. 'Rainbow'	🌱 ●			🌱 🌱		120	180	-15	💧	☀	Cream with pink flushes when young
L. f. 'Rollissonii'	🌱 ●			🌱 🌱		100	120	-15	💧	☀	Narrow leaves. Compact
L. 'Scarletta' syn. 'Zeblid'	🌱 🌱			🌱 🌱		60	60	-15	💧	☀	Glossy red foliage

Ligustrum delavayanum

Looking more like boxwood than privet, this small-leaved evergreen shrub has become a popular topiary plant.

Globe-headed standards and more intricate shapes modelled on frames are now quite common in larger garden centres. Finished specimens have often originated in warm climes and may not be fully acclimatized to cooler regions, so plant in late spring or early summer to give plants the greatest chance of toughening up if you live in an area which has cold winters. Unless you live in a mild area, provide winter protection for plants and pots or move into the conservatory or greenhouse in late autumn. In early summer, tiny white flower clusters appear that are followed by small black berries. Clip lightly between late spring and late summer to keep a neat profile. Borderline hardy – around -15°C.

Ligustrum delavayanum

☀ sunny   ☀ semi-shady   ● shady

Myrtus communis

An aromatic evergreen with an ancient history of cultivation, common myrtle (*Myrtus communis*) is a Mediterranean shrub that will relish spending its summers in the heat and shelter of a sunny patio or terrace.

Myrtus communis

Although compact growing if left to its own devices, its glossy dense and deep green foliage can be clipped into globes or domes. In good summers, plants become studded with attractive spherical flower buds that open to fluffy white scented blooms. These may be followed by small, deep purple berries. 'Variegata' has creamy white variegation and is an eye-catching variant. Grow in soil-less multipurpose compost kept moist in summer but ensure good drainage. Overwinter in a frost free greenhouse or conservatory and reduce watering.

	SPRING	SUMMER	AUTUMN	WINTER	height (cm)	spread (cm)	min. temp °C	moisture	sun/shade	flower colour	
Myrtus communis		flower flower	harvest		90	60	-5	moist	sun		Small, glossy dark green leaves
M. c. 'Variegata'		flower flower	harvest		75	45	-5	moist	sun		Creamy white edged leaves

Osmanthus

The fragrant osmanthus produce their clusters of tiny tubular white flowers from mid- to late spring against a backdrop of dense, small, dark green leathery foliage.

Osmanthus x *burkwoodii* has smaller blooms but a faster growth rate than most osmanthus and can be shaped with shears after flowering to form a more rounded profile. Forms of *O. heterophyllus* could be mistaken for holly with their larger, glossy, prickly leaves. 'Variegatus' has a broad cream margin but the most colourful is 'Goshiki', with bronzed new shoots and leaves marbled creamy yellow. These are somewhat tender and are best sheltered for the winter. Protect from cold, drying winds.

Osmanthus heterophyllus 'Variegatus'

	SPRING	SUMMER	AUTUMN	WINTER	height (cm)	spread (cm)	min. temp °C	moisture	sun/shade	flower colour	
Osmanthus x *burkwoodii*	flower flower		planting planting planting		90	60	-15	well drained	part shade		Fragrant
O. delavayi	flower flower		planting planting harvest		60	60	-15	well drained	part shade		Fragrant. Blue-black autumn fruits
O. heterophyllus 'Goshiki' (syn. 'Tricolor')	planting		flower flower		90	90	-5	well drained	part shade		Leaves splashed cream and yellow
O. h. 'Variegatus' (syn. 'Argenteomarginatus')	planting		flower flower		90	90	-5	well drained	part shade		Broad creamy-white edge

planting   flower   harvest   well drained   moist   wet

Pachysandra terminalis

This tough, shade tolerant creeping ground cover plant has leathery dark green leaves with jagged margins arranged in distinct whorls.

In early summer a tuft of white flowers occurs at the centre of each plant. Combined with variegated lesser periwinkle, Pachysandra forms a useful base for taller shade loving shrubs such as rhododendrons growing in large permanent containers.

'Green Carpet' is a more refined version worth looking out for although not as commonly available, and the pretty white-edged 'Variegata' is especially useful for autumn and winter seasonal containers and baskets. Watch for slugs and snails.

Pachysandra terminalis

	SPRING	SUMMER	AUTUMN	WINTER	height (cm)	spread (cm)	min. temp °C	moisture	sun/shade	flower colour	
Pachysandra terminalis					20	60+	-15		shady		Occasional white fruits
P. t. 'Green Carpet'					15	60	-15		shady		Compact form. Smaller leaves
P. t. 'Variegata'					25	60	-15		shady		White-edged leaves

Pieris
Lily-of-the-valley bush

Pieris japonica

There are numerous compact growing *Pieris japonica* cultivars that are suitable for container gardening and these ericaceous or acid loving woodland shrubs certainly have a lot to offer.

The glossy foliage is attractively arranged in whorls and the new spring growth can be as eye-catching as flowers with some having dark mahogany red or bronze tinting and others bearing scarlet or pink leaves that age prettily.

	SPRING	SUMMER	AUTUMN	WINTER	height (cm)	spread (cm)	min. temp °C	moisture	sun/shade	flower colour	
Pieris japonica 'Debutante'					90	90	-15		semi-shady		Compact. Good flowering form
P. j. 'Little Heath'					90	90	-15		semi-shady		Dwarf. Pink-red flushed new growth
P. j. 'Little Heath Green'					90	90	-15		semi-shady		Deep red young shoots. Flat-topped bush
P. j. 'Purity'					90	90	-15		semi-shady		Compact. Excellent flowering cultivar
P. j. 'Variegata'					120	120	-15		semi-shady		Small, white-edged leaves, pink in spring
P. j. 'White Rim'					90	90	-15		semi-shady		Bold, creamy variegation. Drooping flowers

☀ *sunny*   ◑ *semi-shady*   ● *shady*

P
R

Pittosporum

Kohuhu *or*
Japanese
mock orange

Although most forms of the New Zealand kohuhu (*Pittosporum tenuifolium*) eventually make upright shrubs several metres tall, they are slow growing and compact and will be happy in containers for a number of years.

The leaves are relatively small, glossy and with a wavy margin and the stems are usually a contrasting dark red or black, adding greatly to their ornamental value. Pittosporum's small, black-red flowers release a sweet honey fragrance. 'Tom Thumb', whose pale green leaves darken to purple in winter, makes a naturally low bush and others such as the white variegated 'Silver Queen' can be clipped to a conical form. 'Kohuhu' is somewhat tender, so shelter from cold drying winds. Grow in John Innes No 3 compost and keep well watered. In cold areas wrap plants and pots with insulating material.

Pittosporum tenuifolium 'Abbotsbury Gold'

Pittosporum tenuifolium 'Tom Thumb'

	SPRING	SUMMER	AUTUMN	WINTER	height (cm)	spread (cm)	min. temp °C	moisture	sun/shade	flower colour	
Pittosporum tenuifolium 'Abbotsbury Gold'	planting flower	flower			150	75	-5	well drained	sun	■	Yellow-green with irregular green edge
P. t. 'Purpureum'	planting flower	flower			150	75	1	well drained	sun	■	Purple leaves. More tender
P. t. 'Tom Thumb'	planting flower	flower			100	60	-5	well drained	sun	■	Pale green darkening to purple. Compact
P. t. 'Silver Queen'	planting flower	flower			200	100	-5	well drained	sun/shade	■	Grey-green with white margins. Hardier
P. tobira	flower	planting			120	100	1	well drained	sun/shade	□	Seed capsules open to orange fruits
P. t. 'Variegtum'	flower	planting			120	100	1	well drained	sun/shade	□	Grey-green with cream-white margins

Rhododendron

Rhododendron 'Addy Wery'

Dwarf and compact growing rhododendrons make successful container plants for shade.

Many of the small leaved cultivars will also tolerate full sun. Some of the most useful rhododendron groups for pot work are the Japanese hybrid azaleas, including the low spreading 'Mothers Day' and 'Blue Danube' and the more upright 'Vuyk's Scarlet'. These have small evergreen leaves and masses of late spring or early summer blooms.

	SPRING	SUMMER	AUTUMN	WINTER	height (cm)	spread (cm)	min. temp °C	moisture	sun/shade	flower colour	
Rhododendron 'Addy Wery'	planting flower flower				120	120	-15	well drained	sun/shade	■	Funnel-shaped, vermilion-red flowers
R. 'Curlew'	planting flower flower				60	60	-15	well drained	sun/shade	□	Funnel-shaped with darker speckles
R. 'Doc'	planting flower flower				120	120	-15	well drained	sun/shade	■	Large trusses of funnel-shaped blooms
R. 'Mothers Day'	planting flower flower				30	90	-15	well drained	sun/shade	■	Large flowers
R. 'Vuyk's Scarlet'	planting flower flower				75	120	-15	well drained	sun/shade	■	More hardy than some
R. yakushimanum	planting flower flower				120	150	-15	well drained	sun/shade	□	Coloured felting on leaves. Large flowers

planting   flower   well drained   moist   wet

Rosmarinus
Rosemary

Though chiefly grown as a culinary herb, the Mediterranean shrub rosemary has a number of free-flowering cultivars that are grown for both their richly shaded blue flowers and aromatic foliage.

One of the most hardy is 'Miss Jessopp's Upright', but for an attractive flowering display seek out cultivars like 'Benenden Blue' which is much more ornamental and excellent in pots. Growth habit varies from uprights like 'Primley Blue' to cascading or carpeting cultivars including 'McConnell's Blue'. These more prostrate kinds work well trailing over the edge of a large pot of mixed herbs or silverlings. Grow in gritty well-drained but moisture-retentive compost in full sun.

	SPRING	SUMMER	AUTUMN	WINTER	height (cm)	spread (cm)	min. temp °C	moisture	sun/shade	flower colour	
R. o. var. angustissimus 'Benenden Blue'	● ● ● ✂				90	90	-5	💧	☼	◻	Narrow leaves (syn. 'Collingwood Ingram')
Rosmarinus officinalis 'Fota Blue'	● ● ● ✂				45	90	-5	💧	☼	◼	Semi prostrate
R. o. 'McConnell's Blue'	● ● ✂				40	90	-5	💧	☼	▦	Low, spreading, with broad leaves. Protect
R. o. 'Miss Jessopp's Upright'	● ● ✂				150	120	-5	💧	☼	◼	Upright, vigorous (syn. 'Fastigiatus')
R. o. 'Primley Blue'	● ● ● ●				90	60	-5	💧	☼	◼	Neat, upright. Free flowering
R. o. 'Severn Sea'	● ● ● ● ✂			●	90	100	-5	💧	☼	▦	Spreading with arching shoots

Santolina
Cotton lavender

The silvery-grey leaved cotton lavender (*Santolina chamaecyparissus*) is a woody-based aromatic plant that has long been associated with herb gardens. New shoots are covered in a white wool and the leaves are very finely divided.

When pruned hard in spring it forms a tight bun-shape. The golden yellow, rounded, button-like flowers appear singly on vertical stems. The colour combination is a bit harsh for some tastes and best combined with purple or blue foliage and flowers. Softer alternatives include the creamy-yellow flowered S. c. 'Lemon Queen' and the feathery grey-green leaved S. pinnata subsp. *neapolitana*. Try cotton lavenders with ornamental varieties of culinary sage, or with bright green, small-leaved hebes.

	SPRING	SUMMER	AUTUMN	WINTER	height (cm)	spread (cm)	min. temp °C	moisture	sun/shade	flower colour	
S. chamaecyparissus	✂	●	✂		60	90	-5	💧	☼	▦	Dense silver-grey foliage
S. c. 'Lemon Queen'	✂	●	✂		45	45	-5	💧	☼	◻	Compact. Soft coloured flowers
S. pinnata subsp. neapolitana	✂	●	✂		45	50	-5	💧	☼	▦	Grey-green feathery leaves
S. rosmarinifolia	✂	●	✂		60	90	-5	💧	☼	▦	Vivid green feathery leaves
S. r. subsp. rosmarinifolia 'Primrose Gem'	✂	●	✂		60	90	-5	💧	☼	◻	Pale flowered cultivar

☼ sunny   ☼ semi-shady   ● shady

Senecio
Cineraria

These sub-shrubby plants from the Mediterranean, commonly known as Cineraria, have long been used in summer bedding displays for their felted, grey-white leaves, but were often discarded at the end of the season in the belief that they were half-hardy annuals.

Now garden centres offer varieties of *Senecio cineraria* (syn. *Cineraria maritima*) in the autumn as foliage detail for pot and hanging basket arrangements. When overwintered, plants produce long stems carrying clusters of small, daisy-like flowers the following year, but these stems are best cut back to re-establish strong, bushy growth. The leaves of the popular 'Silver Dust' are almost lace-like, whilst those of 'Cirrus' resemble oak leaves. The secret to their survival is sharp drainage in winter – plants are extremely drought tolerant.

Senecio cineraria 'Silver Dust'

	SPRING	SUMMER	AUTUMN	WINTER	height (cm)	spread (cm)	min. temp °C	moisture	sun/shade	flower colour	
Senecio cineraria 'Cirrus'	planting	flower	planting		30	30	-5	well drained	sun		Broad leaves with toothed edges
S. c. 'Silver Dust'	planting	flower	planting		30	30	-5	well drained	sun		Finely cut leaves
S. c. 'White Diamond'	planting	flower	planting		40	30	-5	well drained	sun		Deeply lobed, silver-white leaves

Skimmia

Some of the most striking plants offered for sale in the autumn are the skimmias – compact, evergreen shrubs having either male or female flowers.

Skimmia japonica

Males like the neat and compact *S. japonica* 'Bowles Dwarf' and the popular *S. j.* 'Rubella' have crimson red flower buds arranged in dense cone shapes that resemble clusters of tiny berries. Meanwhile the buds of *S. x confusa* 'Kew Green' are a bright acid green contrasting with the dark glossy foliage. When skimmia flowers open in spring they are strongly honey scented and the foliage is also aromatic when crushed. Males and females are normally required for fruit but the hermaphrodite, *Skimmia x reevesiana*, produces long-lasting crops of bright scarlet berries on its own. It is superb with gold-variegated evergreens and dwarf daffodils. Grow in soil-less, preferably ericaceous compost (especially for *S. x reevesiana*) and keep moist but well drained.

	SPRING	SUMMER	AUTUMN	WINTER	height (cm)	spread (cm)	min. temp °C	moisture	sun/shade	flower colour	
S. x confusa 'Kew Green'	flower flower		planting		50	90	-15	moist	sun/shade		Acid green flower buds
Skimmia japonica 'Bowles' Dwarf Male'	flower flower		planting		30	45	-15	moist	shade		Crimson flower buds. Compact
S. japonica 'Rubella'	flower flower		planting		120	120	-15	moist	shade		Crimson flower buds
S. j. subsp. *reevesiana*		flower harvest harvest harvest	planting		75	90	-15	moist	shade		Scarlet berries

planting	flower	harvest	well drained	moist	wet

Solanum

Winter cherry,
Christmas
cherry,
Jerusalem
cherry *or*
Madeira cherry

Berry-laden plants of *Solanum pseudocapsicum* come into garden centres in late summer and early autumn.

Once treated almost exclusively as a houseplant, more cold tolerant versions of this species are now offered as autumn patio plants. Buy with a good crop of green berries with just a few beginning to turn cream – these later darken to orange or orange red. This will ensure the maximum period of enjoyment before the berries drop or spoil. Try combining plants with pure white mini cyclamen and white variegated ivy. Plant in containers placed in a sheltered

Solanum pseudocapsicum

spot to protect them from frost for as long as possible. Discard after use. Hardy to 5°C (41°F). Height and spread 30–45cm (12–18in).

Stipa

Pheasant grass
or Mexican
feather grass

Stipa tenuissima

The hair like leaves, delicate flowers and changing colours of these evergreen grasses gives them high ornamental value. Several are sufficiently compact to grow in containers.

In *Stipa arundinacea* or pheasant grass, the arching flower stems reach to the ground and the clumps of shimmering leaves become bronzed and streaked with orange and red towards the end of summer, the colours lasting though the winter. In *S. tenuissima*, the upright tussocks of fine yellow green leaves give rise to arching, gossamer like flowerheads producing a misty haze. And in the Mexican feather grass, *S. t.* 'Pony Tails', the soft tussocks of bright green leaves gradually turn a warm pale brown. All the plants described are happy in loam-based compost, for example John Innes No 3, provided they are kept sufficiently moist.

Stipas work well as specimen plants planted in tall, slim pots so that their cascading foliage and flowers can be properly appreciated.

S

Evergreen Plants

	SPRING	SUMMER	AUTUMN	WINTER	height (cm)	spread (cm)	min. temp °C	moisture	sun/shade	colour	
Stipa arundinacea					45	90	-10				Orange-red foliage from late summer
S. tenuissima					60	30	-15				Delicate flowers. Erect yellow-green leaves
S. t. 'Pony Tails'					65	80	-15				Bright green tufts turning honey coloured

☼ *sunny*   ☼ *semi-shady*   ● *shady*

Thuja
Arborvitae

Many conifers with dense foliage can be used as temporary container plants when young. Good examples include two hedging cultivars, both of which have a narrowly conical profile – *Thuja occidentalis* 'Holmstrup' and *T. o.* 'Smaragd'.

'Holmstrup' has an interesting texture with curving fans of mid-green foliage, whilst the bright green 'Smaragd' has a tight dense form. *T. o.* 'Rheingold' has fluffy juvenile foliage of golden bronze which turns a rich orange in winter. It naturally makes a broad pyramid or globe. Coming down in size, for a really neat green globe try the dwarf arborvitaes, *T. o.* 'Hetz Midget' or 'Tiny Tim'.

Thuja occidentalis 'Tiny Tim'

	SPRING	SUMMER	AUTUMN	WINTER	height (cm)	spread (cm)	min. temp °C	moisture	sun/shade	foliage colour	
T. occidentalis 'Hetz Midget'	planting		planting		30	30	-15	well drained	sun		Green globe. Slow growing
T. o. 'Holmstrup'	planting		planting		180	90	-15	well drained	sun		Textured cone. Mid green
T. o. 'Rheingold'	planting		planting		120	120	-15	well drained	sun		Broad cone or globe
T. o. 'Smaragd'	planting		planting		180	90	-15	well drained	sun		Compact. Narrowly conical. Bright green
T. o. 'Tiny Tim'	planting		planting		60	45	-15	well drained	sun		Syn. *Platycladus orientalis* 'Aurea Nana'

Thymus
Thyme

The drought tolerant, aromatic thymes make wonderful container plants for the hot sunny patio. Creeping types like *Thymus serpyllum* 'Pink Chintz' and the yellow speckled *Thymus* 'Doone Valley' work particularly well.

'Doone Valley' makes an attractive carpet in a large alpine trough or sink. You can also plant coloured leaf thymes such as the yellow-green leaved *T. pulegiodes* 'Archers Gold' and 'Bertram Anderson' in winter hanging baskets along with silver and purple leaf herbs and violas. The lemon-scented *T.* x *citriodorus* 'Silver Queen' has grey-green leaves variegated creamy white, and this bushy plant combines well with pastel shaded sun-lovers like thrift (*Armeria maritima*), *Scabiosa* 'Butterfly Blue' and *Brachyscome* 'Pink Mist'. Grow in gritty, free-draining, loam-based compost. Watch for reversions in coloured leaf and variegated forms.

Thymus 'Doone Valley'

	SPRING	SUMMER	AUTUMN	WINTER	height (cm)	spread (cm)	min. temp °C	moisture	sun/shade	colour	
Thymus x *citriodorus* 'Silver Queen'	planting	flower	planting		30	25	-15	well drained	sun		Grey and creamy white
T. 'Doone Valley'	planting	flower			12	35	-15	well drained	sun		Yellow spotted leaves
T. pulegioides 'Archer's Gold'	planting	flower	planting		23	45	-15	well drained	sun		Yellow green with yellow margins
T. pulegioides 'Bertram Anderson'	planting	flower	planting		23	60	-15	well drained	sun		Yellow green
T. serpyllum 'Pink Chintz'	planting	flower	planting		7	60	-15	well drained	sun		Grey-green. Profuse flowers

planting   ● flower   harvest   well drained   moist   wet

Viburnum tinus
Laurestinus

Forms of the hardy evergreen laurestinus (*Viburnum tinus*) are chiefly grown for their long flowering season, which spans the coldest months of the year. In autumn, clusters of attractive pink buds appear in large numbers and, depending on the weather, these begin to open, continuing the display right through to spring.

Viburnum tinus

In large numbers the flowers give out a sweet honey fragrance and may be followed by metallic, blue-black berries. Certain cultivars have been selected for compact growth and improved flowering, including the early blooming 'Eve Price' and the pink flowered 'Gwenllian'. The bold cream-variegated leaves of 'Variegatum' are very attractive, but this tender plant needs a sheltered site with protection from strong midday sun and cold winds.

	SPRING	SUMMER	AUTUMN	WINTER	height (cm)	spread (cm)	min. temp °C	moisture	sun/shade	flower colour	
Viburnum tinus	● ● ● ◎		✎		● ●	150	120	-15	◊	☀	☐	Blue-black berries
V. t. 'Eve Price'	● ◎		✎ ● ● ● ● ● ●		120	120	-15	◊	☀	☐	Compact. Pink flower buds
V. t. 'Gwenllian'	● ◎		✎ ● ● ● ● ●		120	120	-15	◊	☀	▨	Deep pink buds
V. t. 'Variegatum'	● ● ◎		✎	● ●	120	120	-10	◊	☀	☐	Cream variegated leaves

Vinca
Lesser periwinkle

Whether trailing over the rim of a large permanent container or cascading from a basket of winter flowering pansies, the creeping lesser periwinkles are a useful alternative to English ivy.

The lax stems have pairs of narrow, leathery leaves that are either plain green, white- or gold-variegated. The new cultivar *Vinca minor* 'Illumination' has bright butter yellow leaves with only a fine green margin and it gleams in winter sunshine. Watch for die-back and cut out affected growth immediately. Do not cover the crowns with mulch.

Vinca minor f. *alba*

	SPRING	SUMMER	AUTUMN	WINTER	height (cm)	spread (cm)	min. temp °C	moisture	sun/shade	flower colour	
Vinca minor 'Alba Variegata'	✎ ● ● ● ● ●		✎ ✎ ✎		20	60+	-15	◊	☀	☐	Cream variegated
V. m. 'Argenteovariegata'	✎ ● ● ● ● ●		✎ ✎ ✎		20	60+	-15	◊	☀	▨	Cream variegated
V. m. 'Atropurpurea'	✎ ● ● ● ● ●		✎ ✎ ✎		20	60+	-15	◊	☀	▨	Deep green leaves
V. m. 'Illumination'	✎ ● ● ● ● ●		✎ ✎ ✎		20	60+	-15	◊	☀	▨	Green margin to bright pale yellow leaves
V. m. 'La Grave' (syn. 'Bowles Variety')	✎ ● ● ● ● ●		✎ ✎ ✎		20	60+	-15	◊	☀	▨	Compact. Larger blooms
V. m. f. *alba*	✎ ● ● ● ● ●		✎ ✎ ✎		20	60+	-15	◊	☀	☐	Pure white blooms

☀ sunny   ☀ semi-shady   ● shady

Troubleshooting

The following diagram is designed to help you diagnose problems with your plants from the symptoms you can observe. Starting with the part of the plant that appears to be most affected – flowers, leaves or stems – by answering successive questions 'yes' [✓] or 'no' [✗] you will quickly arrive at a probable cause. Having identified the cause, turn to the relevant entry in the directory of pests and diseases for details of how to treat the condition.

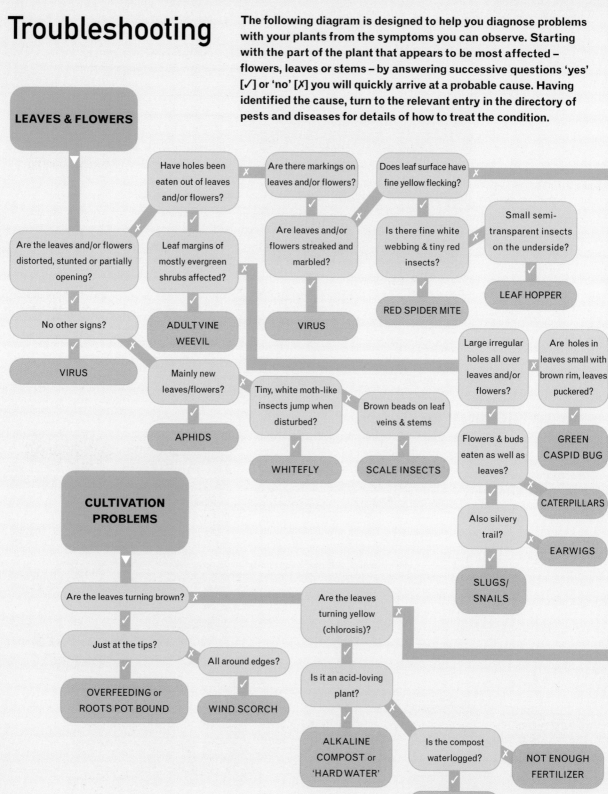

LEAVES & FLOWERS

Have holes been eaten out of leaves and/or flowers?

Are there markings on leaves and/or flowers?

Does leaf surface have fine yellow flecking?

Are the leaves and/or flowers distorted, stunted or partially opening?

Leaf margins of mostly evergreen shrubs affected?

Are leaves and/or flowers streaked and marbled?

Is there fine white webbing & tiny red insects?

Small semi-transparent insects on the underside?

LEAF HOPPER

No other signs?

ADULT VINE WEEVIL

VIRUS

RED SPIDER MITE

VIRUS

Large irregular holes all over leaves and/or flowers?

Are holes in leaves small with brown rim, leaves puckered?

Mainly new leaves/flowers?

Tiny, white moth-like insects jump when disturbed?

Brown beads on leaf veins & stems

APHIDS

WHITEFLY

SCALE INSECTS

Flowers & buds eaten as well as leaves?

GREEN CASPID BUG

CATERPILLARS

Also silvery trail?

EARWIGS

CULTIVATION PROBLEMS

SLUGS/ SNAILS

Are the leaves turning brown?

Are the leaves turning yellow (chlorosis)?

Just at the tips?

All around edges?

Is it an acid-loving plant?

OVERFEEDING or ROOTS POT BOUND

WIND SCORCH

ALKALINE COMPOST or 'HARD WATER'

Is the compost waterlogged?

NOT ENOUGH FERTILIZER

PLANT ROTTING

152

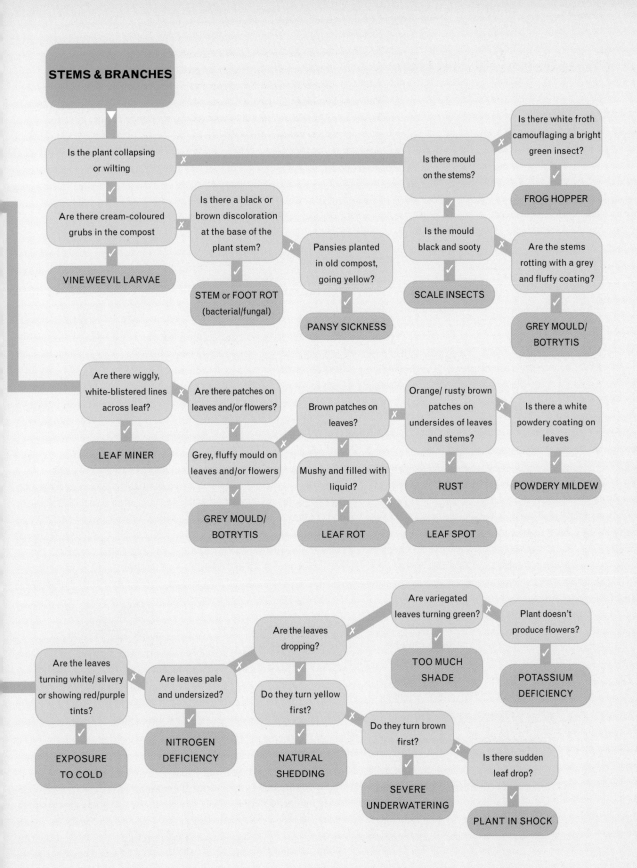

STEMS & BRANCHES

Is the plant collapsing or wilting ✗ → Is there mould on the stems?

Is the plant collapsing or wilting ✓

Are there cream-coloured grubs in the compost ✗ → Is there a black or brown discoloration at the base of the plant stem?

Are there cream-coloured grubs in the compost ✓

VINE WEEVIL LARVAE

Is there a black or brown discoloration at the base of the plant stem? ✓

STEM or FOOT ROT (bacterial/fungal)

Is there a black or brown discoloration at the base of the plant stem? ✗ → Pansies planted in old compost, going yellow?

Pansies planted in old compost, going yellow? ✓

PANSY SICKNESS

Is there mould on the stems? ✗ → Is there white froth camouflaging a bright green insect?

Is there white froth camouflaging a bright green insect? ✓

FROG HOPPER

Is there mould on the stems? ✓

Is the mould black and sooty ✓

SCALE INSECTS

Is the mould black and sooty ✗ → Are the stems rotting with a grey and fluffy coating?

Are the stems rotting with a grey and fluffy coating? ✓

GREY MOULD/ BOTRYTIS

Are there wiggly, white-blistered lines across leaf? ✓

LEAF MINER

Are there patches on leaves and/or flowers? ✓

Grey, fluffy mould on leaves and/or flowers ✓

GREY MOULD/ BOTRYTIS

Are there patches on leaves and/or flowers? ✗ → Brown patches on leaves?

Brown patches on leaves? ✓

Mushy and filled with liquid? ✓

LEAF ROT

Mushy and filled with liquid? ✗ → LEAF SPOT

Brown patches on leaves? ✗ → Orange/ rusty brown patches on undersides of leaves and stems?

Orange/ rusty brown patches on undersides of leaves and stems? ✓

RUST

Orange/ rusty brown patches on undersides of leaves and stems? ✗ → Is there a white powdery coating on leaves

Is there a white powdery coating on leaves ✓

POWDERY MILDEW

Are the leaves turning white/ silvery or showing red/purple tints? ✓

EXPOSURE TO COLD

Are the leaves turning white/ silvery or showing red/purple tints? ✗ → Are leaves pale and undersized?

Are leaves pale and undersized? ✓

NITROGEN DEFICIENCY

Are leaves pale and undersized? ✗ → Are the leaves dropping?

Are the leaves dropping? ✓

Do they turn yellow first? ✓

NATURAL SHEDDING

Do they turn yellow first? ✗ → Do they turn brown first?

Do they turn brown first? ✓

SEVERE UNDERWATERING

Do they turn brown first? ✗ → Is there sudden leaf drop?

Is there sudden leaf drop? ✓

PLANT IN SHOCK

Are the leaves dropping? ✗ → Are variegated leaves turning green?

Are variegated leaves turning green? ✓

TOO MUCH SHADE

Are variegated leaves turning green? ✗ → Plant doesn't produce flowers?

Plant doesn't produce flowers? ✓

POTASSIUM DEFICIENCY

153

Pests & Diseases

So many pest and disease problems are a result of improper care and can often be remedied by better cultivation. The use of chemical sprays really ought to be a last resort rather than routine, especially in an ordinary domestic garden. It pays to check new purchases thoroughly for signs of pest or disease.

Ants

Ants' nests may be found in large containers that are kept on the dry side and though they may not harm the plant directly, they can be aggressive when disturbed – for example, when emptying compost out at the end of the season. Ants also 'farm' aphids, collecting and feeding off their sticky honeydew, and can deliberately put aphids onto previously clean shoots. Do not leave compost in containers that are not planted. Apply ant powder if their activities become a nuisance.

Aphids

One of the most common and troublesome pests, these sap-sucking insects cause distortion of the new sappy shoot tips, leaves and flowers and, more seriously, transmit viruses. Aphids are encouraged by overuse of nitrogen-rich feeds and young or weak plants are most vulnerable. Check daily when watering and deadheading and rub off colonies or nip off affected parts with thumb and forefinger. Encourage hoverflies, ladybirds and lacewings to visit the garden and breed since they and their larvae have voracious appetites for aphids. For bad infestations blast plants with a strong jet of water or spray with insecticidal soap solution if you are gardening organically.

Caterpillars

There are many different kinds of caterpillar. Some feed singly and are so well camouflaged that you don't notice them until you discover large tattered holes in the edges of the leaves. Others appear in large enough numbers to spot them easily, but by then swift action is necessary to prevent leaves becoming stripped or skeletonized. Hand pick and dispose of caterpillars, but be wary of direct contact with caterpillars covered in bristle-like hairs, as these can cause a skin irritation. Organic gardeners can buy a bacterial solution that is sprayed on to infect and kill the caterpillars.

Earwigs

This familiar insect with a pincer at the end of its tail rarely does much damage but can sometimes munch away at Chrysanthemum and Dahlia flowerheads. These nocturnal animals hide in the dense flowers during the day and feed at night. Try trapping the creatures in upturned plant pots filled with straw suspended by a garden cane. Empty them out in the daytime and remember that they are useful aphid killers!

Froghoppers

First spotted by the 'cuckoo spit' that they leave behind, these small, vivid green sap sucking insects camouflage themselves under the foam that they produce in their nymphal stage. Cuckoo spit does little direct damage to plants but, like aphids, it can transmit viral diseases to affected plants. Blast off any signs of cuckoo spit with a strong jet of water, taking care not to damage the plant in the process. Adult froghoppers are so called because of their frog-like shape. If left to their own devices they will also damage plants in the same way as their younger counterparts, although they do not actually produce cuckoo spit.

Leaf miners

Wiggly lines of white blistering in leaves indicates the activities of the leaf miner, a small grub which burrows into the spongy layer between the upper and lower surfaces of leaves. Chrysanthemums and argyranthemums are particularly badly affected by leaf miners; if these pests are not dealt with promptly, their leaves will begin to turn brown. Pick off affected leaves.

Leafhoppers

These small, well-camouflaged sap-sucking insects can be found on the underside of salvia leaves and those of other plants including the herb sage, pelargoniums, primulas and roses. Their activities cause pale mottling on the upper surface of the leaves and, like aphids, they transmit viruses. Adult leafhoppers have almost translucent bodies with dark spots, but the white discarded skins are often easier to spot. If necessary, water or spray with a systemic insecticide after dusk.

Red spider mites

A common pest under glass, these tiny insects rarely become a problem outdoors unless plants are growing in a hot dry environment. The first sign of their presence is a sickly yellow mottling on the upper leaf surface. You might also sometimes notice white webbing on the undersides of leaves. The mites are hard to pick out without a hand lens, as they are so small. Changing the environment for the plants, increasing the humidity by spraying the foliage and ground around pots in dry spells and watering more regularly all lessen the severity of attacks. Control red spider mites with insecticidal soap solution, otherwise water or spray with a systemic insecticide after dusk.

Scale insects

Most often found on evergreen shrubs such as bays, rhododendrons and camellias, the scale insect looks like a small brown blister on the stems and the underside of leaves along the midrib. The first sign is usually black sooty mould on the upper surface of leaves and a sticky honeydew residue. Scale insects can transmit viruses and are difficult to control, because the protective shell repels insecticides. Control small infestations organically by rubbing off scales with a cotton wool bud soaked in methylated spirits. Wipe off the sooty mould and honeydew with a damp cloth. Discard badly infested plants.

Slugs and snails

These familiar pests leave ragged holes in leaves, stems and flowers and a telltale silvery slime trail. Check newly purchased plants for the clusters of transparent slug eggs – often found in the compost at the bottom of the pot – and also seek out the tiny little slugs that are easily missed but which can be very destructive left unnoticed. Slugs and snails are nocturnal so catch them feeding out in the open at night using a torch. Pick off and dispose. Use sharp grit as a mulch deterrent for vulnerable plants like hostas.

Vine weevils

The all-female adult beetles are a dull grey-brown and quite slow moving. They feed at night, favouring evergreen shrubs like Euonymus and Rhododendron, leaving u-shaped notches in the edges of leaves. Pick off and dispose of adults as they are capable of laying thousands of eggs. Their grubs are the most serious problem, causing sudden collapse of plants by eating away entire root systems. Potted ferns, heucheras, ivies and polyanthus are all popular targets.

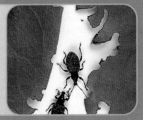

Whitefly

Normally a pest of the greenhouse, whitefly can transfer outdoors for the summer, causing damage to lush, leafy plants like Abutilon and Fuchsia. The tiny white triangular insects flutter into the air when disturbed and the honeydew excreted is colonized with sooty mould. These sapsuckers transmit viruses and are difficult to control, requiring repeated sprays of insecticidal soap to kill off each successive generation, since the eggs and larval stages are resistant to treatment.

Woodlice

These grey, 'armour-plated' pests feed at night and hide in dark places during the day. Mainly they feed on dead plant material, but they may also damage seedlings by feeding on the bases of the stems or even very young leaves. Physical control is not practical, except to ensure that any plant debris is not left lying around. If seedling damage is a major problem, apply ant powder around the seedlings. Woodlice often inhabit the bases of pots.

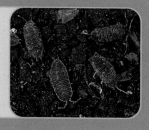

Bulb rot

Bulbs, corms and tubers – for example, dahlias – can easily rot if stored under the wrong conditions over winter. The condition is caused by a variety of fungi and several different bacteria. If it occurs, shoots will fail to emerge and leaves, if they do appear, will most likely be discoloured and weak. When buying new bulbs, test for firmness by gently squeezing them and discard any in storage that have gone soft.

Grey mould

Botrytis or grey mould forms a grey fur over decaying matter and is a particular problem in autumn and winter, when growth slows down and it begins to attack living material weakened by less favourable conditions. Be meticulous with clearing away debris, spent flowers and yellowing leaves, especially around winter flowering primroses and polyanthus, pansies and violas.

Leaf spot

There are many reasons why leaves become discoloured and covered in the rusty brown marks that characterize leaf spot. The cause is often fungal, but may also be linked to sap sucking insects or bulb rot. Overwatering of plants such as fuchsias causes yellowing and blotchiness of the lower leaves in particular, but can easily be remedied by reducing moisture levels.

Mildew

The most common form of mildew in container gardening is powdery mildew, which looks just like a dusty white residue left in patches on the foliage. It is prevalent in hot, dry weather, especially when plants have been stressed by underwatering. Verbenas and *Glechoma hederacea* growing in hanging baskets seem particularly vulnerable to the condition. Cut back plants thoroughly, and give them plenty of water and liquid feed to drive out the problem and encourage regeneration.

Pansy sickness

This is a disease that affects pansies, causing them to rot off and die. The stems of the plants rot at ground level and the top growth wilts, turns yellow and can be lifted easily. However, the condition is easily preventable. Avoid replanting pansies in compost that has already been used to grow them earlier in the season and, to be on the safe side, always pot up with fresh compost.

Rust

This fungal disease which affects a number of plants, including fuchsias and antirrhinums, is identified by the raised orange pustules on the under surface of leaves and along stems. To avoid rust becoming a feature of the plants in your containers, use rust-resistant varieties if possible and control the problem by picking off affected parts and discarding badly affected plants.

Sooty mould

Sooty mould appears as a result of sap sucking insects excreting honeydew. The black mould feeds off the sugar solution and can smother leaves, adversely affecting the plant's ability to photosynthesize. Control the pest by picking off the insects and wash the honeydew and mould off the affected plant.

Stem and foot rot

Plants grown under the wrong conditions – for example, when the compost is too wet or when too much overhead watering has taken place, especially during the cooler months – can become infected with organisms that will cause the stem or base of the stem to rot, leading to the collapse of the plant. Destroy affected plants and re-plant the container using fresh compost.

Virus

Viruses usually occur in plants that have been attacked by sap sucking insects. The foliage and flowers may be distorted and there may be colour breaks in the flowers or foliage – such as yellow streaking on leaves, and colours breaking up on flowers, creating curious effects. Destroy affected plants.

Chilling injury

Curiously, 'chilling injury' is not due to plants being subjected to frost, which usually blackens the foliage. It occurs early in the season when plants have not been properly acclimatized to the cooler outdoor environment (a process known as hardening off), or if the temperatures outdoors or under glass are just too cold for that particular plant to operate normally. The condition is common among sub-tropical plants and fuchsias, whose foliage develops red and purple tones. Other plants may turn white (especially the shoot tips). Nurse the affected plants back to health by spraying them with a foliar feed tonic such as seaweed extract, which contains easily absorbed nutrients.

Chlorosis

Often a result of iron or nitrogen deficiency, though sometimes also magnesium or manganese deficiency, chlorosis is a physiological condition in which the leaves lose green chlorophyll from parts of the leaf – for example, the veins may stay green whilst the parts in between turn yellow. The condition is most common among underfed or improperly fed plants, including roses, hydrangeas and lime-hating or ericaceous plants. For iron deficiency, try a chelated or sequestered iron fertilizer applied as a foliar feed. Use ericaceous compost and avoid using hard water on ericaceous plants, as this introduces lime which affects their ability to take up certain key minerals.

Wilt

Sudden wilting may be a sign of drought, but if all else is normal, it could indicate vine weevil activity or fungal or bacterial wilt, in which the microscopic organism blocks the vessels carrying food and water through the plant's stems. If it is the latter – which is technically known as Fusarium wilt – it will usually occur in affected plants just as they are about to flower. The stems blacken just above ground level or halfway up and develop a pink fungal growth. Destroy any plants affected by bacterial wilt.

Index of Plants

This index lists the plants mentioned in this book by their Latin names. Common names appear in bold type where applicable

General Index

Acknowledgements

The author and publishers would like to thank Coolings Nurseries for their cooperation and assistance with the photography in this book, including the loan of tools and much specialist equipment. Special thanks go to Sandra Gratwick and Nicky Peto. Coolings Nurseries Ltd., Rushmore Hill, Knockholt, Kent, TN14 7NN. Tel: 00 44 1959 532269; Email: coolings@coolings.co.uk; Website: www.coolings.co.uk.

The publishers would also like to thank Thompson & Morgan (UK) Ltd for a number of the plant portraits that appear throughout the A–Z sections of this book and www.TopiaryShop.co.uk for the photograph at the bottom of page 143.